FREEDOM IS A DREAM

A DOCUMENTARY HISTORY OF WOMEN IN THE EPISCOPAL CHURCH

EDITED BY

SHERYL A. KUJAWA-HOLBROOK

 CHURCH

CHURCH PUBLISHING INCORPORATED, NEW YORK

Library of Congress Cataloging-in-Publication Data

Kujawa-Holbrook, Sheryl A.
    Freedom is a Dream / Sheryl A. Kujawa-Holbrook
      p. cm.
    Includes bibliographical references.
    ISBN: 0-89869-387-X (pbk.)
      1. Kujawa-Holbrook, Sheryl A. 2. Women in the Anglican Commu-
nion 2. United States I. Title
BX5182.3 .F74 2002
283'.092'273— B 21

2002073333

Church Publishing Incorporated
445 Fifth Avenue
New York NY 10016

http://www.churchpublishing.org

5 4 3 2 1

For Paul Holbrook

With thanksgiving for all your love and encouragement —
Our first book together!

ACKNOWLEDGMENTS

The depth of the documents assembled here would not have been possible without the contribution of many colleagues and family members of subjects who made suggestions of names and texts. The author would like to extend her sincere thanks to the following persons: Patricia Albright, Phyllis Amenda, Owanah Anderson, Barbara Jean, SHN, Eva Bradham, Martha Birchfield, John L. Bogart, Lawrence H. Bradner Elaine Caldbeck, Jerry Carroon, Bud Cedarholm, Stuart W.H. Ching, Nan Cobbey, Pam Conley, Pamela Darling, Roderick Dibbert, Mary Sudman Donovan, Elizabeth Clay Garlichs, Dick Gillett, Nancy Grandfield, David Green, Marie-Eve Harbec, Carleton Hayden, Suzanne Hiatt, Hilary Mary, CT, Bob James, Ruth Juchter, OSH, Kitty Kawecki, John Kater, Wayne H. Kempton, Margaret Landis, Donald H. Langstraat, Zhenga LaRosa, Elizabeth Chaplin Lloyd, Mark MacDonald, Mary Elizabeth, CHS, Elizabeth Singer Maule, Anca Meret, Fred Neal, Kathleen Nutter, Marguerite Parks, Anna-Brita Perkins, William Perkins, David W. Perry, Edward W. Rodman, Thelma J. Roundtree, Rima Lunin Schultz, David Siegenthaler, Barbara B. Schnorrenberg, Gardiner H. Shattuck, Jr, Eleanor Singer, Edward E. Thompson, Barbara S. Turner, Elizabeth Turner, Mary Whitten, Frederick Boyd Williams

Also, Jennifer Peters and Mark J. Duffy of the Archives of the Episcopal Church were very helpful in tracking and verifying leads.

In addition, the following organizations were particularly helpful: National Episcopal Historians and Archivists, the Episcopal Women's History Project, and the Anglican Bibliopole.

Texts were suggested and/or provided by the following: Magee Anderson, Joanna Bowen Gillespie, Pua Hopkins, Donn Morgan, John Ratti, Linda Stark, Fredrica Harris Thompsett, Fran Toy, Janet Vetter.

Translations provided by David Andrés Álvarez, Pua Hopkins, and Diane Wong.

Research assistance provided by Priscilla Bates. Editorial assistance by Liza Q. Wirtz.

Financial assistance for this project provided by a Conant Fund faculty sabbatical grant, the Theological Writing Fund of the Episcopal Divinity School, and by an Episcopal Women's History Project Travel Grant.

Lastly, the author wishes to convey her deep appreciation for Frank L. Tedeschi, Vice President and Managing Editor of Church Publishing Incorporated, for his support of this project.

CONTENTS

Dedication   iii

Acknowledgments   v

Introduction   x

(in chronological order by date of birth)

Martha Laurens Ramsay (1759-1811)   1
    Memoirs of the Life of Martha Laurens Ramsay

Judith Lomax (1774-1828)   6
    A Sabbath Journal, 1774-1828

Sojourner Truth (c. 1797-1883)   13
    I Suppose I Am About the Only Colored Woman That Goes
    About to Speak for the Rights of Colored Women

Frances Maria Mulligan Hill (1799-1884)   17
    A Letter from Frances M. Hill Concerning the Progress of
    Female Education in Greece

Catharine E. Beecher (1800-1878)   22
    A Letter from the Author to a Mother

Maria W. Stewart (1803-1879)   30
    Farewell Address to Her Friends in the City of Boston

Harriet Beecher Stowe (1811-1896)   39
    Four Ways of Observing The Sabbath

Elizabeth Cady Stanton (1815-1902)   50
    The Woman's Bible

Anne Ayers [Sister Anne] (1816-1896)   59
    Practical Thoughts on Sisterhoods

Amelia Jenks Bloomer (1818-1894)   66
    Alas! Poor Adam

Harriet Ross Tubman (c. 1820-1913)   74
    The Moses of Her People

Lucy Larcom (1824-1883)   78
    Letters on "Religious Changes" and "Membership in the Episcopal Church"

Lili`uokalani (1837-1917)   85
    Hawaii's Story

Lucy Gilmer Breckinridge (1843-1865)   90
    Selections from her journal, 1862-1864

Julia Chester Emery (1852-1922)   96
    St. Mary's, Moiliili

Louise deKoven Bowen (1859-1953)   103
    Growing Up With A City

Anna Julia Hayward Cooper (c. 1859-1964)   110
    A Voice from the South

Vida Dutton Scudder (1861-1954)   119
    On Journey

Susan Trevor Knapp (1862-1941)   128
    The Relation of Social Science to Christianity

Mary Kingsbury Simkhovitch (1867-1951)   137
    The Red Festival

Emily Malbone Morgan (1872-1937)   144
    Letters to Her Companions, 1897, 1904

Harriet Bedell (1875-1969)   152
    Among the Indians of Oklahoma

Frances Perkins (1880-1965)   159
    The Vocation of the Laity

Lucy Randolph Mason (1882-1959)   165
    To Win These Rights: A Personal Story of the CIO In the South

Anna "Eleanor" Roosevelt (1884-1962)   172
    Christmas: A Story

Ella Cara Deloria (1889-1971)   184
    Speaking of Indians

Sarah Louise "Sadie" Delany (1890-1999)   192
    On My Own at 107

King Yoak Won Wu (1890-1982)   198
    Excerpt from the Oral History of King Yoak Won Wu

Annie Elizabeth "Bessie" Delany (1891-1995) 204
 Having Our Say

Ruth Elaine Younger, [Mother Ruth, CHS] (1897-1986) 209
 St. Hilda's and St. Hugh's School:
  Its Philosophy and Ideals

Margaret Mead (1901-1978) 216
 Ritual Expression of the Cosmic Sense

Paula Velázquez de Álvarez (1903-1987) 226
 A Short History of the Organization of the Episcopal
  Church Women in the Diocese of Puerto Rico

Dora Phyllis Meekings Chaplin (1905-1990) 229
 The Privilege of Teaching

Sarah Patton Boyle (1906-1994) 237
 The Desegregated Heart

Elizabeth "Rachel" Hosmer, OSH (1908-1988) 246
 My Life Remembered

Cynthia Clark Wedel (1908-1986) 255
 A God For All People

Emily Gardiner Neal (1910-1989) 263
 The Long Road Begins

Anna Pauline "Pauli" Murray (1911-1985) 272
 Women Seeking Admission to Holy Orders – As Crucifers
  Carrying the Cross

Phyllis Anderson Stark (1911-1993) 280
 I Chose A Parson

Carman St. John Wolff Hunter (1921-2000) 288
 Each Day Brings New Joy

Jeanne Louise McGonigal Vetter (1929-1996) 294
 Selections from her Homilies

Dorothy J. Brittain (1932-2001) 301
 Intimate Friends: Being Single in the 1980s

Alicia "Cristina" Rivera, OSH (1933-1996) 309
 Letter to the Order of St. Helena from Jamaica, c. 1973

Selected Bibliography 314

About the Author/Editor 320

INTRODUCTION

Freedom is a dream
Haunting as amber wine
Or worlds remembered out of time.
Not Eden's gate, but freedom
Lures us down a trail of skulls
Where men forever crush the dreamers—
Never the dream.

I was an Israelite walking a sea bottom,
I was Negro slave following the North Star,
I was an immigrant huddled in ship's belly
I was a Mormon searching for a temple,
I was a refugee clogging roads to nowhere—
Always the dream was freedom.[1]

This anthology bespeaks the spiritual vision and personal testimonies of Anglican and Episcopal women in the history of the church in the United States. Their faith stories—the record of their enactment of their vocations in the world—and the variety of social contexts from which they went forth and in which they ministered, illustrate the deep balance between the intensity of personal intimacy with God and the capacity for prophetic social witness.

The Anglican and Episcopal women included in this collection represent a multiplicity of social locations and vocations—educators, missionaries, social workers, spouses, mothers, clergy, administrators, health care workers. Yet one theme which binds all these women together is their service to the church and their search for freedom, for as Pauli Murray suggests, "Freedom is a Dream." This concept of the struggle for, or *towards*, freedom suggests itself differently depending on the social context of the subject. For while all women have suffered from some form of oppression, all women have not suffered from oppression *equally*. Gender oppression does not stand alone; it is enhanced or mitigated through the complexities of the multiple identities we all incarnate—race, ethnicity, social class, sexual identity, ability—all have everything to do with the way we interact with the world and live out our vocations. Therefore, the fact that I am a white, heterosexual, able-bodied, middle-class, ordained, woman is not incidental to God: it has *everything* to do with how I live, with whom I love, and with the kind of power I exercise in the world. I have experienced injustice, now and then, however I know of women who have struggled through a great deal more. The power of my whiteness, my abilities, my material benefits, are spiritually inescapable. My spirituality is the way my life reflects the love I have for God, other people, and the world, and is consistent with my race, gender, sexual identities, abilities, and limitations.

Howard Thurman believed that it is only through the liberation of our self-identities that we can live our genuine vocations. "Often it is most difficult to accept our fact," he wrote. "It means being very specific about ourselves. This is our face, not another's; it will always be our face exhibiting a countenance that reveals all the laughter and all the tears in our years of living… No substitute can be found for it—go wherever we will, knock at every door, our face remains our face"[2] The assumption here is that when we love our true selves the way God loves us, we open ourselves to a variety of dimensions of liberation, of freedom. Just like many of the women whose witness can be found in this collection, we become empowered in ways we had not heretofore imagined. We also open ourselves, perhaps most genuinely, to vocation, which is our response to God's call to care for others and the world we share.

The truth sets us free. The core gospel truth that reverberates through Pauli Murry's poem is that abundance is not about the accumulation of material goods but about the breadth of our *love* — evidenced in courage, compassion, and the commitment to stand with the unloved and the powerless.

In this sense, spirituality is not limited to recitation of prayers or observing rules, though external practices are important, but the opening of our hearts to love and service. Power isn't the ability to hold power *over* another or the capacity to commit violence, but the courage to speak truthfully and live with integrity come what may.

For the women whose lives and witness have been recorded here, the dream of freedom took on a variety of forms. For those who were born enslaved, or whose loved ones were enslaved, the dream of physical freedom as well as existential and spiritual freedom was alive. For some, the freedom to obtain an education, or to engage in meaningful work or service, was the dream. And still for others, often women of great privilege, freedom existed where and when they were able to exercise that privilege for the freedom of others. All this comes through Jesus Christ. The power of the freedom of Christ implicated the women included in this anthology. It will implicate us in the complicated web of life, and brings with it awesome responsibility, deep compassion, and transforming joy.

For the women in this text, the church was an agent of this freedom by calling them forth into their transcendental mission. The process of living out this calling—vocation—impacted their hearts and minds and spirits and brought about new attitudes regarding God, themselves and the world. God makes use of every aspect of our lives as an integral part of vocation. As the lives of the women here suggest, we need to remember who and whose we are in order to celebrate what we bring to God's service.

Obviously, a variety of choices were made in the compilation of an anthology of this sort. I found the boundaries of a printed volume at times overwhelmingly vast and at times too constraining. While I remain excited about the opportunity to uncover, along with the support of many colleagues, more subjects than could be possibly be included, some hard choices had to be made about who eventually *was* included. Another historian would no doubt make other choices, yet I have attempted to include women from a broad spectrum of racial and ethnic backgrounds, social classes, abilities, sexual identities, ages, and regional backgrounds. I began with the assumption that I could not compile an anthology of this sort without a strong presence of women of color. Obviously, a collection of documents is constructed with a bias toward those who participate largely in written cultures, rather than those from oral cultures. Though my own work is heavily biased toward written culture, I hope to move with this collection toward a more balanced perspective. Thus, I needed to examine throughout the compiling and editing process what type of texts should be included so as not to exclude persons from oral cultures.

However, even with an expanded notion of what constitutes a primary "document" or "text" there are subjects not included in this anthology because of my failure to obtain a document. For instance, I had hoped to include a section on Rosa Judith Cisneros Aguilar, a devout member of her parish in El Salvador and a journalist, lawyer, and family-planning advocate, who was assassinated in of front her home in 1981. Though Planned Parenthood International gives a major award in her name, there are very limited records about her available. Numerous letters and e-mails in English and Spanish across several countries failed to reveal a document. Still, a parish, Santa Rosa Cisneros Church, Chasnigua, Villanueva, Honduras gives witness to her ministry. Kate Turabian, the author of the omnipresent style manual for term papers, theses, and dissertations, with which I spent a great deal of my own life, was also a Sunday school teacher in the diocese of Chicago. Unfortunately, an excerpt from the style manual was not exactly what I needed! Lois Stephens, an educator from the diocese of Massachusetts, and mentor to many, left her legacy in the form of skilled local educators, rather than documents. Similarly, women such as Margaret Hawk, of the diocese of South Dakota, Virginia Ram, of the diocese of Los Angeles, and Ruby Middleton Forsythe, of the diocese of South Carolina, served their people locally, and the Episcopal Church locally and nationally, but left few extant written records for a researcher. However, I know that these women—and many others—will return in the narrative of my future work and that of others.

The women included in this anthology also represent a cross-section of vocations and how they related with the institutional life of the church. Here an attempt was made to achieve a balance between those women who already have a presence within the historical narrative of the church, including those who have held the vocation of "the first…"; those who gained notoriety in other walks of life but who were also Episcopalians; and finally, those women who lived deeply spiritual lives and undertook acts of great courage, but who are not present in the dominant narrative, who are little known in the larger church.

Early on in the process of editing this collection, I made the decision that one non-negotiable criteria for the subjects included here is that they be deceased; there is historical value in our capacity to look backward on a life in order to gain perspective and assess a person's contribution in full context. Similarly, I made an early decision to focus on women who were members of the Episcopal Church in the United States, including Anglican women from the colonial era in regions that became part of the United States and women who lived in other countries that were at one time part of the Episcopal Church, rather than to extend the focus to all Anglicans in North America. Though there would have been value, obviously, in a broader project, the availability of sources, as well as the cultural and ecclesiastical differences between churches in the Anglican Communion, and accounting for these differences, suggested to me that it was more practical to set the narrower focus.

The documents in this collection were selected for their capacity to give an insight into a subject's understanding of her *own* vocation in her *own* time. Thus I have refrained from twenty-first century intrusions into the texts. For instance, though I would evaluate my own writing based on the criteria of fully inclusive language for God and humankind, that criteria does not hold for persons living in another age, whose ethos generated *different* questions about the relationships between God, humankind, and the use of language.

During the course of the research for this project I have been asked, on occasion, why only women were selected for this particular collection? Though the number of sources that document women's participation in the Episcopal Church, or any church for that matter, have increased dramatically over the past twenty-five years, a great deal of work still needs to be done before a balance is effected between the number of women studied in comparison to the number of men.

Further, a collection of documents in particular, stresses the autobiographical basis for contextual theology. "Telling my story is not itself theology but a basis for theology," writes Jung Young Lee, "indeed the primary context for doing my theology. This is why one cannot do theology for another. If theology is contextual, it must certainly be at root autobiographical."[3] Thus these collected voices of Anglican and Episcopal women living in the past are a part of the larger faith story of the Episcopal Church; how God has formed us, nurtured us, and allows us to change over time.

One of the roots of prophetic action is history. A knowledge of the identities, beliefs, ideas, and actions of persons living in the past is vital to those of us who purport to lead the church into the future. Thus the voices of the women collected here not only speak to their own age, but to those of us who share in their humanity; to those of us who also seek a larger freedom through the Episcopal Church, and who strive for justice and peace for all people. As Toni Morrison suggests:

> While it may be true that the future, your future, is in your hands, the past is also in your hands... History has its flexible side. Of course it can be repeated disastrously, or it can be reformed in new guises, but it can also be critiqued... And each time we critique and examine it, it can deliver other information and insight that in fact changes what we already know about it... My point is, you are not bound by the future, and, more important, you are not bound by the past. The past can be more liberating than the future if you are willing to identify its evasions, its distortions, its lies, and unleash its secrets and truths. So I want to wish you not only the brightest of futures but also the best of pasts.[4]

Sheryl A. Kujawa-Holbrook
Cambridge, Massachusetts
Monday in Easter Week, 2002

NOTES

[1] Pauli Murray, *Dark Testament and other Poems* (Norwalk: Silvermine, 1970); 12.

[2] Howard Thurman, *Inward Journey* (Richmond, Indiana: Friends United Press, 1973); 21-22.

[3] Jung Young Lee, *Marginality: The Key to Multicultural Theology* (Augsburg: Minneapolis, 1995); 7.

[4] Toni Morrison, June 1992, Duke University Commencement.

MARTHA LAURENS RAMSAY

(1759-1811)

Martha Laurens Ramsay (1759-1811),[1] wife, mother, spiritual diarist, was born in 1759 to Henry Laurens and Eleanor Ball Lauren. Her father was an important figure in the American Revolution, and one of the most prosperous planters and slave importers in the Carolinas; her mother was also from a planter's family. Martha was the fifth of Henry Laurens' thirteen children. Her mother died in 1770. Though her father encouraged Martha Lauren's academic and artistic gifts—it was said that she could read at three and she was soon proficient in French, geography, and arithmetic, among other subjects—he also insisted that she learn the basics of housekeeping. The Laurens family attended the Anglican Church of St. Philip's in Charles Town, South Carolina, regularly, where Martha was confirmed at the age of twelve.[2]

As a young woman of fourteen, Martha Laurens made a covenant with God, by which she attempted to govern her life. Martha also developed a discipline of daily Bible reading, as well as a regular review of the catechism and other devotional reading, such as seventeenth and eighteenth century divines.[3] She spent her young adulthood in her uncle's home in France, nursing ailing family members and founding a school for village children.

Martha Laurens became the third wife of her father's physician, David Ramsay, in 1787. Ramsay was active in the state legislature and one of the first historians of the American Revolution. Martha Laurens Ramsay bore eleven children in fifteen years; eight survived to adulthood. For the next twenty-four years Martha Laurens Ramsay managed a large household efficiently, supported her husband in his career ventures, and saw to the education of all her children, as well as the training of household slaves. (Though David Ramsay was publicly ambivalent about slavery, Martha's writings are silent.)[4] Both Ramsays were active in the civic life of their community. Martha Laurens Ramsay also assisted her husband in his research and writing. Though she continued to participate in the pastoral offices of the Anglican Church, and had her children baptized there, Martha Laurens Ramsay joined her husband's Independent (Congregational) Church at the time of their marriage. She enjoyed their affiliation with the ministers there, most of who were college friends of David Ramsay.[5]

Martha Laurens Ramsay is one of the few eighteenth-century Southern women who left a written record of her spiritual journey. Her husband had not learned about the existence of her diary until three days before her death; after he read it he was moved to publish it along with a selection of her other writings shortly after her death. While her public life was largely shaped by the men in her life, Martha Laurens Ramsay's interior life—her mind and her soul—showed a deep evolution of consciousness. Certainly, her outward life consisted of the patterns found in the lives of the conventional daughters, wives, and mothers of her era. Martha Laurens Ramsay was also not without her contradictions; her written legacy was largely silent about the domestic life that absorbed most of her years, and slavery, perhaps the largest moral issue of her day. Still, as the record of the spiritual journey of a convicted evangelical Christian, who had absorbed a great deal of scripture in her lifetime, Martha Laurens Ramsay's writings witness to the life of a woman who strove to emulate true discipleship in the midst of life's joys and struggles.

Behind her own Calvinist self-critical worldview, the reader of the *Memoirs of The Life of Martha Laurens Ramsay* is also introduced to a woman of great warmth and substance. The following excerpts allow us to share in a time of great happiness, a day of

Christian worship, and a time of great sorrow after the death of a daughter.

NOTES

[1] The major secondary source on Martha Laurens Ramsay is Joanna Bowen Gillespie, *The Life and Times of Martha Laurens Ramsay, 1759-1811* (Columbia: University of South Carolina Press, 2001). Dr. Gillespie generously provided insights into Martha's life and suggested texts for this collection.

[2] Gillespie, *The Life and Times of Martha Laurens Ramsay,* 1-31.

[3] Ibid, 7-8; 33-34.

[4] Ibid, 173-74; 177.

[5] Ibid, 105-109; 121, 189-90

CR

MARTHA LAURENS RAMSAY
Excerpts from the Memoirs of The Life of Martha Laurens Ramsay[*]

A DAY WELL SPENT

Blessed be God for this day's entertainment. How sweet is the society of lively Christians, when we meet together and spend the hours, not in idle chit chat about dress or weather or such unprofitable themes, but in mutual exhortation and encouragement. How comfortably have I passed this day. In the morning I was at the sanctuary, heard the word of salvation, and sat with pleasure under the teaching of the Gospel. When I returned, met with dear fellow members, and adored together the name of Jesus our Lord. In the afternoon I visited serious friends, and entered on the delightful subject, talked of redeeming love and Christian meekness; and again this evening met with an acquaintance of the same mind, and renewed the delightful converse, and now at night I have been blessed in my retirement, and had great enlargement in prayer both alone and with my servant. I cannot close a day so distinguished for spiritual mercies, without holy elevation, without a song of praise, nor sleep till I have rendered thanks. Praise the Lord, O my soul, and let all that is within me praise his holy name....

NOVEMBER 29, 1797

Since the death of my dear little Jane, which happened the last day of July, after two months of anxiety and suspense, I have been in great weakness of body, and sadness of mind. During the last three weeks of her sickness, I was deeply exercised in soul. Some very especial sins and failures in duty were set home on my conscience; in her sickness I felt the rod due to my departures from God, the unevenness of my walk. I endeavored to seek the Lord by deep contrition, confession of sin, repentance, faith and prayer. I sought the Lord by day, and spent almost every hour of the night (that I could spare from nursing) prostrate before him, taking hardly any bodily rest. I thought if the life of the child should be granted me, it would be an evidence that the Lord, for Christ's sake, had forgiven me those things which with so many tears and such brokenness of spirit, I had bewailed before him; and there were appearances of her recovery. But alas, how vain were my hopes. My child was taken, and I was plunged into the double sorrow of losing a most cherished and beloved infant, and of feeling the stroke as a hiding of the Lord's face, a refusal to be entreated by so great a sinner.

Lord! I desire to be humbled, to acknowledge thy rightful sovereignty over me and mine, to lay my hand upon my mouth and my mouth in the dust before thee...Anything that is not Hell is too good for me...From the death of this baby to the present hour, my body has been in a state of great weakness, and with regard to my soul I have walked in darkness. My will is brought into humble submission to the divine will, but I have had none of the sensible manifestations of the divine presence...which at [other] seasons of affliction have enabled me not only to bow before the Lord but even to rejoice in tribulation. Other trials of a temporal nature I have also undergone at this time, and even now, many things seem to be going against me...yet I would endeavor to...stay myself upon the rock of Israel....

Help me to look back to past experiences, to call to mind thy former answers to prayer, and to trust that thou who has helped me hitherto will not now forsake me…Show me any unrepented sin; discover to me any indulged or hidden iniquity…and give me true repentance which consisteth not only in confessing but in forsaking sin…In all seasons may I walk as becometh a true Christian…Thou knowest my groanings and my sighs and tears are not hid from thee…Make me to dread every sin which might be as a separating wall between my God and my soul. Oh my God, if it be thy will, remove the pressure under which I labor, or give me that thorough resignation of mind that it becometh the creature to exercise toward its Creator.

Oh Father, Son, and Holy Ghost, I give myself up to thee, to be and to do and to bear whatever thou shalt see fit for me during my journey through life…I desire to have my will swallowed up in the divine will…supremely desiring nothing but salvation for me and mine, persuaded that God will order all things better for me than I could by myself…Shall not the Judge of the whole earth do right? O yes, he will…Be not, therefore, cast down O my soul, for whether he gives or takes, he is still my God; and, seeing the whole while I see only in part, will always do better for me than I could for myself.

Resolutions made at this time:

To watch against my easily besetting sin.

To read the word of God with more meditation.

To lift up my heart to the Lord whenever I awake in the night.

To encourage religious conversation in my family on all fit occasions, particularly with my beloved Miss Futerell.

To be more watchful and earnest in inward…prayer…

To be much in prayer for my dear husband, and to endeavor to be to him a useful as well as a loving wife.

To endeavor to see the hand of God in everything, and to undertake nothing without a dependence on and a seeking of his blessing.

Not to let a spirit of indolence get the better of me, in the education of my children. And in this matter, may God most especially help me; for I find when anything presses much on my mind, I am very apt to be listless and inactive in the duty which I owe them.

---

* *Memoirs of The Life of Martha Laurens Ramsay*, David Ramsay, ed. (Boston: S.T. Armstrong, 1812): 82-83; 173-79.

JUDITH LOMAX

(1774-1828)

Judith Lomax (1774-1828), mystic and evangelical, was the first of twelve children born to Thomas and Anne Lomax with prominent family connections in Virginia and Washington, D.C. Her younger brother, John Tayloe Lomax, attended St. John's College in Annapolis and became the first professor of law at the University of Virginia; he eventually became a circuit court judge in Fredericksburg, Virginia.

The Lomax family was torn apart by the deaths of Judith's brother, in 1805, and father, in 1811. Though her father made provisions in his will for his daughters, Judith's financial resources were greatly reduced after his death and were controlled by her brothers. She fled the family home alone for Port Royal, leaving her mother and sisters behind, and boarded in her aunt's home. From this time until the end of her life, Judith Lomax sought to live financially independent from her family. She bought a small house in Port Royal, and later, with her health failing, moved to Fredericksburg to live with her mother and sister.[1]

Although self-described as a "lonely Episcopalian" in Port Royal, Judith Lomax became an active participant in nearly every evangelical religious gathering in town. She was a regular participant at worship services and she taught in the Sabbath Schools. She attended the local conventions of three denominations – Episcopal, Methodist, and Baptist. Judith Lomax was captivated by a good sermon and heard first-hand the preaching of two of the leading evangelicals in antebellum Virginia, Channing Moore and William Meade. Like these two distinguished bishops, Lomax incorporated into her belief system a loyalty to the Episcopal tradition along with a belief in the doctrines of conversion and revivalism. At times, however, she also yearned for Holy Communion and the more liturgical aspects of the Episcopal Church. Her Sabbath Journal is filled with theological discourse. From her home, Judith Lomax grew theologically through reading, education, and connections with the wider church. In turn, she contributed her spirit and energy to the life of her community and charitable endeavors.

Judith Lomax's spirituality was intense and grew more passionate throughout her life. Jesus was her primary companion on earth and in heaven. Gifted with mystical insights, she defined Christ as her "heavenly bridegroom," and herself as the "spouse of God," and "bride of Christ." When her health began to fail, necessitating the move to Fredericksburg, Judith Lomax began to worship regularly at St. George's Church, where she was buried. She prepared to die by continuing to read, to write, to worship, to teach, and to support benevolent causes. She was praised for her spiritual gifts throughout her community at the time of her death in 1828.[2]

In the following excerpts from her Sabbath Journal, Judith Lomax shares her religious activities and reflections over an almost two-mouth period in late 1819.

NOTES

[1] What is known about Judith Lomax's life can be found in the introduction to her journal: *The Sabbath Journal of Judith Lomax* (1774-1828) (Atlanta: Scholars Press, 1999): 7-27. Used with permission of the American Academy of Religion, www.aarweb.org.

[2] Ibid, 15-27.

JUDITH LOMAX
Excerpts from A Sabbath Journal, 1774-1828*

October 28 [1819]

Have met with a disappointment in not being able to get on to a meeting 15 Miles below this.—a meeting of Episcopal Ministers, from whose preaching I anticipated much profit, and expected to have been highly gratified,—but it is all for the best, and I am well convinced that disappointments are not unfrequently beneficial to us.—they serve methinks to humble our proud rebellious spirits, and make us to feel our dependance on that great and omnipotent Being who deals out our portions in due season.—As for me, a poor needy worm of the dust, who every day feel my own imperfect state, it is good I am convinced that I should be kept low in comforts.—my God sees fit that it should be so, were it otherwise, I might perhaps acquire spiritual pride, be vainly puff'd up, and forget how very weak and insufficient a being I am— rather than it should be so, keep me still my heavenly Father humbled low at the foot-stool of thy power, there let me look to Jesus, the divine mediator! from whom cometh every good and perfect gift.—and while I own him as the great high Priest, the rich attoning sacrifice, let me from his fountain, drink endless pleasures in.—Give me to partake of his meek, and lowly spirit.—so may I be ever kept from murmuring, and repining at his all wise dispensations.—and so shall I ever enjoy that peace of mind which passeth all understanding.—Jesus thou great Bishop and Shepherd of Souls! it is thou alone who knowest what is good for me, for thou art the wisest, and the best!—keep me, oh keep me ever thine!—shadow me with thine almighty wings, and let me be still found waiting at thy feet, til all thy will be done.—

[...] again feel that the love of God, a wish to serve him, [preeminent] in my mind,—My Saviour God, fills every avenue of my heart.— Then let me be content, and ever trust in thee my lord, "Sweetly waiting at thy feet, till all thy will be done."—

Sabbath Morn

I have been looking over my last exercise commited to this sheet, and the blush of shame mantles my cheek, to find in it something like a murmuring spirit something like a disgust for Life,—oh, let me guard against a repining spirit! let me not be ungratefully remindful of the numberless blessings daily shower'd upon me by the bountiful hand of a merciful, and omnipotent Father in heaven.—My Life is quite a happy one, at least I think so, when I compare it with the Lot of many,—oh, surely I ought to be happy, and ought to be very thankful, when I remember all that a God, a redeeming Saviour, has done for me,—think of how the Lord has dealt with me, a poor unworthy worm of the dust.—how "he has raised me out of the mire and pit," and placed my feet on a rock,—how he has given me not only temporal comforts, but greater still, spiritual ones, that I trust shall last forever, even when all that is temporal, shall crumble in decay.—oh! when I think of these things, when I think of all his marvelous great kindness, to one who has been unworthy of even his slightest blessing, I feel ready to exclaim in the words of the Psalmist,—"Praise the Lord, oh my soul, and all that is within me, praise his holy name."—But an indulged child, tho it may be very happy while traveling, and wandering abroad, yet will it some-times think of the home of its Father, will sometimes feel a longing desire to be there, not so much, that it feels weary of its pilgrimage, but in the affection of its heart, it sighs to behold the beaming countenance of a fond Parent, to bask forever in the sun-shine of his presence, and in [so] blest a home, to feel safely shelter'd from every storm!

> "Vanish then this world of shadows,
> Pass the former things away;
> Lord appear! appear to glad us,
> With the dawn of endless day.
> O conclude this mortal story;
> Throw the universe aside;
> Come eternal King of glory,
> Now descend—and take thy Bride."

—On Thursday our Venerable Bishop will preach here—[grac]ious is God in sending his chosen servants to this rebell[ious] Village!—oh!

why are the People like the deaf Adder that stoppeth her ears, which refuseth to hear the voice of the charmer, charm [...] never so wisely?"—I had thought the *dear Episcopal* had intirely given us up,—that they had beheld the Village, that they all thought "there was not *one* righteous,—no *not one*." and that they had one, and *all* deserted us *forever*.—and now lo! here comes the very head of the Church.—oh, that his visit may be blest!—It glads my heart to think of his coming!—How the Christian delights to taste of the celestial fountain!—and how having once tasted we thirst for more,—again we thirst,—deeper, and deeper we drink, and still the stream flows on, purer, and more pure, fraught with Nepenthean virtue.

Thursday Morn

Visited on her deathbed the oldest inhabitant of this Village, the dews of death were on her, she was dying fast, but whilst I held her clammy hand, she cast on me an affectionate look, she seem'd truly happy, and addressing me by name, observed, that tho it was hard for the body and soul to part, yet it was a blessed thing to go to Jesus, that she felt she should soon be with him, her countenance was expressive of resignation and triumphant joy.—"Blessed are they who die in the Lord!"—I was call'd from her bed-side to see our dear Bishop, who had just arrived in the Village, I follow'd him to the Sanctuary of God, and heard him deliver an excellent Sermon, his subject was the 3d chapt. of the Gospel of St. John, beginning at the 14th Verse.—"And as Moses lifted up the Serpent in the Wilderness etc."—oh, it was a glorious Sermon!

[...]

November 28

Have [...] return'd from a most delightful visit to King George County, [heard] three more discourses from the dear, excellent Bishop, all of [them] good and melting the heart to good,—oh, how highly favor'd [...]—may all that I have heard from Bishop More, both in and out of the Pulpit, be sanctified to me!—two days did I spend with him at Mr. George Johnson's enjoying the privilege of spiritual conversation, such days, such hours, are not to be effaced from my remembrance,—Ever will I remember my dear spiritual Father, and the

beloved pious People of King George County! oh! it was sweetly gratifying to every feeling of my sensitive mind, after the divine service of
the day, and the excellent sermon was over; to feel my hand alternately
grasp'd by my beloved Mrs. Mason and dear Anne Yates, introducing
me to all their pious Friends,— Thus have I found friends in the People
of God!—But it is to the *great first cause* that I owe it all, it is from the
inexhaustable fountain of Christ's love, that the love of his people
spring,—and "Lord! what am I, that thou art thus mindful of me?"—
But "continue forth thy loving kindness," and let us the people of thy
care, continue to love on, while here on earth, and at the last, be brought
in a holy, and united band, united in Christ, to dwell forevermore in his
presence, in the heaven, of heavens, where there is Life, and joy, and
Love forevermore.— The Bishop return'd with me to the Village, and
comply'd with the request I was commission'd to make to him, namely
to perform the burial service over the Grave of the deceased old Lady,
who had been a member of our Church.

December 1

Have commenced making some improvements in my habitation,
puting a new inclosure, etc.—my mind has been much exercised by
it,—whether might not the money I shall bestow on it, have been better
appropriated by giving to the poor, and in aiding with it religious institutions?—but then I have comfort in thinking that the workman who I
imploy is a poor Man with a family, the money will be the reward of the
industry of an indigent Man, who wants it,—The new inclosure will
secure me from depredations on my little property, so that I can in
leisure moments indulge myself in cultivating my plants etc.. and seeing them bloom beneath my fostering care.—oh, how I love to behold
the power of God exemplified through all his works! I love to watch the
growth of vegetation, and mark how his glory shines in the expanding
of even an infant bud!—I am the most domestic animal alive,—I can
love the rose that entwines itself at my window,—The tree that shades
my dwelling,—and [the] Violet that breathes its perfume around it, as
tho they were objects warm'd by Vitality, for in the affection of my
heart, I exclaim,— "my Father made them all!" and I seem to have a
love for all, both animate, and inanimate, that my heavenly Father has
created.—I adore him through all his works !—I value all his gifts and

the many comforts with which he has bless'd me.—and in the morning when I awake up after refreshing slumbers, I bless him for it, and am thankful for the downy couch on which I have reposed, and dreamt of happiness—it is sweet to be a Christian, and to feel the love of God pervading every avenue of the heart.

---

* *The Sabbath Journal of Judith Lomax (1774-1828)*, Laura Hobgood-Oster, ed. (Atlanta: Scholars Press, 1999): 40-43. Used with permission of the American Academy of Religion, www.aarweb.org.

SOJOURNER TRUTH

(c. 1797-1883)

Sojourner Truth (c. 1797-1883), preacher, abolitionist, reformer, was born in a Dutch settlement in Ulster County, New York. Named Isabella Baumfree at birth, her parents, James and Betsy, were slaves. Truth experienced a great deal of cruelty and was sold to different masters several times during her childhood. Sojourner Truth's first language was Dutch, though she learned English after she was sold to an English-speaking owner at age eleven. From 1810-1827, she lived in a household in New Paltz, New York, and had at least five children with a slave named Thomas; of the four who survived infancy, two were sold away. In 1827—a year before the mandatory emancipation of slaves in New York State—she fled slavery with the assistance of Quaker friends. Sojourner Truth joined the Mother Zion African Methodist Episcopal Church when African-Americans were denied membership in St. George's Church, Philadelphia.[1]

Sojourner Truth was a mystic who had visions and heard voices that she experienced as from God. In 1829, she moved to New York and began a ministry as a street preacher and evangelist, and did missionary work among the poor. In 1843, she had a spiritual experience that inspired her to set out on her own and change her name, from Isabella Baumfree to Sojourner Truth. She set off on a preaching tour, walking from Long Island to Connecticut, eventually ending up in Northampton, Maine. In Maine she joined the Northampton Association for Education and Industry, a community that included abolitionists such as Frederick Douglas, William Lloyd Garrison, and Olive Gilbert. Sojourner Truth supported herself on the proceeds from the publication of her story, *The Narrative of Sojourner Truth,* as dictated to Gilbert. In the 1850s, she undertook a popular speaking tour throughout the Midwest, and eventually settled in Battle Creek, Michigan.[2] Her most famous speech, "Arn't I a Woman?" was given at a woman's rights convention in Akron, Ohio in 1851.

After the Civil War, Sojourner Truth continued in public speaking and worked tirelessly to assist newly freed slaves. She was also known as the "Miriam of the Later Exodus."[3] Sojourner Truth continued her active ministry with reform causes until illness forced her to retire; she died in Michigan in 1883. She is commemorated in the Episcopal calendar on July 20 along with Amelia Bloomer, Elizabeth Cady Stanton, and Harriet Ross Tubman. The following excerpt is from her speech to the Fourth National Woman's Rights Convention in New York City in 1853.

NOTES

[1] *Lesser Feasts and Fasts* (2000) (New York: Church Publishing, 2001): 295-96. The primary source on Sojourner Truth is Olive Gilbert, *The Narrative of Sojourner Truth* (Battle Creek, Michigan, 1878).

[2] Carla L. Peterson, *Doers Of The Word: African-American Women Speakers an Writers in the North* (1830-1880) (New Brunswick: Rutgers University Press, 1998.): 24-28.

[3] LFF, 293.

SOJOURNER TRUTH

"I Suppose I am About the Only Colored Woman That Goes About to Speak for the Rights of Colored Women"*

Is it not good for me to come and draw forth a spirit, to see what kind of spirit people are of? I see that some of you have got the spirit of a goose, and some have got the spirit of a snake. I feel at home here. I come to you, citizens of New York, as I suppose you ought to be. I am a citizen of the state of New York; I was born in it, and I was a slave in the state of New York; and now I am a good citizen of this State. I was born here, and I can tell you I feel at home here. I've been lookin' round and watchin' things, and I know a little mite 'bout Woman's Rights, too. I come forth to speak 'bout Woman's Rights, and want to throw in my little mite, to keep the scales a-movin'. I know that it feels a kind o' hissin' and ticklin' like to see a colored woman get up and tell you about things, and Woman's Rights. We have all been thrown down so low that nobody thought we'd ever get up again; but we have been long enough trodden now; we will come up again, and now I am here.

I was a-thinkin', when I see women contendin' for their rights, I was a-thinkin' what a difference there is now, and what there was in old times. I have only a few minutes to speak; but in the old times the kings of the earth would hear a woman. There was a king in the Scriptures; and then it was the kings of the earth would kill a woman if she come into their presence; but Queen Esther come forth, for she was oppressed, and felt there was a great wrong, and she said I will die or I will bring my complaint before the king. Should the king of the United States be greater, or more crueler, or more harder? But the king, he raised up his sceptre and said: "Thy request shall be granted unto thee—to the half of my kingdom will I grant it to thee!" Then he said he would hang Haman on the gallows he had made up high. But that is not what women come forward to contend. The women want their rights as Esther. She only wanted to explain her rights. And he was so liberal that he said, "the half of my kingdom shall be granted to thee," and he did not wait for her to ask, he was so liberal with her.

Now, women do not ask half of a kingdom, but their rights, and they don't get 'em. When she comes to demand 'em, don't you hear how sons hiss their mothers like snakes, because they ask for their rights; and can they ask for anything less? The king ordered Haman to be hung on the gallows which he prepared to hang others; but I do not want any man to be killed, but I am sorry to see them so short-minded. But we'll have our rights; see if we don't; and you can't stop us from them; see if you can. You may hiss as much as you like, but it is comin'. Women don't get half as much rights as they ought to; we want more, and we will have it. Jesus says: "What I say to one, I say to all—watch!" I'm a-watchin'. God says: "Honor your father and your mother." Sons and daughters ought to behave themselves before their mothers, but they do not. I can see them a-laughin' and pointin' at their mothers up here on the stage. They hiss when an aged woman comes forth. If they'd been brought up proper they'd have known better than hissing like snakes and geese. I'm 'round watchin' these things, and I wanted to come up and say these few things to you, and I'm glad of the hearin' you give me. I wanted to tell you a mite about Woman's Rights, and so I came out and said so. I am sittin' among you to watch; and every once and a while I will come out and tell you what time of night it is.

---

* Sojourner Truth delivered this speech at the Fourth National Woman's Rights Convention in New York City, 1853. Reprinted from *Black Women in White America: A Documentary History*, Gerda Lerner, ed. (New York, 1972): 567-568.

FRANCES MARIA MULLIGAN HILL

(1799-1884)

rances Maria Mulligan Hill (1799-1884), missionary and educator, was born to a prominent family in New York City. Her father, John Mulligan, was a lawyer in the office of Alexander Hamilton and her grandfather served George Washington. Her mother was Elizabeth Winter Mulligan; she and her husband had nine children. The Mulligans owned a mansion on Cedar Street, where Frances was raised. The family probably attended Trinity Church in Manhattan.

In 1821, Frances Mulligan married Henry Hill, a graduate of Columbia College, banker, and superintendent of the Sunday school at St. George's Church. The couple had no children. In 1829, Henry Hill resigned his financial career to enter the Protestant Episcopal Seminary in Virginia. After his ordination in 1830, the couple volunteered for service as educational missionaries in the first foreign mission of the Episcopal Church in Greece.[1]

Once in Greece, the Hills set up a printing press and opened schools. They respected the Orthodox faith of their hosts, but sought "through education and the distribution of good literature in the vernacular, to raise the level of Greek religious life."[2]

Over a five-year period, Frances Hill's school grew from 20 children in a dilapidated building to over 650 children spread throughout a new building. The schools flourished throughout the 1830s, and the Hill's efforts received a great deal of support from the Episcopal mission committee at home, as well as from Greek authorities. Frances Hill's teacher training course gained the support of educator Emma Willard, principal of the Female Seminary in Troy, New York. Willard, also an Episcopalian, formed a Society for the Advancement of Female Education in Greece. Monies raised by the society paid for teacher training for young women in Greece.

Besides the mission schools, the Hills eventually opened a tuition-based boarding school for wealthy girls. Frances Hill became the superintendent of all the girls schools, including the boarding school, an elementary school, and an industrial school, and managed a household of about eighty. During her husband's furlough in the United States during 1841, she had oversight for the entire mission.

After John Henry Hill's return to Greece in 1842, a newspaper in Athens publicly attacked the Hills. While parents and others associated with the school supported the couple, Frances' health suffered and it forced the mission to close temporarily. A year later three of the schools reopened. At the same time, the Episcopal mission committee had shifted its priorities from Greece to Africa and Asia, which threatened to close the mission all together. Despite the reduced level of support from the United States, the Hills rallied their supporters and continued their work on a reduced budget. Under Frances' leadership the girls' elementary school became one of the best in the country, with a curriculum that included ancient Greek, geography, and arithmetic. She also continued her work in teacher training. Frances and John Henry Hill retired in 1869; the mission finally closed in 1882-1883. At the time of her retirement, over 5000 Greek girls from various economic backgrounds had "passed under Mrs. Hill's Christian instruction."[3]

The following document from Frances Hill shares her own perspective on the educational needs of girls.

NOTES

[1] For biographical information on Frances M. Hill see, *Woman's Record*, Sarah Josepha Hale, ed. (New York: Harper & Brothers, Publishers, 1853): 868-70. Both Frances Hill and John Henry Hill, were contributors to *The Spirit of Missions*, 1836-1884.

[2] Ibid.

[3] Ibid.

FRANCES MARIA MULLIGAN HILL*
"A Letter from Frances M. Hill Concerning the Progress of Female Education in Greece."

"We began with the *alphabet!* but even before the point had been reached where elementary education advances to that of a higher order, circumstances already pointed out the necessity of providing for it. Our views were transmitted to some of our friends in the United States—they met with a gratifying response from many ladies of very high character in our own communion; and some ladies of different denominations united in a society, under the direction of Mrs. Emma Willard of Troy, New York, for the avowed purpose of educating female teachers in Greece under our immediate care and superintendence. This department continued in very successful operation from 1834 to 1842. In the meanwhile, and during this period, another progressive change took place. Athens, which had been under the Turkish rule until 1833, became in 1834 the capital of the new kingdom of Greece, and the families of those who were connected with government, came to reside in Athens. No provision having been made in any quarter for the education of the daughters of these families, an appeal to us on the part of the parents of such to permit their daughters to enjoy those privileges of education which we were affording to the native females of Athens exclusively, could not be put aside—and in this manner, the daughters of the most influential and best educated families in Greece, were added to those who were already with us and who were destined to be employed in extending the same benefits to their fellow countrywomen. About the same time, in consequence of the destitution of means which existed nearly throughout the Levant, applications were made to us from the more wealthy families in Smyrna and Constantinople, and Jassy and Bucharest, in the North and East, as well as from the Ionian Islands in the West. And at one period we actually had pupils from all those places congregated under our roof. The domestic establishment of our Mission from 1837 to 1842, embraced 60 pupils, while at the same time there were no less than from 500 to 600 in daily attendance upon the schools, as *externes*. The Greeks, however, with a laudable pride, were not willing to allow strangers to do everything for them. They were not long in setting on foot measures for bearing a part themselves, in the great work of female education. A society was formed ... which had for one of its objects the preparation of female teachers. To this society, in 1842, we made over the whole of our domestic establishment. The necessity which had imposed upon us this duty, had ceaed, and the *impulse* had been given: the work, moreover, had become much too laborious for those who were engaged in it. The funds of that Society are continually increasing by liberal donations from wealthy Greeks residing in Germany, in the Danube provinces, and elsewhere.

With regard to the number of pupils who have been educated in our schools, it would be difficult to make an exact estimate. If we assume 250 for the annual average of such as had completed their education, and gone out into the world; and if we commence our reckoning from 1836, i.e. five years after we commenced our labours here, we may fairly, I think, put down the number at 3500. I have no wish to exaggerate numbers, and I hope I am within the limit of facts.

Although there are no female schools which can, strictly speaking, be called *branches* of the Mission School at Athens, there is scarcely one throughout the Kingdom, of which either the Directresses or some of the Teachers, have not been educated, wholly or in part, by us. For years we had a Normal School for the education of female teachers, sent to us by the Government from different provinces of the Kingdom. Several of these, by the terms of the agreement we made with the Government, after being examined and receiving their Diplomas, were sent into the Morea and other parts to open schools in their respective districts as Government Teachers. One of these laboured most effectually in the island of *Hydra* for seven years, where no school for females had *ever existed*. The school she established is still continued there, and is very flourishing—but she, after seven years' labour there, returned, and is now one of the most efficient of our teachers in the Mission Schools.

The effects of female education here has been most gratifying. We have had the pleasure of observing many of our early pupils in domestic life, as wives and mothers at the head of their families, discharging the high trust reposed in them, with a care and assiduity most exemplary and praiseworthy. We know of many instances where the Mother who had been educated under our eye, has waited with anxiety for the period when she could place her children under the salutary influence of our system of instruction. We have seen the powerful effect of a good and virtuous education overcoming the custom of ages, and the power of *Mammon*. Many parents who have had *no other dowry* to bestow upon their daughters but this—"that they had been educated in our schools,"—have married their daughters to men of education and good sense, able to support them well—and we have seen their mothers coming to us with tears of gratitude, acknowledging the lasting benefits conferred by education, when they found that an instructed mind was prized by men of sense, more than money or lands.

This is a concise summary of the progress of female education in Greece; and I think *I may add* that the female sex has made greater use of their advantages, and greater improvement in proportion to their advantages, than the male sex."

---

* This letter was reprinted in *Woman's Record*, Sarah Josepha Hale, ed. (New York, Harper & Brothers, 1853): 868-69. Sarah Josepha Hale was also an Episcopalian.

CATHARINE E. BEECHER

(1800-1878)

Catharine E. Beecher (1800-1878), author and educator, was the first child of the Presbyterian minister, Lyman Beecher, famous for his evangelical faith, his revivals, and for his support to the temperance and other moral reform movements. Catharine was born in East Hampton, New York in 1800, and, as the oldest, took responsibility for the large Beecher household at age sixteen, upon her mother's death. Though she briefly attended school in Litchfield, Connecticut, Catharine Beecher always considered her home training in the domestic arts and morality as her "true education" and vocation.

As an educator and reformer, Catharine Beecher was concerned about the large numbers of children, particularly girls, throughout the United States who lived unschooled. In 1823, she established a school in Hartford, Connecticut where she was one of the first educators to offer calisthenics and training in teaching and domestic arts for girls. Throughout the 1830s and 40s she traveled extensively through-out the Midwest, opening a school in Cincinnati, Ohio, writing and lecturing on "female education," and supporting the temperance movement.

The strains of Catharine Beecher's religious and intellectual thought came together in her belief in a "woman's sphere." Beecher saw women as the moral saviors of society, and the female vocation as duty and sacrifice to God and to the family. She believed that the "intellectual culture in the female mind, is combined with the spirit of religion which so strongly enforces the appropriate duties of a woman's sphere."[1] Although Beecher was unsympathetic to reformers such as nineteenth-century abolitionists and feminists who she felt agitated in a manner beyond woman's unique domestic role, she was not callous towards the marginalized and the oppressed. Rather, she wrote and spoke passionately against the many conditions that exploited women and left them untrained for their true calling. Moreover, Beecher was indignant about the "national sin of slavery" and the "piracy" of the slave trade.[2] She believed that the appropriate response by Christian females to the sin of slavery was through the "maxims of peace and charity, which it is in the power of the females of our country to advocate, both by example and by entreaties."[3]

Catharine Beecher was in delicate health for most of her life, and experienced several nervous breakdowns. She frequented many different health establishments, and died in Elmira, New York, in 1878, where she traveled to take a water cure. Through her work as an author she supported herself and her numerous causes. Some of her most notable works include *Letters on the Difficulties of Religion* (1836), *A Treatise on Domestic Economy* (1841), and *Common Sense Applied to Religion* (1857).

Uncomfortable with the Calvinism of her father, Catharine Beecher—as did her sister, Harriet Beecher Stowe—converted to the Episcopal Church. Beecher felt more spiritual and intellectual freedom in the Episcopal Church and agreed with its emphasis on religious training and instruction in childhood rather than the Calvinist emphasis on regeneration. Her *Religious Training of Children* was completed in 1864 just as she was confirmed in the Episcopal Church. The document that follows is one example from Catharine's correspondence after the publication of the book in response to her reader's queries about the religious training of children and her own spiritual journey into the Episcopal church.

NOTES

[1] Catharine E. Beecher, *An Essay on Slavery on Slavery and Abolitionism, with reference to the duty of American females* (Philadelphia: Henry Perkins, 1837): 109.

[2] Ibid.

[3] Ibid, 136.

☙

CATHARINE E. BEECHER
"From the Author to a Mother":
An Excerpt from
Religious Training of Children*

My dear friend,—You ask why I have joined the Episcopal Church, and also why, in doing so, I was confirmed. The first question you will find answered in the proof-sheets I send with this. As to the rite of confirmation, I regard it, in reference to one of my character and circumstances, simply as a courteous compliance with the religious rules of the Christian family I enter, which there is no proper cause for refusing. On the same principle, were I a minister of another denomination, on entering, I should comply with the rules of this church as to ordination; not because I do, but because I do not deem any particular form very important, and so could conscientiously yield to the customs of the Christian community I should enter.

In reflecting on my own course in this matter, and also on the religious condition of your dear children, I am led to present, for your and their consideration, some reasons for their following my example.

Your children now are in a false position; one which does them injustice, and makes a false impression on them and on others, which is injurious to their feelings and to their character.

In your religious community they have been trained to feel that those who *profess* religion by "joining a church" are Christians, and those who do not are not Christians. In the Congregational churches the assumption is that young children are not lambs in Christ's fold, but those out of it, whose natures must be new created before they can be taken in.

It is true, your family training has not been after this pattern; but the pulpit ministries, the Sunday-school, the religious books for children, the religious conversation of most with whom they associate, all assume this view. Moreover, no one can be acknowledged as a Christian by access to the Lord's Table till church officers have examined as to evidence of regeneration and of belief in the creed of the church. Now your children do not believe in some important parts of the creed of your church, nor do they regard themselves as "regenerated" in the sense demanded by your church rules and customs.

Meantime, they see among their associates who are members of the church persons with all sorts of faults, from many of which they themselves are free. These are regarded as "regenerated," fitted for heaven, "lights of the world," the "salt of the earth," looking on others out of the church as sinners, destitute of religious principle, and on the way to hell.

The influence of all this is to throw them into an unconscious and almost resentful antagonism with their Christian friends, which has a repelling influence on both sides. No friend who is "a professor" can address them on the subject without an implied assumption of superiority, or as a reprover or adviser.

Now, in the Episcopal Church, all children are assumed to be young Christians—lambs of the fold to be trained to a *higher* Christian life. All regular worshipers and their children are in the church, and entitled to all its privileges on using the appointed forms.

What, then, is confirmation in this church? It is the child assuming the obligations taken by sponsors in its behalf at baptism.

And what is promised at baptism? Not that the sponsors will positively make the child a true spiritual Christian, but that they will see that it is trained to believe the Christian religion, and use other appointed means for the purpose of securing this end by the help of God. At confirmation, the children assume the same obligations; that is, that they will use the appointed means for becoming true spiritual Christians, with the hope and purpose of securing this end by God's help.

Thus "joining the church" in the Congregational denomination is being examined and voted into a close corporation as already true Christians and fitted for heaven. In the Episcopal form all children are in the church, and confirmation is a public acknowledgment of their obligations, and their desire and purpose to fulfill them in future by God's help.

True faith in Christ, or to be "a true Christian," involves, in the first place, the educational belief in Jesus Christ as Lord of our faith and practice, which sponsors can properly promise to secure.

Whoever has this faith has begun to be a true Christian, or taken the first step. Next comes the receiving and understanding of Christ's teachings. This also may be secured by educational training. Lastly, and chiefly, is *obedience* to Christ's teachings in *purpose, feelings,* and *conduct.* The union of all these makes a true spiritual Christian.

But to "feel and act right" and to "obey Christ" are the same thing, so that whoever is habitually trying to feel and act right is really trying to obey Christ, though the purpose may not be conceived of in that form of expression.

Your children are in the position that thousands of the best Christians are now in, who read the Bible, and hear religious teachings concealed in theological theories that veil the character of God and Christ in darkness, or present it in hideous distortions. Owing to this, all that *emotive* part of religious experience, which is usually sought as the chief evidence of piety, is chilled or destroyed. This was my experience for years, and would have continued so through life, had not these false and cruel theories been thrust aside.

Your children are habitually trying to feel and act right, as much so as most of those who are counted good Christians in every sense. Had they been brought up in the English Church, under such training as you have given, they would have grown up consistent and happy Christians from infancy. I know large families in the Episcopal Church where the parents will tell you that they never knew a time from the cradle when each child, according to its measure of mental development, was not a loving and obedient follower of Christ.

What I now would urge is that you influence your children to join the Episcopal Church, not as converted, regenerated saints, as understood in the Congregational sense, but as persons desiring to be good, and seeking the ministries of Christ's religion for this end.

Let them commence the outward acknowledgment of their religious obligations, and their wish and purpose to fulfill them, by the rite of confirmation, and they will feel relieved from all those fretting repellancies that now surround them, and, under more favorable influences, will come out into "the glorious light and liberty of the children of God."

One other point I offer for consideration. To complete a happy Christian character, *veneration*, *devotion*, and *personal love* to the Savior need to be developed, and these also are the result, more or less, of *training*. In the Episcopal Church these elements are *systematically cultivated*. When our Savior gave the Lord's Prayer—for all ages and conditions—he knew that the ignorant and the young could neither understand nor feel half of the sublime and comprehensive truths included in it. We are obliged to begin with *forms* adapted to a higher life than we possess, and by their aid we gradually rise to the spirit which should fill them. The Episcopal Liturgy is based on this principle. It is adapted to the highest stages of Christian life. The young and ignorant are trained to use it when they can neither understand nor feel much that their lips utter. But as years pass, the spiritual element is developed by this and other culture, till, in due time, the heart feels what the lips utter.

When we take those ancient forms, hallowed by so many beautiful and venerable associations—when *we ourselves* speak in our own ears such glorious words of love, devotion, penitence, and thanksgiving, we are taking the surest mode of calling forth and cultivating these beautiful and happifying elements of Christian character.

Through my past life, among my maternal relatives, I have been a frequent attendant on the Episcopal form of worship, but never joined in it except as Congregationalists ordinarily do. The effect of the change, when I began to take part in the responsive service, was very delightful and elevating, and I became a worshiper at church as I never was before. How singular that those sects which demand an emotive experience as the chief evidence of regeneration should have relinquished all the ritual forms most calculated to develop such an experience!

But you may say, "My husband's feelings and his connection with the Congregational denomination are such that I see not how I can go myself or send my children to the Episcopal Church."

If this is an insurmountable difficulty, I would urge another course. Your minister is a truly good man, and the chief desire of his heart is for the salvation of his flock. Go to him with your difficulties, and ask him if he can not contrive some way to take your lambs into the fold. I have known several mothers in the Congregational denomination who have made this plea to their pastor: "Several of my children are as dutiful and conscientious as most adult 'professors.' They wish to be true Christians, and to obey all Christ's teachings, and yet they dare not come out before the 'examining committee' of the church, nor stand up in public profession, to be gazed at as among the converted saints. Can you not so arrange it that they may come into your church privately as those who *wish* to become true spiritual Christians, and are willing to use all the appropriate means of religious training? And if any of them feel that Christ's command, 'This do in remembrance of me,' is obligatory, can not this ordinance be allowed to my children without forsaking your ministry?"

* * * * *

The preceding letter, in modified forms, has been sent to several friends. The following is a specimen of some of the happy results of the course suggested:

> "What a comfort it is to have *all* my children united in religious sympathy! I have never ceased to bless the day when they were confirmed in the Episcopal Church. It has been to them that *gradual education and progression* which they and I hoped for; and I see, every year, how the services and prayers *gain* on them more and more. One of them said to me the other day, that whatever care or trouble she might have when she entered the church, all fell away from her there, and she always came away happy. The *comfort* of it is every thing to her, and I see a steady progress in them all. I know not how to be thankful enough. All cares are light now these heavier cares are lifted."

The author disclaims any invidious comparison as to the *general* results of religious training in the Episcopal Church. The theory of infant depravity has developed its evil tendencies in this as well as in other denominations, especially in undue reliance on church ordinances, perhaps as injurious as undue reliance in other churches on sudden conversions and "revivals."

The distinctive advantage of the Episcopal Church is that young children are regarded as *young Christians* already in the church, and in a course of gradual training to a higher spiritual life. Whenever, therefore, a parent pursues the methods of early training indicated in this work, all the influences of *the church* are adapted to encourage and aid.

But churches that exclude children as aliens, or enemies of God, till re-created, exert an influence disastrous and discouraging to both parents and children.

---

* Catharine E. Beecher, *Religious Education of Children* (New York: Harper & Brothers, 1864): 380-88.

MARIA W. STEWART

(1803-1879)

Maria W. Stewart (1803-1879) was a public speaker and a teacher. She was the first African American woman to speak publicly on behalf of women's rights. Her addresses were delivered in Boston during a time when women did not speak in public—with the exception of Frances Wright and women in Quaker meetings—and when African American women as public speakers were unknown. Maria W. Stewart was a brilliant orator who challenged African American women to develop their full intellectual capacities and to participate in all walks of life, including religion, business, and politics. During her three-year public career in Boston, she delivered four lectures, was published in *The Liberator,* completed a political pamphlet and a collection of meditations; after her move to New York she compiled a collection of her complete works that was published in by William Lloyd Garrison 1835.[1]

After her retirement from public life, Maria W. Stewart moved to New York City where she eventually found work as a teacher in Manhattan and Brooklyn. In 1852 she moved to Baltimore and taught African American children before relocating to Washington, D.C. in 1861. She eventually became matron of the Freedmen's Hospital. In 1871, she founded a Sunday school near Howard University. Denied funding for the Sunday school from the Episcopal Church because she was black, and from black churches because she was

Episcopalian, Stewart was forced to hold prayer meetings in her home. With the support of a few other African American women, the school was eventually moved to St. Mary's, Washington D.C., then pastored by Alexander Crummel.[2]

Maria W. Stewart was born in Hartford, Connecticut in 1803; little is know of her family origin except that her parents were African American and had the name of Miller. Maria was orphaned at the age of five, and "bound out" in the household of a minister until the age of fifteen. Afterwards, she supported herself as a domestic servant. She received little formal education in her childhood and youth, with the exception of Sabbath school classes. Much of the education she did receive, however, was religious instruction and based in biblical teachings. It is not known whether Stewart actually read the texts or had them read to her, however, as a person of an oral culture, it is likely that she had memorized large portions of the bible.[3]

In 1826, Maria Miller married James W. Stewart, a former prisoner of war and veteran of the War of 1812. At the time of their marriage, James W. Stewart was an independent shipping agent. The couple was part of Boston's African American middle class. It was at her husband's suggestion that Maria added his middle initial to her name. Maria W. Stewart was widowed in 1829, and was defrauded of her inheritance by her husband's executors.[4]

Her husband's death caused Maria W. Stewart to reassess her spiritual life. In 1831, she underwent a conversion experience and made a public profession of her faith in Christ. From the beginning Stewart understood that her newfound religious commitment would place her in conflict with the world. For Stewart religion and social justice were inextricably linked; she was an opponent of not only slavery, but of oppression against women and of all political and economic exploitation. Though she was affiliated with a number of denominations, she appears to have settled in the Episcopal Church later in life: "I have suffered martyrdom for the church in one sense; and rejoice that I now feel that I have a home not only in the Protestant Episcopal Church, but in the Holy Catholic Church in the world," she said. Her funeral was held at St. Luke's Episcopal Church, Washington D.C. in 1879.[5]

The following document represents most of the farewell address that marked the end of Maria W. Stewart's public career. Though condemned for speaking in public, she profoundly believed that God consistently spoke through women throughout history.

NOTES

[1] For a discussion of Maria W. Stewarts life and influence see *Maria W. Stewart: America's First Black Women Political Writer*, Marilyn Richardson, ed. (Bloomington: Indiana University Press, 1987): xiii-xvii

[2] Ibid, xvi.

[3] Ibid, 3.

[4] Ibid, 3-8.

[5] Ibid, 8-9; Quoted from page 108.

സ

MARIA W. STEWART
An Excerpt from her Farewell Address to Her Friends in the City of Boston, September 21, 1833[*]

My Respected Friends,

You have heard me observe that the shortness of time, the certainty of death, and the instability of all things here, induce me to turn my thoughts from earth to heaven. Borne down with a heavy load of sin and shame, my conscience filled with remorse; considering the throne of God forever guiltless, and my own eternal condemnation as just, I was at last brought to accept salvation as a free gift, in and through the merits of a crucified Redeemer. I was brought to see...we are saved by grace alone abounding through the Son...

I found that religion was full of benevolence. I found there was joy and peace in believing. I felt as though I had been commanded to come out from the world, be separate, go forward and be baptized. I thought I heard a spiritual interrogation that asked, "Are you able to drink of the cup that I drank? Can you be baptized with the baptism I underwent?"

My heart made the reply, "Yes, Lord, I am able!" Yet, amid these bright hopes, I was filled with fears, lest my hopes were false. I found that sin still lurked within me. It was hard for me to renounce all for Christ when I saw my earthly prospects blasted. It was a bitter cup but I drank it. It was hard for me to say, "Thy will be done," yet I bent my knee and accepted all for my Redeemer's sake. Like so many, I was anxious to retain the world in one hand and religion in the other. "You cannot serve God and evil," sounded in my right ear. With great strength, I plucked out my right hand and eye—as it were—thinking it better to enter the kingdom of God without them rather than have everything cast into hell. Conflicts ended and I received the heart cheering promise, "Neither death, nor life, nor principalities, nor powers, nor things present, nor things to come, shall be able to separate us from the love of Christ Jesus, our Lord."

Truly I could say with St. Paul that at my conversion, I came to the people in the fullness of the gospel of grace. In one city where I visited previously, I saw the flourishing condition of the churches and the progress made in the Sunday schools. I visited Bible Classes and heard of the union that existed in the Female Associations. When I returned later, I could find very few individuals still interested in these things, except Mr. Garrison, and his friend, Mr. Knapp. Hearing that those gentlemen had observed that female influence was powerful, my soul became fired with a holy zeal for your cause. Every nerve and muscle in me was engaged in your behalf. I felt that I had a great work to perform. I was in haste to make a profession of my faith in Christ that I might be about my Father's business. Soon after I made this profession, the Spirit of God was upon me and I stood to speak before many!

When I went home, reflecting upon what I had said, I felt ashamed and did not know where I could hide myself. Something said within me, "Press on and I will be with you." My heart replied, "Lord, if you will be with me, then I will speak for you as long as I live." So far, I have every reason to believe that it is the Holy Spirit operating within my heart that has led me to have any success in the feeble and unworthy efforts I have made.

But let me begin my subject. You have heard that it was said, "Whoever is angry with brothers or sisters without cause shall be in danger at the judgment. But whoever calls another 'fool' is in danger of hell fire." I believe that the Almighty saw the affliction with which I was suffering, the false representations of me, and there was no one to help. I cried unto the Lord in these troubles. For wise and holy purposes known best to God, I was delivered from the hands of my enemies and God vindicated the wrongs in the sight of the people....

I believe that God has put divine testimony within me, and sealed my forehead. With these weapons I have been able to conquer the evil ones of the earth and hell. What if I am a woman? Is not the God of the ancient times still the God of these days of ours? Did God not raise up Deborah to be a mother and a judge in Israel? Did not Queen Esther save the lives of many Jews? Was not Mary Magdalene the first to declare the resurrection of the Lord Jesus? "Come," said the woman of Samaria, "see a man who has told me all things. Is he not the Christ?"

St. Paul declared that it was shameful for a woman to speak in public. Yet our great High Priest Jesus did not condemn any woman for this. Neither will he condemn me, for God will not break the bruised reed, nor quench the smoking flax until judgment is sent forth on all the earth. If St. Paul could know today of our deprivations and our sufferings, I presume he would make no objection to us pleading in public for our rights.

Holy women ministered to Christ and to the apostles. Women of refinement in all ages, more or less, have had some voice in moral, religious, and political subjects. Why the Almighty God has given me the power to speak like this I do not know. Jesus lifted up his head to the Father and said, "I thank you for hiding things from the wise and the prudent that you have revealed to the little ones. It has seemed to be good in your sight."

[...]

Genius and talent will not be hidden by skin.

To return to my theme, I say again that the mighty work of reformation has already begun among our people. The dark clouds of ignorance are being dispersed. The light of science is bursting forth. Knowledge is beginning to flow, and its moral influence will not be extinguished until its refulgent rays have spread over us from East to West, from North to South. This mighty work has begun but it has not yet finished. Christians must awake from their slumbers. True Christianity must flourish before the church will be built up in unity and immorality be suppressed.

Yet, knowing your own prospects are bright, I am about to leave you and perhaps never to return. For I find it is of no use for me as an individual to try to make myself useful among my own in this city. It was contempt for my moral and religious opinions in private that drove me to speak publicly. Had experience shown me more plainly that it was the nature of human beings to crush each other, I would not have thought it so hard.

But my respected friends, let us no longer talk about prejudice of others until prejudice becomes extinct at home. Let us no longer talk of opposition of others until we cease to oppose our own. For as long as these evils exist, to talk about them only is to do no more than to give breath to the air. Though wealth is more highly prized than humble goodness, none of these things move me. With God as my friend and my portion, what do I have to fear? Promotion comes neither from the East nor from the West; I rejoice that I am as I am as long as this is the will of God. Humans in their most important feelings can be but vanity.

Some people have risen from obscurity to eminence. I, although a female of darker hue, far more obscure than the men of whom I speak, will prove virtuous in spite of the fact that I hang my harp upon the willows and bend my head. If it is the will of my heavenly Father to reduce me to a state of poverty and want, I am still ready to say "Amen, so be it." "The foxes have holes and the birds of the air have nests, but the Son of Man has nowhere to lay his head."

During the short period of my Christian warfare, I have indeed had to contend with the fiery darts of the devil. If it were not for the truth that the righteous are kept by the mighty power of God for faith unto salvation, I should have been like the seed on the wayside long ago. There were times when it actually seemed like the powers of earth and hell have combined to overthrow me. Yet, in the midst of these powers, I found the Almighty God to be a friend that is closer to me than anyone. God does not forsake those who lean upon that Love. The Lord may chasten and correct, but that is for our best interest. "As a father has mercy upon his children, so the Lord has mercy on those who fear our God."

Some of you have said, "Do not talk so much about religion. People do not wish to hear you, for we all know these things. Tell us something we do not know." If you knew these things, my friends, you would be much happier and far more prosperous than you are now....Religion is the most glorious of the themes about which mortals speak. The older it grows, the more new beauty it shows. Earth, with its brilliant attractions, appears as nothing by comparison with religion. Religion is a fountain that never dries up. Those who drink of it shall never thirst. It is a well of water springing up in the spirit for everlasting life.

Those ideas of greatness that are held up to us are no more than delusions, airy visions that we shall never realize. All that we say or do can never elevate us, for the important things are those that we and God do together. How?

Let us stop all political discussion in our behalf, for these, in my opinion, sow only discord and strengthen the seeds of prejudice. A spirit of animosity has already arisen, and unless it is quenched, it will burst forth as a fire and devour us. Our young will be slain by the sword. It is God's will that our condition should be in such a way....Shall the clay say to the creator, "Why have you created me thus?" It is time to stop the political discussions and when our day comes for deliverance, God will provide a way for us to escape and fight our own battles.

Finally, my people, let us follow in God's ways and in the way of peace. Cultivate your own minds and morals. Real merit will elevate you! Pure religion will burst your fetters. Turn your attention to industry, and try to please your employers. Save what you earn; remember that in the grave all distinction withers. High and low are equal.

I draw to my conclusion now. I will long remember the sympathy and kindness of my friends, especially those who have stood by me in the midst of difficulties. May many blessings rest upon them. Gratitude is the only gift I have to offer, but a rich reward awaits them.

To my friends who remain unconverted, I say that my frame will shortly be laid to rest in the ground and lie in ruins. O solemn thought! But why should I revolt, for it is the glorious hope of blessed immortality beyond the grave that has supported me through this vale of tears.

Who among you will strive to meet me at the right hand of Christ? The great day of retribution is fast approaching and who shall abide that coming? You are forming characters for eternity. As you live, so shall you die. As death leaves you, so judgment will find you.

Then shall we receive the glorious welcome, "Come you blessed of my Father, inherit the kingdom prepared for you from before the foundation of the world." Or hear the heart rendering curse, "Depart from me you wicked into the everlasting fire prepared for the devil and his angels." When thrice ten thousand years have rolled away, eternity will be but just begun. Your ideas will just have begun to expand. O eternity, who can fathom thine end or comprehend thy beginning?

Dearly beloved, I have made myself contemptible in some eyes that I may win over some others. It has been like labor in vain. "Paul may plant, and Apollos water, but God alone giveth the increase." To my brothers and sisters in the church, I say, Be clothed with the breastplate of righteousness and have yourself wrapped with the garment of truth, prepared to meet your Bridegroom at his coming. Blessed are those servants who are found watching.

Farewell! In a few short years from now, we shall meet in those upper regions where parting will be no more. There we will sing and shout and shout and sing, and make heaven's high arches ring. There we shall range in rich pastures, and partake of those living streams that shall never dry. O, blissful thought! Hatred and contention shall cease, and we shall join with the redeemed millions of people in giving glory to the Lamb that was slain and to the One who sits upon the throne! Eye has not seen, ear has not heard, nor has it yet entered into the heart of anyone to conceive of the joys that are prepared for those who love God.

Thus far, my life has been almost a life of total disappointment. God has tried me as if by fire. Well was I aware that if I contended boldly for the cause of God, I would suffer. Yet I chose to suffer affliction with my people rather than to enjoy the pleasures of sin for such a short time. I believe that the glorious declaration is about to be made for me that was made to God's ancient covenant people by the prophet, "Comfort, take comfort my people. Say unto her that her warfare is accomplished and her iniquities are pardoned." I believe that a rich reward awaits me, if not in this world, then in the world to come.

Oh, blessed hope. The bitterness of my soul has departed from those who endeavored to discourage and prevent me from Christian progress. I can now forgive my enemies and bless those who hated me. Cheerfully can I pray for those who have despitefully used and persecuted me.

May you fare well!

---

* The essay is taken from a copy of the *Productions of Mrs. Maria W. Stewart* (Boston: Friends of Freedom and Virtue, 1835), found in the Boston Public Library and the Schomberg Center for Research in Afro-American Culture, New York.

HARRIET BEECHER STOWE

(1811-1896)

Harriet Beecher Stowe (1811-1896)[1], author, was born in Litchfield, Connecticut, in 1811, into one of the most prominent religious and reform-minded families of her day. Her father was a renowned Congregational minister, Lyman Beecher. Her mother, Roxana Foote Beecher, died when Harriet was four. His wife's death left Lyman Beecher in despair; Harriet and the younger children were raised by a combination of their sisters, aunts, and their grandmother Foote, an Episcopalian. It was through the influence of her grandmother and her aunt and godmother, Harriet Foote, that Harriet Beecher was first introduced to the Book of Common Prayer and the catechism.[2]

Lyman Beecher remarried a few years later, though his second wife never became a strong maternal presence to his children. As a child, Harriet Beecher attended an exclusive girls' school in Litchfield; at thirteen she enrolled in the school founded by her sister Catharine E. Beecher in Hartford. From 1832 to 1850 Harriet Beecher Stowe lived in Cincinnati, Ohio, where her father was president of Lane Theological Seminary.

In 1836, Harriet married the widowed Lane seminary professor Calvin Stowe, and within the first seven years of marriage bore five children. In order to supplement the family's income, Harriet began to write short stories. In 1850, when the South threatened to secede from the union, Harriet Beecher Stowe began to write a serial denouncing slavery. The serial was published as a novel in 1852, *Uncle Tom's Cabin,* and became one of the more influential works in American History. The novel analyzed slavery in New England, the Midwest, and the South during the time of the Fugitive Slave Law. Stowe stressed the cruelty, dehumanization, and moral depravity of slavery for the slaves, as well as for those who tolerated and profited from it. Although Stowe wrote other novels during her career, none of her later works had the impact of *Uncle Tom's Cabin.* A prolific writer, between 1862 and 1884 Harriet Beecher Stowe wrote more than a book a year.

Calvin and Harriet Beecher Stowe had a loving partnership, though they suffered many financial losses and the deaths of four of their seven children. The couple's commitment to each other and their common causes deepened over time. They sheltered fugitive slaves in their home until they moved to Maine in 1850.

After the death of Lyman Beecher and her move back to Hartford in 1864, Harriet Beecher Stowe joined the Episcopal Church, as did her son Frederick. She was drawn to eucharistic worship and had attended the Episcopal Church for some years previous to her membership. Her older sister Catherine and her three daughters had been confirmed in 1862. Although Harriet Beecher Stowe criticized what she perceived to be some of the shortcomings of the Episcopal Church—its association with affluence and its ambiguity about slavery—she appreciated Anglican aesthetics, liturgy, and theology. She supported an Episcopal missionary project to help educate and minister to newly freed African Americans in Florida, and was honored to serve at the altar in Mandarin (today part of Jacksonville).[3] She died in 1896.

Although Harriett Beecher Stowe turned to the Episcopal Church, her writing continued to reflect her concern with the themes of more Calvinistic New England theology. The following document is an excerpt from a pamphlet, *Four Ways of Observing the Sabbath.* In this excerpt, Stowe argues not only for the importance of keeping the Sabbath, but for the responsibility of parents in the religious formation of their children.

NOTES

[1] For biographical information on Harriet Beecher Stowe, see Joan D. Hedrick, *Harriet Beecher Stowe: A Life* (New York: Oxford University Press, 1994).

[2] John Gatta, "Harriet Beecher Stowe," *The Living Church* (May 20, 2001): 10; Hendrick, 3-30.

[3] Gatta, 10; Hendrick, 340-41.

HARRIET BEECHER STOWE*
An Excerpt from Four Ways of Observing The Sabbath

WAY THE FOURTH

It was near the close of a pleasant Saturday afternoon that I drew up my weary horse in front of a neat little dwelling in the village of N———. This, a near as I could gather from description, was the house of my cousin William Fletcher, the identical rogue of Bill Fletcher of whom we have aforetime spoken. Bill had always been a thriving, push-ahead sort of a character, and during the course of my rambling life I had improved every occasional opportunity of keeping up our early acquaintance. The last time I returned to my native country, after some years of absence, I heard of him as married and settled in the village of N———, where he was conducting a very prosperous course of business, and I shortly after received a pressing invitation to visit him at his own home. Now, as I had gathered from experience the fact that it is of very little use to rap one's knuckles off on the front door of a country house without any knocker, I therefore made the best of my way along a little path, bordered with marigolds and balsams, that led to the back part of the dwelling. The sound of a number of childish voices made me stop, and looking through the bushes, I saw the very image of my cousin Bill Fletcher, as he used to be twenty years ago; the same bold forehead, the same dark eyes, the smart, saucy mouth, and the same "who cares for that" toss of his head. "There, now," exclaimed the boy, setting down a pair of shoes that he had been blacking, and arranging them at the head of a long row of all sizes and sorts, from those which might have fitted a two-year-old foot upwards, "there, I've blacked every single one of them, and made them shine too, and done it all in twenty minutes; if anybody thinks they can do it quicker than that, I'd just like to have them try, that's all."

"I know they couldn't, though," said a fair-haired little girl, who stood admiring the sight, evidently impressed with the utmost reverence for her brother's ability; "and, Bill, I've been putting up all the play-things in the big chest, and I want you to come and turn the lock—the key hurts my fingers."

"Poh! I can turn it easier than that," said the boy, snapping his fingers; "have you got them all in?"

"Yes, all; only I left out the soft bales, and the string of red beads, and the great rag baby for Fanny to play with—you know mother says babies must have their playthings on Sunday."

"Oh, to be sure," said the brother, very considerately, "babies can't read, you know, as we can, nor hear Bible stories, nor look at pictures." At this moment I stepped forward, for the spell of former times was so powerfully on me, that I was on the very point of springing forward, with a "halloo, there, Bill!" as I used to meet the father in older time; but the look of surprise that greeted my appearance brought me to myself.

"Father and mother are both gone out, but I think, sir, they will be home in a few moments: won't you walk in?"

I accepted the invitation, and the little girl showed me into a small and very prettily furnished parlour. There was a piano, with music books, on one side of the room, some fine pictures hung about the walls, and a little, neat center-table was plentifully strewn with books. Besides these, the two recesses on each side of the fire-place contained each a book-case with a glass locked door.

The little girl offered me a chair, and then lingered a moment, as if she felt some disposition to entertain me if she could only think of something to say, and at last, looking up in my face, she said, in a confidential tone, "Mother," says she, "left Willie and me to keep house this afternoon while she was gone, and we are putting up all the things for Sunday, so as to get everything done before she comes home. Willie has gone to put away the playthings, and I'm going to put up the books." So saying, she opened the doors of one of the bookcases, and began busily carrying the books from the center-table to deposit them on the shelves, in which employment she was soon assisted by Willie, who took the matter in hand in a very masterly manner, showing his sister what were and what were not "Sunday books" with the air of a person entirely at home in the business. Robinson Crusoe and the many volumed Peter Parley were put by without hesitation; there was, however, a short demurring over a North American Review, because Willie said he was sure his father read something one Sunday out of one of them, while Susan averred that he did not commonly read in it, and only read in it then because the piece was something about the Bible; but as nothing could be settled definitely on the point, the review was "laid on the table," like knotty questions in Congress. Then followed a long discussion over an extract book, which, as usual, contained all sorts, both sacred, serious, comic, and profane, and at last Willie, with much gravity, decided to lock it up, on the principle that it was best to be on the *safe side*, in support of which he appealed to me. I was saved from deciding the question by the entrance of the father and mother. My old friend knew me at once, and presented his pretty wife to me with the same look of exultation with which he used to hold up a string of trout, or an uncommon fine perch of his own catching, for my admiration, and then looking round on his fine family of children, two more of which he had brought home with him, seemed to say to me, "There! What do you think of that now?"

And, in truth, a very pretty sight it was—enough to make any one's old bachelor coat sit very uneasily on him. Indeed, there is nothing that gives one such a startling idea of the tricks that old Father Time has been playing on us, as to meet some boyish or girlish companions with half a dozen or so of thriving children about them. My old friend, I found, was in essence just what the boy had been, only instead of "not caring tho' the Sabbath would come but once a year," he now called it a delight, *"the best of all the seven."* There was the same upright bearing, the same confident, cheerful tone to his voice, and the same fire in his eye; only that the hand of manhood had slightly touched some of the lines of his face, giving him a staidness of expression becoming the man and the father.

"Very well, my children," said Mrs. Fletcher, as, after tea, William and Susan finished recounting to her the various matters that they had set in order that afternoon. "I believe now we can say that our week's work is finished, and that we have nothing to do but rest and enjoy ourselves."

"Oh, and papa will show us the pictures in those great books that he brought home for us last Monday, will he not?" said little Robert.

"And, mother, you will tell us some more about Solomon's Temple and his palaces, won't you?" said Susan.

"And I should like to know if Father has found out the answer to that hard question I gave him last Sunday?" said Willie.

"All will come in good time," said Mrs. Fletcher. ["]But, tell me, my dear children, are you sure that you are quite ready for the Sabbath? You say you have put away the books and the playthings; have you put away, too, all wrong and unkind feelings? Do you feel kindly and pleasantly towards everybody?"

"Yes, mother," said Willie, who appeared to have taken a great part of this speech to himself: "I went over to Tom Walters this very morning to ask him about that chicken of mine, and he said that he did not mean to hit it, and did not know he had till I told him of it; and so we made all up again, and I am glad I went."

"I am inclined to think, Willie," said his father, "that if everybody would make it a rule to settle up all their differences *before Sunday*, that there would be very few long quarrels and lawsuits. In about half the cases, a quarrel is founded on some misunderstanding that would be got over in five minutes if one would go directly to the person for explanation."

"I suppose I need not ask you," said Mrs. Fletcher, "whether you have fully learned your Sunday-school lessons?"

"Oh, to be sure," said William. "You know, mother, that Susan and I were busy about them through Monday and Tuesday, and then this afternoon, we looked them over again, and wrote down some questions."

"And I heard Robert say his all through, and showed him all the places on the Bible Atlas," said Susan.

"Well, then," said my friend, "if everything is done, let us begin Sunday with some music."

Thanks to the recent improvements in the musical instruction of the young, every family can now form a domestic concert, with words and tunes adapted to the capacity and the voices of children; and while these little ones, full of animation, pressed round their mother, and accompanied her music with the words of some beautiful hymns, I thought that, though I might have heard finer music, I had never listened to any that answered the purpose of music so well.

It was a custom at my friend's to retire at an early hour on Saturday evening, in order that there might be abundant time for rest, and no excuse for late rising on the Sabbath; and, accordingly, when the children had done singing, after a short season of family devotion, we all betook ourselves to our chambers, and I, for one, fell asleep with the impression of having finished the week most agreeably, and with the anticipations of very great pleasure on the morrow.

Early in the morning I was roused from my sleep by the sound of little voices singing with great animation in the room next to mine, and, listening, I caught the following words:—

"Awake! Awake! Your bed forsake,

To God your praises pay;

The morning sun is clear and bright,

With joy we hail his cheerful light.

In songs of love

Praise God above—

It is the Sabbath day!"

The last words were repeated, and prolonged most vehemently by a voice that I knew were Master William's.

"Now, Willie, I like the other one best," said the soft voice of little Susan; and immediately she began,

"How sweet is the day,

When leaving our play,

The Saviour we seek;

The fair morning glows

When Jesus arose—
The best in the week."

Master William helped along with great spirit in the singing of this tune, though I heard him observing, at the end of the first verse, that he liked the other one better, because "it seemed to step off so kind o' lively;" and his accommodating sister followed him as he began singing it again with redoubled animation.

It was a beautiful summer morning, and the voices of the children within accorded well with the notes of birds and bleating flocks without,—a cheerful, yet Sabbath-like and quieting sound.

"Blessed be children's music!" said I to myself; ["]how much more better this is than the solitary tic-tic of old Uncle Fletcher's tall mahogany clock!"

The family bell summoned us to the breakfast-room just as the children had finished their hymn. The little breakfast-parlour had been swept and garnished expressly for the day, and a vase of beautiful flowers, which the children had the day before collected from their gardens adorned the center-table. The door of one of the bookcases by the fire-place was thrown open, presenting to view a collection of prettily bound books, over the top of which appeared, in gilt letters, the inscription, "Sabbath Library." The windows were thrown open to let in the invigorating breath of the early morning, and the birds that flitted among the rose-bushes without, seemed scarcely lighter and more buoyant than did the children as they entered the room. It was legibly written on every face in the house, that the happiest day in the week had arrived, and each one seemed to enter into its duties with a whole soul. It was still early when the breakfast and the season of family devotion was over, which was regularly attended to both morning and evening, every day, but I was struck with the appropriateness of the psalm, which was, cxvii.24,—

"This is the day God made, in it
We'll joy triumphantly,"

And the portion read, was the twentieth chapter of the Gospel of John. Then the children eagerly gathered round the table to get a sight of the pictures in the new books which their father had purchased in New York the week before, and which had been reserved as a Sunday treat. They were a beautiful edition of Calmet's Dictionary, in several large volumes, with very superior engravings.

"It seems to me that this work must be very expensive," I remarked to my friend, as we were turning the leaves.

"Indeed, it is so," he replied; "but here is one place where I am less withheld by considerations of expense, than in any other. In all that concerns making a show in the world, I am perfectly ready to economize. I can do very well without expensive clothing or fashionable furniture, and am willing that we should be looked on as very plain sort of people in all such matters; but in all that relates to the cultivation of the mind, and the improvement of the hearts of my children, I am willing to go to the extent of my ability. Whatever will give my children a better knowledge of, or deeper interest in, the Bible, or enable them to spend a Sabbath profitably and without weariness, stands first on my list among things to be purchased. I have spent in this way one third as much as the furnishing of my house costs me." On looking over the shelves of the Sabbath library, I perceived that my friend had been at no small pains in this selection. It comprised all the popular standard works for the illustration of the Bible, together with the best of the modern religious publications adapted to the capacity of young children. Two large drawers below were filled with maps and scriptural engravings, some of them of a very superior character.

"We have been collecting these things gradually, ever since we have been at housekeeping," said my friend; "the children take an interest in this library, as something more particularly belonging to them, and some of the books are donations from their little earnings."

"Yes," said Willie, "I bought Helon's Pilgrimage with my egg-money, and Susan bought the Life of David, and little Robert is going to buy one, too, next New year."

"But," said I, "would not the Sunday-school library answer all the purpose of this?"

"The Sabbath-school library is an admirable thing," said my friend; "but this does more fully and perfectly what that was intended to do. It makes a sort of central attraction at home on the Sabbath, and makes the acquisition of religious knowledge and the proper observance of the Sabbath a sort of family enterprise. You know," he added, smiling, "that people always feel interested for an object in which they have invested money."

The sound of the first Sabbath-school bell put an end to this conversation. The children promptly made themselves ready, and, as their father was the superintendent of the school, and their mother one of the teachers, it was quite a family party.

One part of every Sabbath at my friend's was spent by one or both parents, with the children, in a sort of review of the week. The attention of the little ones was directed to their own characters, the various defects or improvements of the past week, were pointed out, and they were stimulated to be on their guard in the time to come, and the whole was closed by earnest prayer for such heavenly aid as the temptations and faults of each particular one might need. After church in the evening, while the children were thus withdrawn to their mother's apartment, I could not forbear reminding my friend of old times, and of the rather anti-Sabbatical turn of his mind in our boyish days.

"Now, William," said I, "do you know that you were the last boy of whom such an enterprise in Sabbath-keeping as this was to have been expected? I suppose you remember Sunday at the 'old place.'"

"Nay, now, I think I was the very one," said he, smiling, "for I had sense enough to see, as I grew up, that the day must be kept *thoroughly* or not at all, and I had enough blood and motion in my composition to see that something must be done to enliven and make it interesting; so I set myself about it. It was one of the first of our housekeeping resolutions, that the Sabbath should be made a pleasant day, and yet be as inviolably kept as in the strictest times of our good father; and we have brought things to run in that channel for so long, that it seems to be the natural order."

"I have always supposed," said I, "that it required a peculiar talent, and more than common information in a parent, to accomplish this to any extent."

"It requires nothing," replied my friend, "but common sense, and a strong *determination to do it.* Parents who make a definite object of the religious instruction of their children, if they have common sense, can very soon see what is necessary in order to interest them; and, if they find themselves wanting in the requisite information, they can, in these days, very readily acquire it. The sources of religious knowledge are so numerous, and so popular in their form, that all can avail themselves of them. The only difficulty, after all, is, that the keeping of the Sabbath and the imparting of religious instruction is not made enough of a *home* object. Parents pass off the responsibility on the Sunday-school teacher, and suppose, of course, if they send their children to Sunday-school, they do the best they can for them. Now I am satisfied, from my experience as a Sabbath-school teacher, that the best religious instruction imparted abroad still stands in need of the co-operation of a systematic plan of religious discipline and instruction at home; for after all, God gives a power to the efforts of a *parent* that can never be transferred to other hands."

"But, do you suppose," said I, "that the *common* class of minds, with ordinary advantages, can do what you have done?"

"I think, in most cases, they could, *if they begin* right. But when both parents and children have formed *habits*, it is more difficult to change than to begin right at first. However, I think *all* might accomplish a great deal if they would give time, money, and effort towards it. It is because the object is regarded of so little value, compared with other things of a worldly nature, that so little is done."

My friend was here interrupted by the entrance of Mrs. Fletcher with the children. Then the Sabbath was closed with the happy songs of the little ones; nor could I notice a single anxious eye turning to the window to see if the sun was not almost down. The tender and softened expression of each countenance bore witness to the subduing power of those instructions which had hallowed the last hour, and their sweet, bird-like voices harmonized well with the beautiful words,

> "How sweet the light of Sabbath eve,
> How soft the sunbeam lingering there;
> Those holy hours this low earth leave,
> And rise on wings of faith and prayer."

---

* Harriet Beecher Stowe, *Four Ways of Observing the Sabbath* (Glasglow: George Gallie, 1854).

ELIZABETH CADY STANTON

(1815-1902)

Elizabeth Cady Stanton (1815-1902)[1], woman's rights leader, was born to an affluent family in Johnstown, New York in 1815. She was the daughter of Judge Daniel Cady and Margaret Livingston Cady. In an attempt to earn her father's acceptance after the death of her brother, Elizabeth Cady excelled in scholarship. Judge Cady arranged for his daughter to attend the all-male-Johnstown academy, where she was honored in Greek, and also excelled in Latin and mathematics. A brilliant student, Elizabeth attended Emma Willard's Female Seminary in Troy, New York. She studied law for seven years in her father's law office, but was denied a legal career because she was a woman. She soon became active in the abolitionist and temperance movements.

In 1840, Elizabeth Cady married Henry Stanton, a lawyer and an abolitionist. The couple removed the word "obey" from the wedding service at Elizabeth's insistence, and attended the World's Anti-Slavery Convention on their honeymoon. The couple returned and moved from Johnstown to Boston to Seneca Falls, New York to Brooklyn and, finally, to Manhattan to follow Henry's career and to raise seven children.

In 1847, Elizabeth Cady Stanton once again met Lucretia Mott, a Quaker with whom the following year she organized the first woman's rights convention in Seneca Falls, New York. (Judge Cady heard of the plan and feared his daughter had gone insane.) At the Seneca Falls Convention in 1848, Elizabeth Cady Stanton read her famous Declaration of Sentiments, modeled after the Declaration of Independence. Three years later Stanton met Unitarian activist Susan B. Anthony, with whom she began a long collaboration. Elizabeth Cady Stanton worked tirelessly for woman's rights the rest of her life, often enduring ridicule and threats of violence.

During the Civil War, Elizabeth Cady Stanton and Susan B. Anthony founded the Women's Loyal National League, which pressed for the immediate abolition of slavery by constitutional amendment. However, after the war, her primary interest in the woman's movement re-emerged and both she and Anthony refused to support the Fourteen or Fifteenth Amendments. Stanton went on to found the National Woman Suffrage Association in 1869. She died in New York in 1902—eighteen years before ratification of the Nineteenth Amendment which allowed women the right to vote.[2] She is commemorated in the Episcopal Church calendar on July 20 along with Amelia Jenks Bloomer, Sojourner Truth, and Harriet Ross Tubman.

Elizabeth Cady Stanton did not accept the use of organized religion or scripture as means to enforce the subordination of women. She believed that male clergy and the church used scripture to perpetuate the oppression of women and keep them out of the ranks of the clergy. Still, she attended Trinity Episcopal Church in Seneca Falls with Amelia Jenks Bloomer and preached hundreds of sermons throughout the country. After the release in 1881 of the Revised Version of the Bible—published by a committee with no women scholars—Elizabeth Cady Stanton organized her own committee. The *Woman's Bible*, published in two volumes in 1895 and 1898, is a commentary on biblical passages commonly used to oppress women.[3] The following except from the *Woman's Bible* is from the introduction.

NOTES

[1] The primary sources for biographical information is Elizabeth Cady Stanton, *Eighty Years & More: Reminiscences, 1815-1897* (New York: Schocken Books, 1971; rpt. 1898).

[2] Elizabeth Cady Stanton, *The Woman's Bible* Amherst, (New York: Prometheus Books, 1999; rpt. 1895), vii-viii.

[3] *Lesser Feasts and Fasts* (2000) (New York: Church Publishing, 2001) 294.

℘

ELIZABETH CADY STANTON
An Excerpt from The Woman's Bible*

INTRODUCTION—

From the inauguration of the movement for woman's emancipation the Bible has been used to hold her in the "divinely ordained sphere," prescribed in the Old and New Testaments.

The canon and civil law; church and state; priests and legislators; all political parties and religious denominations have alike taught that woman was made after man, of man, and for man, an inferior being, subject to man. Creeds, codes, Scriptures and statutes, are all based on this idea. The fashions, forms, ceremonies and customs of society, church ordinances and discipline all grow out of this idea.

Of the old English common law, responsible for woman's civil and political status, Lord Brougham said, "it is a disgrace to the civilization and Christianity of the Nineteenth Century." Of the canon law, which is responsible for woman's status in the church, Charles Kingsley said, "this will never be a good world for women until the last remnant of the canon law is swept from the face of the earth."

The Bible teaches that woman brought sin and death into the world, that she precipitated the fall of the race, that she was arraigned before the judgment seat of Heaven, tried, condemned and sentenced. Marriage for her was to be a condition of bondage, maternity a period of suffering and anguish, and in silence and subjection, she was to play the role of a dependent on man's bounty for all her material wants, and for all the information she might desire on the vital questions of the hour, she was commanded to ask her husband at home. Here is the Bible position of woman briefly summed up.

Those who have the divine insight to translate, transpose and transfigure this mournful object of pity into an exalted, dignified personage, worthy our worship as the mother of the race, are to be congratulated as having a share of the occult mystic power of the eastern Mahatmas.

The plain English to the ordinary mind admits of no such liberal interpretation. The unvarnished texts speak for themselves. The canon law, church ordinances and Scriptures, are homogeneous, and all reflect the same spirit and sentiments.

These familiar texts are quoted by clergymen in their pulpits, by statesmen in the halls of legislation, by lawyers in the courts, and are echoed by the press of all civilized nations, and accepted by woman herself as "The Word of God." So perverted is the religious element in her nature, that with faith and works she is the chief support of the church and clergy; the very powers that make her emancipation impossible. When, in the early part of the Nineteenth Century, women began to protest against their civil and political degradation, they were referred to the Bible for an answer. When they protested against their unequal position in the church, they were referred to the Bible for an answer.

This led to a general and critical study of the Scriptures. Some, having made a fetish of these books and believing them to be the veritable "Word of God," with liberal translations, interpretations, allegories and symbols, glossed over the most objectionable features of the various books and clung to them as divinely inspired. Others, seeing the family resemblance between the Mosaic code, the canon law, and the old English common law, came to the conclusion that all alike emanated from the same source; wholly human in their origin and inspired by the natural love of domination in the historians. Others, bewildered with their doubts and fears, came to no conclusion. While their clergymen told them on the one hand, that they owed all the blessings and freedom they enjoyed to the Bible, on the other, they said it clearly marked out their circumscribed sphere of action that the demands for political and civil rights were irreligious, dangerous to the stability of the home, the state and the church. Clerical appeals were circulated from time to time conjuring members of their churches to take no part in the anti-slavery or woman suffrage movements, as they were infidel in their tendencies, undermining the very foundations of society. No wonder the majority of women stood still, and with bowed heads, accepted the situation.

Listening to the varied opinions of women, I have long thought it would be interesting and profitable to get them clearly stated in book form. To this end six years ago I proposed to a committee of women to issue a Woman's Bible, that we might have women's commentaries on women's position in the Old and New Testaments. It was agreed on by several leading women in England and America and the work was begun, but from various causes it has been delayed, until now the idea is received with renewed enthusiasm, and a large committee has been formed, and we hope to complete the work within a year.

Those who have undertaken the labor are desirous to have some Hebrew and Greek scholars, versed in Biblical criticism, to gild our pages with their learning. Several distinguished women have been urged to do so, but they are afraid that their high reputation and scholarly attainments might be compromised by taking part in an enterprise that for a time may prove very unpopular. Hence we may not be able to get help from that class.

Others fear that they might compromise their evangelical faith by affiliating with those of more liberal views, who do not regard the Bible as the "Word of God," but like any other book, to be judged by its merits. If the Bible teaches the equality of Woman, why does the church refuse to ordain women to preach the gospel, to fill the offices of deacons and elders, and to administer the Sacraments, or to admit them as delegates to the Synods, General Assemblies and Conferences of the different denominations? They have never yet invited a woman to join one of their Revising Committees, nor tried to mitigate the sentence pronounced on her by changing one count in the indictment served on her in Paradise. The large number of letters received, highly appreciative of the undertaking, is very encouraging to those who have inaugurated the movement, and indicate a growing self-respect and self-assertion in the women of this generation. But we have the usual array of objectors to meet and answer. One correspondent conjures us to suspend the work, as it is "ridiculous" for "women to attempt the revision of the Scriptures." I wonder if any man wrote to the late revising committee of Divines to stop their work on the ground that it was ridiculous for men to revise the Bible. Why is it more ridiculous for women to protest against her present status in the Old and New Testament, in the ordinances and discipline of the church, than in the statutes and constitution of the state? Why is it more ridiculous to arraign ecclesiastics for their false teaching and acts of injustice to women, than members of Congress and the House of Commons? Why is it more audacious to review Moses than Blackstone, the Jewish code of laws, than the English system of jurisprudence? Women have compelled their legislators in every state in this Union to so modify their statutes for women that the old common law is now almost a dead letter. Why not compel Bishops and Revising Committees to modify their creeds and dogmas? Forty years ago it seemed as ridiculous to timid, time-serving and retrograde folk for women to demand an expurgated edition of the laws, as it now does to demand an expurgated edition of the Liturgies and the Scriptures. Come, come, my conservative friend, wipe the dew off your spectacles, and see that the world is moving. Whatever your views may be as to the importance of the proposed work, your political and social degradation are but an outgrowth of your status in the Bible. When you express your aversion, based on a blind feeling of reverence in which reason has no control, to the revision of the Scriptures, you do but echo Cowper, who, when asked to read Paine's "Rights of Man," exclaimed, "No man shall convince me that I am improperly governed while I *feel* the contrary."

Others say it is not *politic* to rouse religious opposition. This much-lauded policy is but another word for *cowardice*. How can woman's position be changed from that of a subordinate to an equal, without opposition, without the broadest discussion of all the questions involved in her present degradation? For so far-reaching and momentous a reform as her complete independence, an entire revolution in all existing institutions is inevitable.

Let us remember that all reforms are interdependent, and that whatever is done to establish one principle on a solid basis, strengthens all. Reformers who are always compromising, have not yet grasped the idea that truth is the only safe ground to stand upon. The object of an individual life is not to carry one fragmentary measure in human progress, but to utter the highest truth clearly seen in all directions, and thus to round out and perfect a well balanced character. Was not the sum of influence exerted by John Stuart Mill on political, religious and social questions far greater than that of any statesman or reformer who has sedulously limited his sympathies and activities to carrying one specific measure? We have many women abundantly endowed with capabilities to understand and revise what men have thus far written. But they are all suffering from inherited ideas of their inferiority; they do not perceive it, yet such is the true explanation of their solicitude, lest they should seem to be too self-asserting.

Again there are some who write us that our work is a useless expenditure of force over a book that has lost its hold on the human mind. Most intelligent women, they say, regard it simply as the history of a rude people in a barbarous age, and have no more reverence for the Scriptures than any other work. So long as tens of thousands of Bibles are printed every year, and circulated over the whole habitable globe, and the masses in all English-speaking nations revere it as the word of God, it is vain to belittle its influence. The sentimental feelings we all have for those things we were educated to believe sacred, do not readily yield to pure reason. I distinctly remember the shudder that passed over me on seeing a mother take our family Bible to make a high seat for her child at table. It seemed such a desecration. I was tempted to protest against its use for such a purpose, and this, too, long after my reason had repudiated its divine authority.

To women still believing in the plenary inspiration of the Scriptures, we say give us by all means your exegesis in the light of the higher criticism learned men are now making, and illumine the Woman's Bible, with your inspiration.

Bible historians claim special inspiration for the Old and New Testaments containing most contradictory records of the same events, of miracles opposed to all known laws, of customs that degrade the female sex of all human and animal life, stated in most questionable language that could not be read in a promiscuous assembly, and call all this "The Word of God."

The only points in which I differ from all ecclesiastical teaching is that I do not believe that any man ever saw or talked with God, I do not believe that God inspired the Mosaic code, or told the historians what they say he did about woman, for all the religions on the face of the earth degrade her, and so long as woman accepts the position that they assign her, her emancipation is impossible. Whatever the Bible may be made to do in Hebrew or Greek, in plain English it does not exalt and dignify woman. My standpoint for criticism is the revised edition of 1888. I will so far honor the revising committee of wise men who have given us the best exegesis they can according to their ability, although Disraeli said the last one before he died, contained 150,000 blunders in the Hebrew, and 7,000 in the Greek.

But the verbal criticism in regard to woman's position amounts to little. The spirit is the same in all periods and languages, hostile to her as an equal.

There are some general principles in the holy books of all religions that teach love, charity, liberty, justice and equality for all the human family, there are many grand and beautiful passages, the golden rule has been echoed and re-echoed around the world. There are lofty examples of good and true men and women, all worthy our acceptance and imitation whose lustre cannot be dimmed by the false sentiments and vicious characters bound up in the same volume. The Bible cannot be accepted or rejected as a whole, its teachings are varied and its lessons differ widely from each other. In criticising the peccadilloes of Sarah, Rebecca and Rachel, we would not shadow the virtues of Deborah, Huldah and Vashti. In criticising the Mosaic code we would not question the wisdom of the golden rule and the fifth Commandment. Again the church claims special consecration for its cathedrals and priesthood, parts of these aristocratic churches are too holy for women to enter, boys were early introduced into the choirs for this reason, woman singing in an obscure corner closely veiled. A few of the more democratic denominations accord women some privileges, but invidious discriminations of sex are found in all religious organizations, and the most bitter outspoken enemies of women are found among clergymen and bishops of the Protestant religion.

The canon law, the Scriptures, the creeds and codes and church discipline of the leading religions bear the impress of fallible man, and not of our ideal great first cause, "the Spirit of all Good," that set the universe of matter and mind in motion, and by immutable law holds the land, the sea, the planets, revolving round the great centre of light and heat, each in its own elliptic, with millions of stars in harmony all singing together, the glory of creation forever and ever.

---

* Elizabeth Cady Stanton, *The Woman's Bible* (Amherst, New York: Prometheus Books, 1999; rpt. 1895): 7-13.

ANNE AYERS
[SISTER ANNE]

(1816-1896)

Anne Ayers (1816-1896), religious and founder of the Sisterhood of the Holy Communion, was born in London, England in 1816 and moved to New York City with her parents in 1845. While working as a teacher to supplement the family income, Ayers heard a sermon on "Jephtha's Vow" by William Augustus Muhlenberg and discerned a call to a life of religious service. On All Saints Day, November 1, 1845, Sister Anne was formally consecrated a "sister of the Holy Communion" by Muhlenberg in a private ceremony.

Anne Ayers pursued her vocation to the religious life at a time when there were no existing sisterhoods in the Episcopal Church or the Church of England. "So far as it was known, not a single sister had been professed anywhere in the Anglican Communion for nearly three hundred years,"[1] and there was considerable public opinion against it. Yet two contemporary religious movements—the deaconess movement in Germany and the Oxford Movement of the 1830s and 40s paved the way for the revival of sisterhoods. A few women who joined Sister Anne were formally organized into the Sisterhood of the Holy Communion in 1852. The order remained active until 1940.

Sister Anne was William Augustus Muhlenberg's primary collaborator and, under their leadership, the Sisterhood of the Holy Communion embarked on a variety of ministries. These included teaching, social work among the poor, and perhaps most notably, nursing and hospital administration. From 1858 to 1877, Ayers directed both nursing and housekeeping at St. Luke's Hospital in New York City, originally founded by Muhlenberg. In 1865 the two founded St. Johnland on Long Island, a facility for the rural poor, orphaned, homeless, and handicapped. Though some of her sisters found Ayers' leadership to be autocratic, her zeal for the religious life and service to the sick and needy was unquestionable. She died in New York City at St. Luke's Hospital in 1896.

In contrast to Roman Catholic orders, the Sisterhood of the Holy Communion took no lifetime vows, but rather, pledged themselves to three-year, renewable, terms. Members of the Sisterhood of the Holy Communion also wore a prescribed form of secular dress rather than religious habits, refrained from marriage during their term of service, and lived under the direction of the "First Sister," rather than under a formal rule of life.

Many of Anne Ayers' writings are linked to her long ministry with Muhlenberg. She published *Evangelical Sisterhoods* (1867), *Evangelical Catholic Papers* (1875-77), and *The Life and Work of William Augustus Muhlenberg* (1880). *Practical Thoughts on Sister-hoods*, was published anonymously in 1864 and is Ayers' reply to a letter from a friend anxious "to see some way of enlisting the more earnest of our unmarried women to co-operate in such labors with better system and efficiency than has hitherto, to any extent, been found among us."[2] Written while Anne Ayers labored under the pressures of her multiple responsibilities at St. Luke's Hospital, she conveys her thoughts on the possibilities for women called to lives of service.

NOTES

[1] Boone Porter, Jr. *Sister Anne: Pioneer in Women's Work* (New York: National Council, 1960): 6.

[2] [Anne Ayers], *Practical Thoughts on Sisterhoods: In Reply to a Letter of Inquiry* (New York, T. Whittaker, 1864): iii.

ANNE AYERS
Practical Thoughts on Sisterhoods[1]

My Dear Friend –

A brief absence from my usual duties affords the opportunity I have so long desired for answering, at some length, the various thoughts and questions contained in your letter, on the organization of the voluntary labors of Christian women.

You say that you have thrown out these questions "in the hope that they will elicit from me some hints which may guide those who are groping after light, how best to systematize and employ the services of such of our sex as desire to give a larger portion of their time to the Lord who bought them." I do not know how well qualified I am to be of use in this way, but your special interest in the subject makes it very agreeable to me to sit down for a talk with you of things which might be, if the unmarried female communicants of our Church were ready, in any number, to give themselves to the service of charity as a vocation.

Would that the companying together of Christian women, in the way we are thinking of, and for the purpose of carrying on the different charitable institutions among us, were not still so much in the future. Look at your own experience in this regard. You are making your initiation in a field of unquestioned usefulness and excellence,[2] one too which pre-eminently demands the sisterly co-operation and devotion of refined and intelligent women. Now how many of such women have come to your assistance during the year that has passed? I do not mean as transient helpers and sympathizers, doing just so much as is easy, convenient, or agreeable; but how many, giving their time and energies unreservedly and ungrudgingly, can you count upon to share your toils and your cares? Perhaps, scarce one. And why? Is it not because our Christianity is of so low an order, because we are so entangled with the world, so uninstructed, not only in the spirit of sacrifice, but in the spirit of gospel brotherhood, so used to loving our neighbors a little, and ourselves, very much, and so content with just getting to Heaven, not perceiving that "there are many gains and many losses in Christ, over and above that unappreciable one of the soul?"

In thus speaking, I am not forgetting the excellent women who, in our age, as in all others of the Church, are found here and there, in singleness of heart, going about doing good. But these are often matrons, with households of their own, and are always the few, not the many; not the numbers we are thinking of, who gathered into societies as ministering sisters, deaconesses, lady-nurses, or whatever else they may call themselves, are to be the life and soul of our different hospitals and asylums, and the best security against the deterioration of such institutions into mere *machines of charity.*

You say that many earnest minds in our Church are turning inquiringly to a consideration of the systematic employment of devout women in labors of this kind. I wish I could think this were so, to any extent, likely to lead to practical results; but I do not. In your immediate neighborhood, and in connection with the inception of the new hospital work there, I can understand that a certain sort of interest has been excited; but elsewhere, and throughout the Church at large, we hear of little of the kind. On the contrary, I think that, in some respects, the present is a period very adverse to the formation of such communities. The war-spirit, which we all, more or less, breathe, is directly opposed to the discipline and order indispensable to the last restricted and most simple of these organizations; and the luxury and extravagance all around us, increasing rather than diminishing under the calamities of the land, are wholly hardening in their general effect; while the strange unfeminine attire, to which our eyes are growing but too accustomed, both evinces and induces a state of public sentiment greatly at variance with the meek and lowly virtues of the life we are considering, not to speak of other antagonist influences, which your own mind will readily suggest, as essentially damaging to the higher developments of Christian faith and obedience.

But, I allow, there is another and a less discouraging view to be taken of these very evils; one which, by turning them upon themselves, so to speak, may make them actually conducive to the ends which they seem ready to subvert; and, perhaps, it is thus that God's good providence will solve some of the sorrowful problems of our day. I mean, for example, that the very excess and extravagance of the times may act upon certain minds with a repulsion which will drive them far beyond the line of that moderate, compromising Christianity, which they once made their boundary, into those stricter spheres of Christian love and duty where there are no reservations for selfish indulgence, and no entanglements of worldly aims.

We may look for sisters, too, from among the multitude of women whose hearts the sword is daily making desolate; some of these will soon forget their losses in new delights, but others, of greater depth of nature, with whom to love once is to love for ever, will be able to find a solace for their griefs only in sharing and consoling the griefs of others.

And, further, we may believe that many a single woman of culture and leisure who, before this terrible war broke out, was wont to spend her time, for the most part, in idleness and self-indulgence, having tasted in her ministrations to the sick and wounded of our armies the sweets of usefulness and self-sacrifice, will shrink from returning to her former empty life, and that the generous patriotism which led her to make the wards of a military hospital a familiar haunt, might be converted, under good teaching and proper leadership, into hearty zeal for the work before us. Think of the numbers of such who, at the present time, at large cost of ease and comfort, are ministering to our soldiers in every direction; and when they are no longer needed for this service, what would be more natural than that they should accept kindred employment in the way we are supposing? "The happiest life," says Dr. Chalmers, "is that which has the fullest occupation with the highest aim." Having once proved the truth of this, they will not readily resign themselves again to the vapidness of doing nothing.

And here I cannot help wishing that our bishops and pastors would speak more directly to us women, on these points than they do. It is customary to urge men to the work of the ministry, missions, etc., and should not holy arguments be sometimes addressed to us, also, to stir us up to something in the Christian life more distinct and impressive than that now common to us? Yet when do we hear a word from the pulpit to this effect? We women have a little faith, we have warm affections and pure impulses, we have heads and hands; why not show us that we are not living up to our vocation, not turning to good account the powers we are indued with, that communicants though we be, we are frittering away our lives, "spending our money for that which is not bread, and our labor for that which satisfieth not;" or, at the best, allowing ourselves to be dwarfed and cramped into the niches of custom and worldly conformity, when we might be developing, by healthful exercise in pure Christian air, toward perfect stature in Christ?

Our reverend teachers must forgive me if I seem to speak undutifully. I do not mean to be presumptuous, but I feel that, if they would set these things forth, as they know how to do, and if all would pray earnestly for the outpouring of larger grace upon us, there would be some hope of an answer to that almost audible groan of yours, when, after relating to me your rescue of the unhappy child from its wretched, drunken mother, you cry out, "What can we women do?"

It is not without strong reason that I attach importance to preaching of this kind; for it was a sermon, delivered now nearly twenty years ago,[3] which gave the first impulse to the formation of the community to which I belong. The faithful words entered "as a nail in a sure place," and from them sprang, in due time, the first Protestant Sisterhood in this country.

[...]

I need hardly tell you, either, that the Sisterhood of the Holy Communion, thus originating, has grown up, and continues to work on, under a peculiar conjuncture of favoring circumstances not likely to reproduce themselves elsewhere, and that therefore it is not calculated to serve, altogether, as a precedent for another institution.

Still it is true, as you say, that we have made experiences, in all these years, which cannot but be valuable to others as well as ourselves, and it is upon these experiences I am going to draw for my replies to your further questions. We were formally organized into a Sisterhood in the year 1852, and from that date forward there has always been a company of us, larger or smaller, living together, and working by rule, first in the Parish School, among the parish poor, in the Church Dispensary and the Church Infirmary, and, of late years, in St. Luke's Hospital.

You ask me, "What are the advantages of such organization, or combination, over the ordinary system of ministration among the poor?"

In answering you, let me turn to a paper I have at hand, containing a summary of the work of one of those years preceding our transfer to

St. Luke's Hospital—the year 1856. It is an account of our stewardship rendered to those who had made us their almoners that year. Our company at this time consisted of three full Sisters, two probationary ones, and two associate, or non-resident Sisters. We were living in the house built for us adjoining the Church of the Holy Communion, and which was also the Dispensary, and had hired the house next to it, and made to communicate with it, for the Infirmary and School.

The work accomplished was as follows: In the Infirmary (seventeen beds), eighty patients, principally incurables; no hired nurse. Out-patients of the Dispensary, over fourteen hundred; medicine, sick diet, and nursing at their homes, as needed. In the Parish School, seventy children taught every day, and in part clothed; one hired teacher. Poor families cared for, one hundred and fifty; one hundred of whom belonged to the Church of the Holy Communion, and were regularly visited accordingly....

---

[1] Excerpted from [Anne Ayers], *Practical Thoughts on Sisterhoods*. (New York: T. Whittaker, 1864): 5-10, 12-13.

[2] The Protestant Episcopal Hospital, Philadelphia.

[3] By the Rev. Dr. Mulenberg, July, 1845.

AMELIA JENKS BLOOMER

(1818-1894)

Amelia Jenks Bloomer (1818-1894), reformer and suffragist, is celebrated in the calendar of the Episcopal Church on July 20, along with Elizabeth Cady Stanton, Sojurner Truth, and Harriet Ross Tubman.[1] Bloomer was a largely self-educated woman, active in a variety of the reform movements of her age, including temperance, anti-slavery, and woman's rights. She attended the pivotal woman's rights convention at Seneca Falls in July 1848. Active in the temperance movement and editor of the Ladies Temperance Society's newspaper the *Lily*, Bloomer soon began to write and speak on woman's rights. Though she never intended to champion the cause of more practical clothing for women, her defense of loose-fitting Turkish "pantelettes" for women in the *Lily* was picked up by several newspapers and thus became known as the "Bloomer Costume." As clergy attacked women who wore the new fashion, Ameila's popularity soared as she debated them publicly on the issue.[2] Propelled into the national press by the issue of dress reform, Bloomer felt that the furor it caused detracted from more important aspects of the woman's rights struggle.

By the early 1850s Amelia Bloomer and her husband, attorney and anti-slavery reformer Dexter Chamberlain Bloomer, moved to the Midwest, first to Mount Vernon, Ohio, and then in 1855 to Council Bluffs, Iowa where they remained for the rest of their lives.

In Council Bluffs, Amelia Bloomer worked to establish churches, schools, and hospitals. The Bloomer's home offered hospitality to reformers and clergy of all denominations. As a working mother to two adopted children, Amelia Bloomer had a rich home life; she was an avid gardener and competed for culinary prizes at the local fair. Earnest and with a limited sense of humor, Bloomer nonetheless was thoroughly committed to the causes she espoused. She died of a heart attack in 1894 shortly after undergoing electrical treatments for a serious ailment.

Though raised a Presbyterian, Amelia Bloomer became an Episcopalian in the early 1840s and was baptized at Trinity Church, Seneca Falls. An active Episcopalian for the rest of her life, she was deeply concerned about the implications of scriptural interpretation for women. Drawn into reform efforts from the perspective of deep religious commitment, Bloomer did not hesitate to respond to "biblical" arguments against woman's suffrage. She gave several versions of the speech in the following document in which she re-examines several biblical passages as they relate to women, believing that "God has placed no ruler between woman and himself."[3] The speech was delivered at the first woman's suffrage meeting in Des Moines, Iowa in 1870.

NOTES

[1] *Lesser Feasts and Fasts* (2000) (New York: Church Publishing, 2001): 294-295.

[2] Ibid.

[3] Amelia Jenks Bloomer, "Alas! Poor Adam," in *Here Me Patiently: The Reform Speeches of Amelia Jenks Bloomer*, Anne C. Coon, ed. (Westport: Greenwood Press, 1994): 139.

Amelia Jenks Bloomer
An Excerpt from the Speech,
"Alas! Poor Adam"*

Among the many obstacles thrown in the way of woman's progress and enfranchisement, there is a very serious one in the minds of many which I wish briefly to consider this evening. It is one that has not only made her submissive and in a measure contented in her inferior, subject state, but has in numberless instances caused her untold sorrow and made her life one of extreme bitterness. I allude to the prevalent idea and teaching that woman was created subject to man—an inferior being, incapable of self government—needing a protector and supporter, and that man was to rule over and govern her for all time. That the Bible not only sanctions but teaches this doctrine, and that woman must not question either its truth or its justice.

This idea and this teaching has, in my view, brought untold misery into the world by making that relation which should be an equal partnership, where the rights and feelings and interests of each should be considered and respected, a relation instead of master and slave—of tyrant and subject—of superior and inferior. Made the woman, who is often superior in intellect, in morals, in benevolence, in every good thing, to her husband, the victim of his whims and caprices, of his blows and curses and lusts.

You may believe all this teaching right and ordained of God, but I confess I do not believe it. It is contrary to all my ideas of the goodness and justice of the All Father, and I believe it cannot be sustained by the Bible. I do not know as I shall be able to throw any light on the subject or convince you, or those of you who believe, and teach, and act out this doctrine, that you have been misreading and misquoting the scriptures, but I wish you to examine with me some of the leading passages which are such a law to many and which are ever threateningly held over woman's head.

First, then, we will go back to Genesis, where, in the very first account given of the creation of man, "God said, 'let us make man in our image, after our likeness, and let them have dominion over the fish of the sea, and over the fowl of the air, and over every creeping thing that creepeth upon the earth.' So God created man in his own image, in the image of God created He him; male and female created He them. And God blessed them, and God said unto them, 'be fruitful and multiply, and replenish the earth, and subdue it, and have dominion over the fish of the sea, and over the fowl of the air, and over every living thing that moveth upon the earth'" [Genesis 1:26-28].

In all this we find nothing to show that God created the man superior to the woman, or that he gave him greater right, or power, or dominion than he gave to her, or that he assigned them to different spheres of action. On the contrary, we are clearly told that he gave her equal power and dominion, and united her jointly and equally with him in the great commission given for the temporal government of the earth.

But farther on we are told (in a chapter said to have been written and added several hundred years after the first account of the creation of man), of the fall of this first pair—of Eve eating of the forbidden fruit, after the serpent had overcome her scruples by promises of great knowledge and good to follow—and of Adam, who was with her, also eating, without any scruples of conscience or promises from her of great reward [Genesis Chapter 3]. Certainly in this transaction he manifested no superiority of intellect or goodness.

In reading this account of the fall of Adam and Eve, I cannot see wherein Eve committed the greater sin or showed the greater weakness. The command not to eat of the tree of knowledge was given to Adam by God himself before the creation of Eve, and we have no evidence that this command was repeated to her by the Creator. She probably received it secondhand from Adam. He being the one to whom the command was directly given, first created, and according to popular belief, endowed with superior intelligence, it was doubly binding on him to observe and keep it. But how stands the record? Alas! poor Adam, while it required all the persuasive powers and eloquence of the subtle tempter, all the promises of wisdom, and knowledge, and power to seduce the so-called "weaker vessel" from the right path, all that was necessary to secure his downfall was simply to offer him the apple. He not only stood by and saw her eat, without a warning word, but ate himself without remonstrance or objection. And then, when enquired of by God concerning what he had done, instead of standing up like a man and honestly acknowledging his fault, he weakly tried to shield himself by throwing the blame on his wife—and his descendants of this day too often follow his example. How anyone can read the history of the fall and gather from it that the woman displayed the weaker intellect I cannot understand. I do not so read it.

The punishment inflicted upon our first parents for this transgression was certainly heavier upon the man than upon the woman. Her sorrows were to be multiplied—but he, too, was to eat his bread in sorrow and to earn it in the sweat of his face, amid thorns and thistles [Genesis 3:16–19]. To her no command to labor was given, upon her no toil was imposed, and no ground cursed for her sake. So far in the account of the creation and fall, surely man can claim no superiority over woman.

But we now come to the consideration of the first passage which seems to give woman a subordinate place, and which men have used as a warrant to humble and crush her, through all the ages that have passed since Adam and Eve were driven from the garden of Eden.

To the woman he said, "Thy desire shall be to thy husband and he shall rule over thee" [Genesis 3:16]. This is generally regarded as a command, and binding for all time, as if He had said, "every woman henceforth who takes to herself a husband shall be in subjection to him as to a master, and every husband who takes a wife shall regard her as a subject and servant, not as a companion and equal, and shall rule over her." Can we believe that it was God's will, and pleasure, and command that such a state of things should exist in the marriage relation? If so, then we make Him responsible for all the quarrels and contentions and murders that ensue between husband and wife, for it is but following up the command that man shall rule his wife, and there is no limit fixed to his power over her. It can hardly be claimed that the Creator intended the woman to be always the meek, patient, silent subject—obeying implicitly and answering not—else He would have made her more patient under wrongs and dumb before her master, instead of endowing her with intellect, a keen sense of right, and in all respects like passions with man.

But I deny that there is any evidence to show that the words we have been considering had any binding force any farther than upon the parties to whom they were addressed. To Eve he said, "thy desire shall be to thy husband and he shall rule over thee." Not a word of the future. Not a word of this law following her seed, as was the case when talking to the serpent. Then again these words were addressed to *her,* and not to her husband, and there is no evidence to show that he heard or knew of them. There is no command given to Adam to rule over his wife, and nowhere in the Bible can a passage be found where the husband is commanded to rule the wife—as we should suppose would be the case if such rule was intended.

In my view, the passages quoted are to be regarded in the light of prophecy or prediction and not of command. Substitute *will* in place of *shall,* which translators tell us may with equal propriety be done and often is done, and all is clear enough. "He *will* rule over thee." God foresaw what would follow and foretold it as a result. Eve would naturally feel humbled under a sense of wrong committed, sin incurred, the banishment imposed, and the lost favor of her husband, and would desire to regain that favor and make peace with him. This would lead her to cringe to and subject herself unto him; and he, laying all the blame of the fall on her, and accusing her to her Maker to shield himself—to hide his own weakness and sin—was ready to vent his anger upon her, and to punish her with his tyranny. And so it has come that his male descendants, following his example, have ruled over woman through all past ages and still continue that rule, though in a lesser degree, at the present time. And woman has submitted—just as weak nations submit to stronger—not because she believes it just, not because she feels herself inferior, but because man has the power and chooses to exercise it, and because he has made her believe that he so rules by Divine command.

God has placed no ruler between woman and himself. If this were so—if it be true that man is her ruler and master, to whom she is to yield obedience, then she is answerable to man and not to God for her actions. Her own conscience and the will of her husband may sometimes conflict—who then is she to serve? Her husband, of course, if he is her ruler and she bound to obey him. It is a question with some whether woman has a soul! This has grown out of this same idea of woman being created solely for man—his subject and servant—to minister to his passions and pleasures. If she has a soul, and if this doctrine of implicit obedience to the husband be true, then the husband must be answerable to God for her. She cannot justly be held accountable to two masters.

We pass to the New Testament, and there we find several passages from St. Paul, which in the minds of the opponents of woman's cause condemn woman to everlasting silence, submission, and nonentity. "Let the woman learn in silence with all subjection. I suffer not a woman to teach nor to usurp authority over the man, but to be in silence" [I Timothy 2:11–12]. "Let your women keep silence in the churches, for it is not permitted unto them to speak, but to be under obedience, and if they will learn anything let them ask their husbands at home, for it is a shame for women to speak in the church" [I Corinthians 14:34-35]. "Wives obey your husbands. The man is head of the wife as Christ is head of the Church" [Ephesians 5:22–23].

These I believe comprise all the utterances and rules laid down to govern woman's action, and they have been a terror to awe her into a state of fear and submission during all the centuries that have passed since they were proclaimed. To me they have no such terror, for I regard none of them as spoken to, or of, me. Whatever rules may have been necessary for the action of women eighteen hundred years ago, has [sic] little to do with the women of our day. As well say that the men of this generation shall be, and do, as were, and did, the men of that olden time, as to say that the women of these days shall be bound by laws and customs in force eighteen centuries before their existence...

...While many of the clergy still hold these injunctions warningly over our heads and think it an abomination for a woman to speak or preach, yet they have constantly violated them and caused them to be violated. They hold up St. Paul against a woman preaching or teaching, yet they not only suffer but they encourage and urge her to teach the scriptures in Sunday Schools and in tract visitations. By a late report in a religious paper we learn that Bible classes, on Sunday afternoon, have been started by certain women in the metropolis of London for the instruction of young men and young women. The services at these Bible meetings are usually conducted entirely by the women, but occasionally they invite some clergyman to deliver an address—and strange as it may seem, the clergy cheerfully respond to such invitations, and never once tell the women that they are violating St. Paul's command, "I suffer not a woman to teach." And so all over the world we find men inviting women into various fields of religious labor in disregard of St. Paul. There is really more teaching the gospel by women in Sunday schools and Bible classes than by ministers in their sermons.

[...]

But, my friends, the passages we have been reviewing have nothing whatever to do with the question of Woman Suffrage—nothing to do with her talking and acting outside the church. Search the Bible through and you can find nothing against her sharing in political affairs, or enjoying political rights. They relate only to the church—and to the church of other times. Let woman set her heart at rest on this point, and cease to feel that God created her an inferior and subject, and that she must not claim her rights and hope to better her condition in this life. That condition has been steadily improving since the introduction of Christianity, and the end is not yet....

---

* As published in *Hear Me Patiently: the Reform Speeches of Amelia Jenks Bloomer*, Anne C. Coon, eds. (Westport: Greenwood Press, 1994): 136-45.

HARRIET ROSS TUBMAN

(c. 1820-1913)

Harriet Ross Tubman (c. 1820-1913), leader in the Underground Railroad, abolitionist, Civil War scout and nurse, was born sometime during 1820 to Ben Ross and Harriet Green on a plantation on Maryland's Eastern Shore. She was the sixth of eleven children born to the enslaved couple. Though her parents named her Araminta, she later chose the name of her mother. Though Harriet performed various duties while she was a slave, she did not make an ideal servant. While a teenager, she was struck in the head by an overseer. The blow fractured Harriet's skull and she was subject to somnolence for the rest of her life. Around 1844 she married a free man named John Tubman. The couple had no children.

In 1849 Harriet feared that she would be shipped away after her masters' death and decided to make her escape. She successfully reached Philadelphia and found work in a hotel. In 1850 and 1851 she also guided members of her family and others out of slavery. She attempted to assist her husband, however, he had remarried and declined her assistance. Tubman was successful, however, in rescuing her parents and several of her siblings. Overall, it is believed that Harriet Tubman made nineteen trips into Maryland between 1851 and 1861 and delivered between sixty and three hundred persons from slavery by leading them into Canada. A reward of $40,000 was offered for her capture. On occasion she worked with other antislavery advocates active with the Underground Railroad, and was given the name "Moses" in appreciation of her work to guide others to freedom.[1]

In 1858/9, Harriet Tubman moved to a farm in Auburn, New York where she offered counsel and shelter to African Americans in need. This site remained her home for the rest of her life. Tubman's work brought her praise from many of the prominent abolitionists of her day, including Frederick Douglass and Oliver Johnson. In addition, she worked with Elizabeth Cady Stanton and Susan B. Anthony for the cause of woman's rights, though she always supported African-American women in founding their own organizations. Having foreseen the Civil War in a vision, Harriet Ross Tubman quickly joined the Union Army, where she served in a variety of roles including scout, spy, cook, and nurse to both Union and Confederate soldiers. She was the first American woman to lead troops into military action when she led 300 black troops on a raid that subsequently freed over 750 slaves.[2]

Harriet Ross Tubman was a deeply religious woman who was guided by her faith in all that she undertook. She took a leading role in the African Methodist Episcopal Zion Church and is commemorated in the calendar of the Episcopal Church on July 20 along with Amelia Bloomer, Elizabeth Cady Stanton, and Sojourner Truth. Her life and work came to the attention of the general public in 1869 after the publication of Sarah Bradford's *Harriet Tubman: The Moses of Her People,* the proceeds of which went to Tubman to pay for her farm. The following excerpts are Harriet Ross Tubman's statements about her life as a slave and her feelings upon obtaining freedom.

NOTES

[1] *Lesser Feasts and Fasts* (2000) (New York: Church Publishing, 2001), 296.

[2] Ibid.

Harriet Ross Tubman
Excerpts from Harriet Tubman:
The Moses of Her People*

"And so," she said to me, "as I lay so sick on my bed, from Christmas till March, I was always praying for poor ole master. 'Pears like I din't do nothing but pray for ole master. 'Oh, Lord, convert ole master,' 'Oh, dear Lord, change dat man's heart, and make him a Christian.' And all the time he was bring men to look at me, and dey stood there saying what dey would give, and what dey would take, and all I could say, 'Oh, Lord, convert ole master.' Den I heard dat as soon as I was able to move I was to be sent with my brudders, in the chain-gang to de far South. Then I changed my prayer, and I said, 'Lord, if you ain't never goint to change dat man's heart, *kill him*, Lord, and take him out de way, so he won't do no more mischief.' Next ting I heard ole master was dead; and he died just as he had lived, a wicked, bad man. Oh, den it 'peared like I would give de world full of silver and gold, if I had to, to bring dat pore soul back, I would give *myself*; I would give eberyting! But he was gone, I couldn't pray for him no more."

[...]

"I knew of a man," she said, "who was sent to the State Prison for twenty-five years. All these years he was always thinking of his home, and counting by years, months, and days, the time till he should be free, and see his family and friends once more. The years roll on, the time of imprisonment is over, the man is free. He leaves the prison gates, he makes him way to his old home, but his old home is not there. The house in which he had dwelt in his childhood had been torn down, and a new one had been put up in its place; his family were gone, their very name was forgotten, there was no one to take him by the hand to welcome him back to life."

"So it was wid me," said Harriet, "I had crossed de line of which I had so long been dreaming. I was free; but dere was no one to welcome [me] to de land of freedom, I was a stranger in a strange land, and my home after all was down In de old cabin quarter, wid de old folks, and my brudders and sisters. But to dis solemn resolution I came: I was free, and dey should be free also; I would make a home for dem in the North, and de Lord helping me, I would bring dem all dere. Oh, how I prayed den, lying all alone on de cold, damp ground; 'Oh, dear Lord,' I said, 'I haint got no friend but you. Come to my help, Lord, for I'm in trouble.'"

---

* Both selections quoted in Sarah Bradford, *Harriet Ross Tubman: The Moses of Her People* (New York: Corinth Books, 1961), 23-25.

LUCY LARCOM

(1824-1883)

ucy Larcom (1824-1883)[1], mill worker, writer, poet, was born in Beverly, Massachusetts, the daughter of Benjamin Larcom, a sea captain, and Lois Barrett Larcom, who ran a boarding house for mill girls. When Benjamin Larcom died, Lucy's mother moved her large family to Lowell, Massachusetts, where she took a job as a supervisor in one of the dormitories in a mill. Lucy Larcom's formal schooling ended shortly thereafter and she, too, joined her sisters in the mill. Lucy began work as a "doffer," that is, the one who replaced the empty bobbins on the machine. Lucy Larcom worked in the mills for the next decade.[2]

Though Lucy Larcom had little formal schooling, she had a love of learning at an early age. She avidly read and wrote poetry; "Pilgrim's Progress" was a favorite. Her love of poetry was fostered by hymnody that she read in church during the sermon. "I was told to listen by the minister," she wrote, "but as I did not understand a word he was saying, I gave it up and took refuge in the hymn-book, with the conscientious purpose of trying to sit still...and sometimes I learned two or three hymns in a forenoon or an afternoon. Finding it so easy, I thought I would begin at the beginning, and learn the whole."[3]

Lucy Larcom also had a thorough knowledge of scripture, though as a child she was somewhat skeptical of the gospel message: "I heard the talk about Jesus as if he were a dead man, one who died a great while ago, whose death made a great difference to us, I could not understand how." She avoided reading Calvin's *Institutes*, preferring English poetry. When her father was alive, Lucy was instructed in the bible every Sunday afternoon. But it took a visiting minister's children's sermon on "Jesus is not dead. He is alive and he loves you," that moved Lucy Larcom's heart. "The stranger never knew how his loving word touched a child's heart," she wrote.[4]

When she was about twenty, Lucy Larcom traveled to Illinois with her sister Emiline to teach in a school housed in a log building. She continued to teach there for three years until she could enroll at Monticello Female Seminary in Godfrey, Illinois, in 1849. Afterwards, she returned to Massachusetts to teach and eventually was hired to teach at Wheaten Female Seminary. Lucy Larcom taught a broad range of subjects at Wheaten, including English literature, rhetoric, moral philosophy, logic, history and botany. Exhausted after eight years with a heavy teaching load, she resigned in 1862. Larcom spent most of the rest of her life as a writer and editor.[5] She died of a heart ailment in 1893, and was buried in an unmarked grave in Beverly, Massachusets.

The central theme in Lucy Larcom's life was her deep commitment to the Christian faith. Though she valued her religious inheritance from her Puritan forebears, she struggled in adulthood with the preaching, worship, and doctrines that she accepted when she became a member of the church in Lowell at the age of thirteen. "I went to the meeting, expecting and needing spiritual food," she wrote, "and received only burning coal and ashes."[6] Though she felt alienated from the church, Lucy Larcom also felt that her love for Jesus increased each year. "She felt herself a member of the Invisible Church, being contented with the thought that the visible churches had no claim on her, because of her errors."[7]

Lucy Larcom's spiritual life was revitalized when she began to attend services at Trinity Church, Boston. The preaching of the rector, Phillips Brooks, touched her deeply. Though Larcom admitted some discomfort with Prayer Book worship—she wished for more opportunity for participation—she loved the availability of the free pews.

She knew little about the Episcopal Church, yet grew to appreciate the liturgical year and the works of Frederick Dennison Maurice.[8]

Phillips Brooks encouraged Lucy Larcom's questions and participation at Trinity, even though she was reluctant to actually become a member for several years. Brooks offered her the Episcopal Church as a "helpful friend," and gracefully responded to her inquiries.[9] Finally, longing for a "home" within the "visible" church, Lucy Larcom received Holy Communion at Trinity Church, Boston, on Easter 1887. The following letters speak to her growing commitment to the Episcopal Church.

NOTES

[1] Lucy Larcom's early life until 1852 is the subject of her most popular book, *A New England Girlhood* (Gloucester: Peter Smith, 1973). *Lucy Larcom: Life, Letters, and Diary*, Daniel Dulany Addison, ed. (Boston: Houghton Mifflin, 1984), is a sequel.

[2] Larcom, *Life and Letters*, 1-20.

[3] Larcom, *New England Girlhood*, 58-62.

[4] Ibid, 64-65.

[5] Ibid, 204-25; *Life, Letters, and Diary*, 21-82.

[6] Ibid, *Life, Letters, and Diary*, 200-02.

[7] Ibid, 203.

[8] Ibid, 206-09.

[9] Ibid, 220-21.

LUCY LARCOM
Letters on "Religious Changes" and "Membership in the Episcopal Church."*

TO PHILLIPS BROOKS

12 Concord Square, March 26, 1885.

Dear Mr. Brooks, I called at the chapel yesterday afternoon, but others were waiting to see you, and it was getting late in the day, so I did not stay. I had, indeed, no good excuse for taking your time; but it would have been a great pleasure to speak to you, after my winter's imprisonment with illness.

It is only within a week or two that I have come to Boston, or been out to church at all. I have enjoyed, almost to pain, the few services I have attended, for I am not sure that I hold myself in the right manner towards God's people, with whom I so fully sympathize in spirit. I wonder if I really am in the Church! My childish consecration was sincere; I entered the communion of the sect in which I was baptized and brought up, from an earnest longing to come nearer to Christ,—a desire which has grown with me through all the years; only now it reaches out beyond all names and groupings, towards the whole Communion of Saints in Him. Nothing less than this is the real Church to me. Some narrowness I find in every denomination, and this distresses and repels me, so that I cannot tell where I belong. Yet when I go to Trinity Church, I feel myself taken possession of, borne upward on the tide of loving loyalty to Christ; and I know that it has not been well for me to live apart from my kindred.

I wish I could find myself among the group who consecrate themselves to-night: but, as you once said to me, if that were the way for me, it would be made plain. And I shall consider Trinity as home, whenever I am in Boston.

I did have one little request to make,—it was liberty to use some paragraphs from your printed sermons in a compilation which I may prepare this year. I shall take it that I have permission, unless forbidden.

Faithfully yours, Lucy Larcom

[…]
JUNE 6.

Canon Wilberforce and the great temperance meeting at Tremont Temple. A most eloquent man, and he goes to the very root of the matter,—no real temperance without spirituality. "Not drunken with wine, but filled with the Holy Ghost,"—he made that infinite contrast clear. His sermon yesterday was most impressive,—from the text, "What seest thou?" It was a Trinity Sunday sermon, and the thought was that in Jesus we see God most perfectly. But emphasis was placed upon the attitude and condition of the soul, for the seeing. It was Canon Wilberforce's first sermon in Boston, and I think this is his first visit to America. It is good to have such neighbors come to see us.

In the afternoon Mr. Brooks spoke from the text, "He that hat the Son hat life." I have seldom heard him speak with more fervor, of what life is, and of the dreadful thing it is to lack life, the life that comes to us and is in us through Christ,—the life of God in human souls. It is his last sermon for the summer, and the text itself is one to keep close at heart all through the year. "Not merely the knowledge of Christ, but Christ Himself with us, we must have," he said: and with the thought comes the suggestion of all true relations of spirit with spirit, the human and the divine interblended, God the soul of our souls and the children one with the Father through the Son. I thank God for what I have found at Trinity Church this winter: I begin to know more what the true Church is,—nothing exclusive or separating, but the coming together of all souls in Christ.
[…]

MARCH 1, 1890.

The same questionings,—yet a clearer light upon the meaning of the Church has gradually come to me. It is as if there were many doors of entrance into one vast temple, some of them opened a little way, and with much scrutiny from within of applicants for admission; some swung wide with welcome. But there is one united worship inside, only some prefer to group themselves in cloisters or corners; but there is freedom and light for all who will receive them.

The Episcopal Church seems to have several doors of its own,— some wide and some narrow; it is not *the* Church,—only one way of entering Christ's Church. If I can enter it that way, I am already there. And I believe more positively than ever, that we should say, in some distinct, personal way, that Christ is the center and head of humanity, and that our whole life, earthly and heavenly, is hid in Him.

What belongs to me in Puritanism I shall never lay aside; I could not, if I would. But I do see more of a hope for future unity in the Church service than in any other way; and if I can see therein for myself the perfect freedom of Christ's service, I am ready to make a new profession there. I am waiting only for His guidance, now.

I see more and more how much the writings of Maurice have been to me for the past twenty years. He is continually unfolding my own thoughts to me,—his absolute sincerity is contagious. I want no pretenses, no subterfuges or concessions in the spiritual life. He speaks to me more clearly than almost any audible voice. And his words seem the expression of the mind of Christ.

MARCH 5.

My birthday. And the world seems as if it were dimly dawning anew to me. Everything in my life has taken a touch of awe,—of strangeness.

I do not know that there is any new gladness in the decision I made yesterday, to be "confirmed" at Trinity Church, but there is a settled feeling that may grow into happiness. I can say that my "heart is fixed," and my life will be firmer and more settled, for having found a place for itself. The church itself seemed a different and more beautiful place, as I sat there and listened to the story of the Woman of Samaria, and of the separateness of souls in consecrated work. "Mean to eat that ye know not of," the doing of God's will,—the hidden manna and the white stone, with the new name known only to him who receives it. Yes, this one little decision has opened closed doors to me already—everything looks sacred.

MARCH 20.

Last night I knelt in the chancel at Trinity Church, and received, with many others, the benediction of consecrated hands; and to-day I can think of myself as avowedly in the visible Church once more. I have been in a false position all these years,—I see it now. It does mean something to name the name of Christ in the presence of His people, as one of their company. I have not been an unbeliever, ever; He has been dear to me always, and most real to my heart.

It was tranquillizing, to be bending there with all that young life,— (no other older life), the snow falling without, soft and white as doves' wings, and the quiet consecration filling all hearts within. I was not wholly happy; I have had too many struggles with myself, and misapprehension between my own heart and others, perhaps, to feel glad or uplifted,—but I was calm and thankful, and felt the atmosphere of blessing surrounding us all.

It is good to have taken this position; I shall feel stronger and richer in life and spirit for it, I trust and believe.

The few words of Mr. Brooks this morning at the church seemed to carry out the spirit of last night's service. We climb up the great mountain-tops, he said, but we cannot live there, though we may keep their inspiration within us. But the high table-lands which we have gained by long gradual ascent,—we can live and breathe there; and can grow hopeful in the broad outlook before us. Such are the consecrations of life to which we have grown step by step, out of which greater developments are to open for us, and above which the loftier summits are always overhanging.

---

* These letters were written shortly after Lucy Larcom first heart the preaching of Phillips Brooks and during her early membership in the Epscopal Church, see *Lucy Larcom: Life, Letters, and Diary*, Daniel Dulany Addison, ed. (Boston: Houghton Mifflin, 1894): 225-26; 247-48; 51-53.

LILI`UOKALANI

(1837-1917)

ili`uokalani (1837-1917)[1], composer, author, philanthropist, was the last sovereign of the Hawaiian Islands from 1891-1895. She was born Lydia Kamaka `eha Loloku Lili `u Walaniaikeiki `i `onohi Ka `alaniali `i Neweweli `i Paki Dominis to High Chief Caesar Kapa ` akea and High Chiefess Keohohaloe, and according to Hawaiian custom was raised by High Chief Abner Paki and Chiefess Kunia. She was also the adopted sister of princess Bernice Pauahi Paki Bishop, to whom she was especially close. During this time, Lydia Kamakaha Paki, as she was known, was educated from 1842-1849 at the American missionary Chiefs' Children's School, where she learned English. She was known as Lili`uokalani after her designation as heir to the throne in 1877. After an engagement to Prince William Lunalilo, she married John Owen Dominis, the Italian-American son of an Italian sea captain who made his home in Hawaii. The marriage was childless and Dominis died the same year Lili`uokalani became queen.[2]

Lili`uokalani became queen of the Kingdom of Hawaii in January 1891 after her brother's death. As queen she attempted to restore some of the power the monarchy had lost under her brother's rule. These actions precipitated rebellion by the American colonists who controlled Hawaii's economy. In 1893, the U.S. Marines occupied government buildings in Honolulu and deposed the queen. Under the leadership of Sanfold Dole, the colonists applied for annexation from the United States. Lili`uokalani applied to President Grover Cleveland for reinstatement, and although the president opposed annexation, Dole set up a provisional government. In 1895 Queen Lili`uokalani was placed under house arrest for eight months; she later abdicated in exchange for the release of her supporters. After her forced abdication, Lili`uokalani was released and lived in Honolulu as a private citizen until her death.

Queen Lili`uokalani was supported by the Anglican bishop and religious orders throughout her imprisonment in 1895 and afterwards. She was later confirmed at St. Andrew's Cathedral, Honolulu, in May 1896. Lili`uokalani was active in Anglican charitable organizations. An accomplished musician and composer of Hawaiian hymns and songs, the queen translated and arranged the service for Holy Communion into a Hawaiian setting. At the time of her death in 1917, Queen Lili`uokalani was buried according to the rites of the Episcopal Church. She left her estate for the establishment of an orphanage for poor children, with a preference for those of aboriginal birth from the islands[3]

The following document is from Queen Lili`uokalani's *Hawaii's Story by Hawaii's Queen*. Originally published in 1898, it is her personal account of the last years of the monarchy. This excerpt is from the chapter on "Hawaiian Autonomy."

NOTES

[1] Biographical information and translation from Pua Hopkins. Additional information on Lili`uokalani found in Barbara Bennett Peterson, *Notable Women of Hawaii* (Honolulu: Univerity of Hawaii Press, 1984) 240-44. Also, see Lili`uokalani, *Hawaii's Story by Hawaii's Queen* (Rutland: Charles Tuttle and Company, 1964).

[2] Bennett, Notable *Women of Hawaii*, 240.

[3] Information provided by Pua Hopkins, 2001.

LILI'UOKALANI OF HAWAII
An Excerpt from Hawaii's Story
By Hawaii's Queen*

I shall not claim that in the days of captain Cook our people were civilized. I shall not claim anything more for their progress in civilization and Christian morality than has already been attested by missionary writers. Perhaps I may safely claim even less, admitting the criticism of some intelligent visitors who were *not* missionaries—that the habits and prejudices of New England Puritans were not well adapted to the genius of a tropical people, not capable of being thoroughly grafted upon them.

Christianity in substance they [the Hawaiians] have accepted; and I know of no people who have developed a tenderer Christian conscience, or who have shown themselves more ready to obey its behests. Nor has any people known to history shown a greater reverence and love for their Christian teachers, or filled the measure of a grateful return more overflowingly. And where else in the world's history is it written that a savage people, pagan for ages, with fixed hereditary customs and beliefs, have made equal progress in civilization and Christianity in the same space of time? And what people has ever been subjected during such an evolution to such a flood of external demoralizing influences?

Does it make nothing for us that we have always recognized our Christian teachers as worthy of authority in our councils, and repudiated those whose influence or character was vicious or irreligious? That while four-fifths of the population of our Islands was swept out of existence by the vices introduced by foreigners, the ruling class clung to Christian morality, and gave its unvarying support and service to the work of saving and civilizing the masses? Has not this class loyally clung to the brotherly alliance made with the better element of foreign settlers, giving freely of its authority and its substance, its sons and daughters, to cement and to prosper it?

But will it also be thought strange that education and knowledge of the world have enabled us to perceive that as a race we have some special mental and physical requirements not shared by the other races that have come among us? That certain habits and modes of living are better for our health and happiness than others? And that a separate nationality, and a particular form of government, as well as special laws, are, at least for the present, best for us? And these things remained to us, until the pitiless and tireless "annexation policy" was effectively backed by the naval power of the United States...

To other usurpations of authority on the part of those whose love for the institutions of their native land we could understand and forgive we submitted. We have allowed them to virtually give us a constitution, and control the offices of state. Not without protest, indeed; for the usurpation was unrighteous, and cost us much humiliation and distress. But we did not resist it by force. It had not entered into our hearts to believe that these friends and allies from the United States, even with all their foreign affinities, would ever go so far as to absolutely overthrow our form of government, seize our nation by the throat, and pass it over to an alien power.

And while we sought by peaceful political means to maintain the dignity of the throne, and to advance national feeling among the native people, we never sought to rob any citizen, wherever born, of either property, franchise, or social standing.

[...]

But for the Hawaiian people, for the forty thousand of my own race and blood, descendents of those who welcomed the devoted missionaries of seventy years ago, — for them has this mission of mine accomplished anything?

Oh, honest Americans, as Christians hear me for my down-trodden people! Their form of government is as dear to them as yours is precious to you. Quite as warmly as you love your country, so they love theirs. With all your goodly possessions, covering a territory so immense that there yet remain parts unexplored, possessing islands that, although near at hand, had to be neutral ground in time of war, do not covet the little vineyard of Naboth's, so far from your shores, lest the punishment of Ahab fall upon you, if not in your day, in that of your children, for "be not deceived, God is not mocked." The people to whom your fathers told of the living God, and taught to call "Father," and whom the sons now seek to despoil and destroy, are crying aloud to Him in their time of trouble; and He will keep His promise, and will listen to the voices of His Hawaiian children lamenting for their homes....

---

* Lili'uokalani, Hawaii's Story By Hawaii's Queen (Rutland: Charles E. Tuttle Company, 1964): 366-68; 373-74. The source and document were provided by Pua Hopkins.

LUCY GILMER BRECKINRIDGE

(1843-1865)

Lucy Gilmer Breckinridge (1843-1865) was the daughter of Virginia gentry. Her grandfather, General James Breckinridge was a close associate of Thomas Jefferson. Shortly after his marriage, James Breckinridge built the elegant family estate, Grove Hill on 4000 acres in Botetourt County. Lucy's father, Cary, was the General's eldest son. Though educated at William and Mary and the recipient of local appointments, Cary Breckinridge devoted most of his career to the management of Grove Hill. By the middle of the nineteenth-century, Cary Breckinbridge was the second largest slaveholder in the county. Lucy's mother, Emma Walker Breckinridge, directed the household as well as the education of the children. Emma not only was a powerful influence over her daughter Lucy, she was a force that permeated all aspects of life at Grove Hill.[1]

The extant documents relating to Lucy Gilmer Breckinridge is a journal that she kept between the years 1862-1864, during the Civil War. The war was a time of immense uncertainty and loneliness for Lucy—most of the men in her family were called away. Like her contemporaries, Lucy Breckinridge spent her days during wartime sewing, making bandages, nursing the sick, reading, writing, and praying. Her journal reveals her perceptions on the issues of war, the life of the church, and the concerns of young womanhood. She died of typhoid fever in 1865, just weeks after the surrender of the last of the Confederacy and within five months of marrying her beloved Thomas Jefferson Bassett.[2] In the following excerpts from her journal, Lucy shares her observations about daily life at Grove Hill.

Notes

[1] Mary D. Robertson, *Lucy Breckinridge of Grove Hill: the Journal of a Virginia Girl, 1862-1864*. (Kent: Kent State University Press, 1979): 1-5.

[2] Ibid, 6, 215-16.

CR

LUCY BRECKINRIDGE
Selections from her journal, 1862-1864[1]

MONDAY, AUGUST 11, 1862

[…]

So, it has been five years since you were at Grove Hill! A great many changes have taken place since then. There have been two marriages in the family and ever so many babies. But, as I am going to write you every day now. I shall let my recitations concerning the family be gradual.

On this day we are very much scattered. Mamma and George are over at Glencary helping Sister to make arrangements to come over here to stay during the war. Brother Lewis is a surgeon and away from home constantly, so that the farm has been under Mr. Mahan's direction, but he has not proved a faithful steward. He entertains deserters at the expense of Brother Lewis' flocks of sheep. etc., and steals things generally. I am glad that Sister is coming over here to live. That she has a very sweet little home is true, but there never was a wilder and more desolate country. The three eldest children are here, and very sweet, interesting little things they are. Though Jimmy is *my* boy. I think Gary is my pet; he talks so sweetly and indistinctly.

We always feel very desolate without Mamma, but tried to amuse ourselves with some books Sister sent over.

We went to the Episcopal Church yesterday, expecting to hear a poor sermon from Mr. McGuire,[2] and were delightfully surprised when our old tutor, Mr. F. Martin, walked into the pulpit—not that he is a very interesting preacher, *au contraire,* but anything is better than Mr. McGuire. We are not satisfied with Mr. McGuire. He is not an Episcopalian at all. Yesterday, he administered communion and left out all of the morning service. Mr. Martin remonstrated with him about it, but his excuse was that the service was so long that the Presbyterians and Methodists get tired. I wish he would read the service and omit his sermon!

On Sunday, he preached a sermon on the subject, "Too late for repentance," and compared a man's putting off religion to a traveler. These are his words: "The traveler arises late in the morning. He reaches the station. Just as he arrives there, he hears the whistle, 'Toot! toot!' and the cars have left him! He runs after them (a long and impressive pause) but they are too fast for him! My friends, (leaning over the pulpit. stretching and winking his bright, blue eyes, and pointing that long, terrible first finger to the congregation) my friends, he is— *TOO—late!!*"

I need scarcely tell you that he is killing out the church here completely—poor man, he has broken up every congregation he ever had anything to do with. After church we went up to speak to Mr. Martin and begged him to come out to see us, which he promised to do that evening. So, after dinner, he arrived and we enjoyed his visit very much. Brother Gilmer and himself got to discussing the doctrines of the different churches. I always drink in anything doctrinal very eagerly. He spoke of predestination, but I have never met anyone yet who could throw any light on that subject. I am sorry I ever thought of it, it puzzles me so.

Then Brother Gilmer spoke of a Carmelitish doctrine. Some man in Tennessee told him about it. He argues that the thief who was crucified with Jesus was not saved. His arguments are these: If the thief was saved it is one of the most important events mentioned in the New Testament, and it is very singular that Luke was the only one of the Evangelists who gives that version of it. The others say that the thieves reviled Him, and if Luke's account is true the sentence may be differently construed from the way it is generally received. The soldiers mocking Jesus, called Him, "King of the Jews," so the thief might have mocked when he said, "Lord, remember me when thou comest into thy Kingdom," and Jesus said, "Today shalt thou sup with me in Paradise." The man argues that Jesus slept in the grave three days and Paradise means a "hidden place," so that Jesus did not mean Heaven, but the grave. The argument is too weak to take the trouble to confute.

Mr. Martin left soon after breakfast this morning. I amused myself during the day reading, *Alone*,[3] quite an interesting novel, but not very well written. Late in the evening Miss Fannie Burwell, who has been with us for the last three weeks, Eliza, Emma, the three children and myself walked to the garden and from there to the stable. I went in to see Little Dorrit, who in spite of my neglect, knows and loves me still. She tried very hard to talk to me, bless her little heart. When we came back to the house we found Cousin George Carr here. We had gone out walking in our dressing wrappers; and to show how cunning girls are, Eliza and Miss Fannie slipped upstairs and dressed, then put on their hats and walked in at the front door as if they had just returned from walking. We sat up quite late discussing the war, generals. etc., and then Monday ended.

[...]

SUNDAY, SEPT. 7, 1862[4]

Soon after breakfast fourteen of us arranged ourselves in the two carriages and two buggies with a few riding horses and went to church. Mr. Woodbridge preached a beautiful sermon and read the whole service which we Episcopalians enjoyed very much. After church Mr. Godwin assembled us around him and read the news. And glorious news it is. Our army at Munson's Hill in sight of Washington! But the Yankees have been as near Richmond! We were so distressed to hear that Mr. Charles Spears had been killed. They told his poor wife about it just as she was coming out of church. Brother James sent a telegraphic dispatch. He was a fine young man and a good soldier.

After dinner we all went to church again and heard another splendid sermon from Dr. Woodbridge. Miss Fannie Burwell left us today. We shall miss her terribly. Tonight Mr. McGuire came. He certainly does not show off to advantage beside Mr. Woodbridge. After tea Mr. Woodbridge had services for the servants. He had quite a good congregation. Mr. McGuire, being our pastor, had to have prayers. Sister Julia and Cousin Kate sang some hymns.

[...]

SUNDAY, JULY 5TH, 1863[5]

Little Emma and I spent the day together reading the bible and learning hymns. She wrote a note to her Mamma, but the poor child shows very little literary taste and cares for nothing but Ella. She has depreciated very much of late. I missed Ma, Eliza and Emma very much. I read all of Capt. H.'s letters. I ought to destroy them, but cannot make up my mind to do so. I wonder if I shall ever love anyone as much as I did him. I am afraid to think of him much, the old love comes back; but I am so thankful that our engagement is broken off, for all of my family objected so strongly to the match, and I should not have been happy if I had married him. Ma came late this evening having had a pleasant visit. Poor Johnny Clarke was drowned in the river on Thursday; two of his brothers met with a similar fate. Mr. Anthony sent me the only ripe apricot, dear, old gentleman! Oh, dear! how dismally the frogs are singing. There is something in the idea that ever since I or anyone else can remember those or some other frogs have been singing that very same song, which always reminds me of eternity. I love to hear them, but it has the same effect on me that drowning is said to have— recalling all the incidents of the past, more particularly those of my childhood, to my mind, and it is impossible to think of the past without being melancholy—even when we remember happy things. We are generally alone and in some private place when we indulge in the pleasures of memory, and the very contrast between what we are recalling and our present position produces melancholy. It is very sweet to look upon "the blue mountains of our dim childhood" as Richter calls the past, and a very good little simile it is. The farther we get from the mountain the more softened is the outline, the less distinct the rocks and rugged places. The mountain is not *blue* enough yet for me to be thinking so sadly. What will my reflections be 10 years hence if I begin so early to moralize, then I'll have cause, I expect, for mournfulness, being quite a desolate old maid or still worse a married woman with ever so many crying babies and a cross, horrid husband as all husbands are. Oh, dear! Oh, dear!! How gloomy the prospect.

[...]

SUNDAY NIGHT, JULY 3RD, 1864[6]

My mind has been so full of doubts of God's goodness and mercy today. I have been so sinful. I read my Bible and prayed, but the light of God's countenance was withdrawn from me. I longed so for some kind friend or pastor to guide and comfort me. Tonight I sat out here in the hail, writing all my sinful doubts, when I heard Eliza and Sister Julia talking about Jesus and the quietness and loveliness of his character until my heart was touched—and I believed. Sorrows are too apt to harden my heart against God, yet, I must reconcile myself to a life of hardship and sorrow. We are born to suffer and to die. The gloomy state of the country depresses me so terribly I cannot see the dawn of peace that I hear some people talk about. They cry, "Peace, peace, when there is no peace." But I *will* try to believe that "He doeth all things well." I had three letters from Tommy this week and wrote one to him. We have heard from George several times. No news yet from dear, Brother Gilmer. I still hope he may recover.

It is late. I must stop writing and go to bed. I have been sick in bed all day.

---

[1] As published in Mary D. Robertson, ed., *Lucy Breckinridge of Grove Hill: The Journal of a Virginia Girl*, 1862-1864 (Kent: Kent State University Press, 1979): 18-20.

[2] The Reverend Mr. William McGuire was rector of the Episcopal Church in Fincastle.

[3] A novel by Marion Harland (pen name of Mary Virginia Terhune, 1830–1922), published in 1854.

[4] Robertson, *Lucy Breckinridge*, 40.

[5] Ibid, 123-24.

[6] Ibid., 188-89.

JULIA CHESTER EMERY

(1852-1922)

Julia Chester Emery (1852-1922), pioneer in missions and women's ministries, is commemorated in the Episcopal calendar on January 9. For forty years, 1876-1916, she served as the Secretary of the Woman's Auxiliary of the Board of Missions established by the General Convention in 1871. She succeeded her sister Mary Abbott Emery Twing to the post. "During the forty years she served as Secretary, Julia helped the Church to recognize its call to proclaim the Gospel both at home and overseas. Her faith, her courage, her spirit of adventure and her ability to inspire others combined to make her a leader respected and valued by the whole church."[1]

During her tenure as Secretary of the Woman's Auxiliary of the Board of Missions, Julia Chester Emery traveled across the United States and the world—often under difficult conditions in remote areas—promoting the work of the auxiliary, raising funds, and offering encouragement to missionaries and their supporters at home. Julia Chester Emery's work was key to the expansion of the work of the Woman's Auxiliary within the Episcopal Church and abroad. In 1897, she addressed the women's missionary conference held in conjunction with the Lambeth Conference. Not only was Emery a delegate from the diocese of New York to the Pan-American Congress in London in 1908; on the way home she traveled around the world to missions in China, Japan, Hawaii, the Philippines, and all the dioceses on the West Coast.[2] By the time Emery retired in 1916, every diocese and missionary district, including Africa, China, Japan, Alaska, Brazil, and Hawaii participated in the Woman's Auxiliary.[3]

Julia Chester Emery was born in Dorchester, Massachusetts in 1852. Her father was a sea captain. Though Captain Charles Emery was a Unitarian, and his wife, Susan Hilton Kelly a Congregationalist, the couple were confirmed and became communicants of the Episcopal Church at the same time as their eldest daughter, Mary Abbott. The couple eventually had eleven children. Julia Chester Emery graduated from Dorchester High School and briefly attended the Normal School in Boston and St. Catherine's Hall in Augusta, Maine. [4]

Besides her sister Mary Abbott Emery Twing, Julia Chester Emery had two other sisters active in the work of the Woman's Auxiliary—Margaret Theresa and Susan Lavinia. Another sister, Helen, supported missionary efforts by providing hospitality in her New York City home to visiting missionaries. In addition, two of Julia Chester Emery's brothers were priests, the elder of whom became Archdeacon of California.[5]

Perhaps one of Julia Chester Emery's most significant contributions to the Episcopal Church still present in many parishes is the United Thank Offering. Founded under the name the "United Offering" in 1889, contributions expanded to approximately $300,000 by 1916.[6] Due to Julia Chester Emery's skilled leadership and ability to inspire women in local parishes, the Woman's Auxiliary grew into an extensive network. Women active in the network received missionary publications and interacted with missionary families. Besides collecting funds, local parish groups made and collected clothing and other items needed by missionaries and their families.

Julia Chester Emery recorded her experiences in the periodical *The Spirit of Missions*. She also wrote the centenary history of the Domestic and Foreign Missionary Society, *A Century of Endeavor, 1821-1921*, as well as biographies of John Henry Hobart and Alexander Viets Griswold. The following article published in *The Spirit of Missions* in 1910 describes Julia Chester Emery's trip to St. Mary's Mission, Moiliili, Hawaii.

NOTES

[1] *Lesser Feasts and Fasts (2000)* (New York: Church Publishing, 2000): 118.

[2] Ibid.

[3] Willeen Smith, "Inspirational Endeavors: The Emery Sisters, "*The Living Church* (February 14, 1999): 15

[4] Margaret A. Tomes, *Julia Chester Emery: Being the Story of Her Life and Work* (New York: The Woman's Auxiliary, 1924): 16-19

[5] Ibid.

[6] Ibid.

CR

JULIA CHESTER EMERY
St. Mary's, Moiliili*

It was on such a beautiful, bright day last April that I took the street car near Bishop Restarick's home in Honolulu, and rode out to the suburb called Moiliili. You pass the aquarium, where are the brightest colored, most fascinating of sea creatures, and by the shore along which many Hawaiians—some of the old royal race–have built their summer cottages. You see stones dug up from the beach on which human sacrifices were once offered to false gods, and banyan trees under which chiefs used to meet in council; and then you come to the hired house standing in its garden under the quiet shade of the algarroba trees, and visit the work that is helping to rear soldiers and servants of the true and gentle Christ. This is called St. Mary's Mission, and there our work has gone on since May, 1907.

The mission really began with Mrs. Folsom in charge, in what had been one of the worst opium haunts in Honolulu. But the poor, mean place had been cleaned and whitewashed, and before the change to the present place was made, so many prayers and praises had arisen there, that somehow it had taken on a homey look.

With it were associated the magic lantern exhibitions, when eager spectators thronged the room and crowded doors and windows; the Moon Feast, when the people's minds were led from the moon to its Creator; Thanksgiving with its harvest hymns and games and feast; Christmas with its decorations and Christmas service; Holy Innocents' with the children's first *real* tree, who had been satisfied heretofore with branches left over from the decorations at the cathedral, tied together to make the semblance of a tree. No wonder the room was crowded full again, and mothers with babies on their backs stood looking in through door and windows on the novel, pretty sight. And as they looked their children were their teachers, reciting, as had been taught to them, the story of the Annunciation and of the birth of our Blessed Lord. Again, there was the night when, through the kindness of a friend, electricity was introduced. On a Sunday evening the kerosene lights were turned out, and as all knelt in the darkness in silent prayer, the leader of the little congregation, turning on the electric light, said solemnly, "And God said, 'Let their be light, and there was light,'" thus making this gift to the mission a reminder of God's wonder-working power in the past, a symbol of the power with which He is ever working in turning darkened souls to glorious light. At another time the phonograph was the mystery, and when Mrs. Folsom started it at the back of the mission, one tiny tot wanted to see for himself where the talking and music came from; but on being lifted up to investigate seemed to get no satisfaction.

These first buildings of St. Mary's were in the midst of a fluctuating population of Japanese and Chinese, and into their homes the missionary went, in sickness ministering to them under her doctor's advice to acceptably that from camp and district generally came the verdict, "Mama's doctor and *haole* medicine too much good *kaukau*," and no matter what the trouble, they always came for "some good, kind medicine, all same like before!"

But at last the mission crowded the mission buildings beyond their utmost capacity, and it was then that the new St. Mary's was found, about ten minutes' walk away, and was rented and occupied.

But remembering the first year of the mission, it was not strange that in leaving it, Mrs. Folsom felt sad, and doubtful if it were the best thing to do. She said to herself, "How shall I know this?" when picking up a little text card, she read, "My presence shall go with you," and felt as though an answer had been given to her questioning prayers. In the old house the school-mother lived in one little building and the school gathered in another; in the new St. Mary's all are under one roof. And the sweet influences of this new home center in the little chapel where the children meet each morning and where Sunday night service is always held. In this new home was formerly an elaborate heathen altar with beautiful adornments, where worship had often been offered to heathen gods; now in the same room, made larger by tearing down a partition, and neatly painted and papered at the expense of the night-school, worship goes up daily to the One True God. The chapel is made beautiful by the memorials which it contains. One who was a friend to the mission from the first gave the altar in memory of his father and mother; the reredos, which he also designed, was made from *koa* wood taken from panels and doors of buildings formerly standing on the palace grounds, in which archives had been kept for many years. It is a memorial to Mrs. Mackintosh, whose memory lingers fragrant and blessed in the islands where she made her home. The cross on the altar is another memorial. The night-school men gave vases, and the Babies' Branch in Rochester the font, and with other gifts the chapel is made a beautiful place in which to draw near to the Heavenly Father.

And it was there that I first met the children of St. Mary's that April morning of last year. They had just filed in from the garden, singing as they went, for their morning prayers. Mrs. Folsom had left them for other work in Hilo, and Miss Van Deerlin was in charge, with Miss Chung, the young Chinese woman who went from Honolulu to New York, where she and Miss Van Deerlin both studied in the Training-School for Deaconesses and became fitted to do this mission work at Moiliili.

They showed their visitors over their mission home and told them of their work, of their neighbors, of the many Japanese near by, of the Portuguese just back of them, of the Chinese a little farther off; of their very small homes, some just in camps; the Japanese tidy, and Portuguese untidy and dirty, with many chickens, ducks and pigs. They told how the Portuguese children love St. Mary's, and will come each morning by seven o'clock, and want no vacations. The missionaries' hardest work is to get rid of them when school hours are past. There have been as many as ninety-five of the day-school children, fifty Hawaiians, others Chinese, Japanese, and Portuguese; and at night twenty-seven men and boys, Japanese, Chinese and Korean, were coming to the evening classes. The day is a busy one: 6:30 a.m., prayers in chapel; 7 to 9, cooking and housework; 9, short service for children; 9:15 to 12, school; 10:45 to 11, dispensary. In the afternoon comes sewing-school, visiting Chinese and Japanese in their homes, dispensary, cooking. From 7 to 9 is night-school, and at 9 comes a short service for the night-school men. On Sunday, Sunday-school is from 9 to 10; dispensary is from 10 to 10:30. From 7 to 8 P.M. there is reading with night-school men, and this is followed from 8 to 9 by an evening service for them, with instruction.

Thus Miss Van Deerlin and Miss Chung are kept busy from day to day. They took me through their living rooms, in which they have been able to gather only such few and simple furnishings; out on the veranda, where they often eat the simple meals which they themselves have prepared; into the room where the older children were at work with their books, and among the kindergarten children who have so few of those little tricks and toys, playing with which makes so many kindergarten children here wise about many useful things. I saw the picture-books sent by our missionary in Salt Lake to help amuse and instruct these children; I heard of the friend who sends a dollar every month to give these missionaries at St. Mary's something to work with; I saw the little dispensary, with its slimly-equipped shelves, in which so much pain is relieved; and then I heard that the children for whom these small things are done at St. Mary's, themselves sent $17 last Easter, that missionaries as loving as Miss Van Deerlin and Miss Chung might minister to children elsewhere, who have no mission house and school and dispensary and chapel.

As I looked at these smallest children and saw how much their school-room lacked, I promised that they should have a blackboard with some colored crayons. These were soon procured and sent, and in return came to me this little note:

St. Mary's Mission,
Moiliili, Honolulu,

May 3, 1909.

My dear Miss Emery:

We want to thank you for the nice blackboards.

This was signed by thirty-nine names. These are some of them: Lo Ah Sin, Manuel, Kanita, Man Wo Kim, Ishero, Rosie, Sizue.

Such names as these show the different races from which the children of St. Mary's come. Some of them will remain in the Hawaiian Islands, some will come to the United States, some of them will return to those distant lands in which their fathers were at home. And we who have spent a few moments where faithful friends and teachers have spent months and years may well pray that wherever, as men and women, they may go, these children may take with them a loving faith in a loving Saviour and a willing readiness to walk in His holy ways, which they learned in St. Mary's, Moiliili.

A Western business man, a communicant of the Church, was asked by a news agency to give his impressions of the Laymen's Movement, to be sent to a large list of daily papers. This is what he wrote: "The Laymen's Missionary Movement evidences a recognition by men of their plain, and in many cases long-neglected, duty, to 'tell it out among the heathen that the Lord is King.' It is a hopeful sign in these days of large doings in business and national affairs that men are having large visions and rising to greater activity in the business of the Church. Our aims hitherto have been altogether too small and low—we have been content with nickels where dollars would hardly suffice. We have allowed the women to man our churches and to supplement our short-comings. The Laymen's Missionary Movement, I believe, is changing these conditions, and under God's guidance and with His blessing the change will be lasting and of ever-increasing value. Every man who can possible attend a Laymen's Missionary Movement Convention ought to do so without fail; otherwise he will miss a rare opportunity to get information, education and inspiration that are of untold value to every one of us. The sincerity, earnestness and deep convictions of the speakers and executive officers of the Laymen's Missionary Movement and the spirit of prayer that prevails at their conventions can never be forgotten by any man who has the privilege of being present."

---

* Julia C. Emery, "St. Mary's Moiliili," *Spirit of Missions* 81 (April 1910): 275-278.

LOUISE DEKOVEN BOWEN

(1859-1953)

Louise deKoven Bowen (1859-1953), reformer and political activist, was a long-time colleague of Jane Addams at Hull House and consistently exercised her great wealth and influence to improve the welfare of women, children, and families in Chicago and the state of Illinois. Her long-time positions included president of the Juvenile Protective Association and treasurer of Hull House for over forty years. After Addams' death in 1935, Bowen became acting president of Hull House.

As a young woman, Louise deKoven—as did many of her contemporaries—considered church work as an acceptable outlet for social service. She taught Sunday school to boys for over eleven years; a ministry that grew to include family visits, job placement, and the establishment of the first Boys Club of Chicago. Though Bowen experienced frustration with what she saw as the limited role women had in the Episcopal Church, her early church work set her reform agenda in motion.

Louise deKoven Bowen was one of the first reformers to recognize the needs of the African American community of Chicago. In her book *The Colored People of Chicago* (1913), Bowen decried the effects of racism on African Americans, describing children's lives as "so circumscribed on every hand by race limitations."[1] She worked with other reformers to establish the first juvenile court in the United

States in Chicago in 1899, and supported the national woman's suffrage movement as a means of social reform.

Throughout her long career, Louise deKoven Bowen developed powerful social and political networks. During World War I she was the first and only woman appointed to the Illinois Council of Defense. During the 1920s Bowen was considered to be a possible mayoral candidate, and eventually became one of three women on the Republican National Committee. Politically, during her last twenty years as an activist, she supported both Democratic and Republican candidates who she believed would further her reform agenda.

Louise deKoven Bowen wrote several autobiographical works, among them, *Growing Up With a City* (1926). The excerpt here focuses on her early reform efforts at St. James Episcopal Church, Chicago.

NOTES

[1] Quoted in Sharon Z. Alter, "Louise deKoven Bowen," in *Women Building Chicago 1790-1990: A Biographical Dictionary*, Rima Kunin Schultz, Adele Hast, eds. (Bloomington: Indiana University Press, 2001): 103.

∞

LOUISE DEKOVEN BOWEN
"Churches, Hospitals, Nurses": An Except from Growing Up With a City*

I always went to church every Sunday with my parents. We lived on the South Side, and we drove north in a buggy, the horse being hitched while we were at church. After church I always lunched at the house of my Sunday School teacher to whom I was passionately devoted.

I was also allowed to help my mother, who was chairman of the Chancel Committee, and every Sunday I assisted her in arranging two vases of flowers for the altar, finding the Lessons for the day and, during the week, mending the cassocks worn by the boy choir. Later I was made chairman of this Committee, and every Easter, Christmas and Holy Day I was at church at five or six o'clock in the morning to get my work done and floral decorations in place before the early service at eight o'clock. It was perhaps good discipline for a young girl thus to get up early and to have responsibility, but I was always very sleepy and tired before night.

The church at that time was the only outlet for social work. The girls taught in sewing and Sunday schools, they visited the poor, they trimmed the church at Christmas and Easter. This church trimming was a matter of great importance, and work began two or three weeks before Christmas, as the greens had to be made into wreaths. The work was done in the basement of the church, and so absorbed the attention of all the young people in the parish that no social entertainment was given during the two weeks preceding Christmas. The young men were always on hand in the evenings to help with the heavy work. It was, altogether, a joyful time. Later in life, when I had had a good deal of experience in social work, I had a pang of conscience that I was doing no church work. I went to my rector and asked for something to do. After thinking the matter over he offered me the chairmanship of the Chancel Committee, the same work I had done when I was an inexperienced girl. This work I declined on the ground that my experience should have fitted me for something more responsible.

When I was sixteen years old I felt I ought to take a Sunday School class, and one Sunday afternoon, with much sinking of the heart, I presented myself to the superintendent of the Sunday School and asked for a class. He told me that there was none without a teacher that day except a class of big boys which had been given up the former week, because their teacher felt she could not manage them. Disappointed that I was not to teach, I asked if I could not try this class of bad boys. I was told that I could, but that they were quite unmanageable. When I was escorted to the class the boys sat in a semi-circle around me; my heart failed me as they were boys of fourteen and sixteen years of age, very rough looking, and certainly very rough acting. I was consoled, however, by the fact that the sons of the sexton, the rector of the parish, and the bishop of the diocese were in the class. To my disappointment, however, they did not prove to be a soothing factor. When I sat down I said I had never had a class before and knew nothing of the rules of the school, but that I intended to be obeyed and that I would not tolerate any rough-housing—that any boy who was not quiet I would put out of the room. One big boy immediately kicked the boy next to him. I told him to be quiet, but as he kicked again I thought it was time for action, and seizing the big boy by the collar I pulled him off the bench and out into the aisle down toward the door, which, when I reached, I opened and cast him out. The whole affair was so unexpected—that is, being seized by a girl and dragged down the aisle before the whole school—that the boy did nothing but kick, but as I was a strong young person I had no difficulty in putting him out. When I returned to the class everyone was as quiet as a mouse. I began the lesson, and from that time on I never had one bit of trouble with the boys. I held this Sunday School class for eleven years. The boys grew into young men, but stayed with me, and brought in others until I had a class of one hundred. The Sunday School room was too small for them, and I had them in the transept of the church itself. I always had the lesson and then told a story which illustrated somewhat, or was intended to illustrate, the subject on which I had been talking. I called the class "The Soldiers of Christ," and if a boy was perfect in attendance and deportment for three months he had a yellow card given him, stating that he had been made a Corporal in the "Soldiers of Christ"; six months made him a Sergeant, nine months a third Lieutenant, etc., and when he became a General he received a gold watch.

When I was holding the class in the transept of the church, the body of the church was occupied by deaf mutes who were holding their regular service there. It was very upsetting to see them rise, kneel and pray, and go through the ritual of the Episcopal Church, and I was always glad to see the clergyman begin his sermon, because then it was less confusing and I did not feel we were interrupting. One day these deaf mutes were, by mistake, locked in the chapel; being unable to make any sound, they spent the night there before they were discovered.

I found that the young men in my class had very little opportunity for recreation, and I had them at my house three times a week to play billiards with me in the billiard room which was in the basement of the house. I also tried to keep in close touch with the boys, so visited their families frequently, heard their troubles and learned to know something about them from their parents. As the boys grew older I found places for them when they went to work. I almost ran an employment agency, for any young man that I knew who did not send to me the information that the store or firm in which he worked wanted a boy never heard the last of it, and I made myself a great nuisance to my friends. I have never experienced in any other way the satisfaction I felt when I was told that some boy I had placed had made good and was promoted. When one boy who had promised well stole something and would have been sent to the penitentiary had it not been for my interference, I was quite broken-hearted. On the whole, the boys did very well, and not long ago I had a letter from one of them telling me that he wanted an appointment as Federal Judge, and hoped to get it.

My billiard room was so unequal to accommodating the young men who came to my house that I determined to find a club house for them. I accordingly secured an old studio on Huron Street which had two large rooms downstairs that were used for lounge and card rooms, and two rooms upstairs for billiard and pool rooms. I put the place in good order, furnished it and found a man who said he would take care of it and be there every night; and this was the first boys' club, to my knowledge, in Chicago. Later I built a large club for boys at Hull-House, fitted up with shops, games and pool rooms, and every convenience, but this club never gave me the real pleasure I got out of the Huron Street Club, which seemed to be all my own. This club was kept up until after I was married and my children were born. During this period I had not been able to devote much time to it, and it seemed best to abandon it as there was no one to take charge of it.

While I was a Sunday School teacher I was also a teacher in the sewing school. I knew very little about sewing and when I was given my first class I found that they were making flannel petticoats, and in my ignorance I had them sew up each side of the petticoat, so that there was no way of getting into it.

One day some money had been missed from the collection plate at sewing school, and I was told by the superintendent that I must search each child to see if it could be found. This was such a disagreeable undertaking that I gave up the sewing school and never returned to it.

[...]

During this time there was very little outlet for anyone who was interested in social work. I had been brought up with the idea that some day I would inherit a fortune, and I was always taught that the responsibility of money was great, and that God would hold me accountable for the manner in which I used my talents. I was, therefore, most eager to learn how to spend what I had in a proper way. My visiting among the hundred families of my Sunday School boys had become so extensive and so many demands for help came to me that I felt I must have some assistance. The old Relief and Aid Society was functioning and it gave aid to worthy people, but did not follow up nor attempt any rehabilitation of the family, and I always had a very strong feeling that something must be done to put a family upon its feet and not just to give temporary aid. I, therefore, employed a Swedish widow whom I knew, and when I had a call for help she would visit the family and try to do very much as the modern investigators for the United Charities do today. She found where the man of the family worked, what he was earning, looked after the health of the children, showed the mother how to purchase, and how to spend her money economically, gave advice on home keeping matters, and then reported to me the sum she thought the family needed, either temporarily or as a permanent stipend. She worked for me in this way for several years, and although she never had any instructions in modern methods of administering relief, yet she had rare common sense, was a good housekeeper, and had the practical experience which enabled her to judge wisely in giving assistance.

I was twenty-seven years old when I was married, and my four children were born during the next six years. I missed the visits I had formerly made among the families of my Sunday School class. When I was making these visits, up and down the most disreputable streets of the North Side, climbing over ash heaps and piles of garbage into old buildings in back yards, I often felt that when I had more money of my own, some of it would be spent in erecting homes for the poor.

[...]

My experience in visiting the poor had shown me how much they needed the ministrations of a trained person when they were ill. I had visited many children who were not well cared for by their parents, and who so much needed nursing and scientific care. I remember one day being very much distressed by going into a house built in the rear of a yard; I climbed up a long flight of wooden stairs on the outside of the house, and was then taken through a kitchen where at least twenty women sat making buttonholes and sewing on buttons on countless pairs of trousers which were piled in heaps on table and chairs. For this work these women received a beggarly pittance.

The mother whom I had gone to see, took me into a bedroom which was perfectly dark, and on the bed, covered with newspapers, lay a little child so emaciated that it seemed as though her bones were sticking through her skin. On a chair by the bed was a lighted candle, the only light in the room, and beside it lay a hunk of bread, the child's food for the day. The little girl, with dirty face, matted and unkempt hair, was holding in her clawlike fingers a long iron spike which she was dressing in a soiled piece of tissue paper and which she told me was her doll. If that child could only have had a visiting nurse she would have been much more comfortable, and with this incident in mind I was very glad to go to a meeting a little later, held at the house of Mrs. John R. Lyon on Michigan Avenue, where a number of us formed the Visiting Nurse Association of Chicago, that fine charity, whose ministering fingers have been laid in sympathy and healing on thousands of our sick poor....

---

* Louise deKoven Bowen, *Growing Up With A City* (New York: Macmillan, 1926): 45-53; 57-58.

ANNA JULIA HAYWOOD COOPER

(c. 1859-1964)

Anna Julia Haywood Cooper (c. 1859-1964),[1] educator and scholar, was born in Raleigh, North Carolina, to Hannah Stanley Haywood, an enslaved woman, and George Washington Haywood, a white man and presumably her mother's master. Cooper's writings suggest little about her childhood—she was a child at the time of the Emancipation Proclamation—though it was known that she had two brothers and that she was devoted to her mother. An academically gifted child, from an early age "Annie" expressed a passion for scholarship. In 1868 she received a scholarship to attend St. Augustine Normal School and Collegiate Institute in Raleigh, North Carolina. The school had been founded by the Board of Missions of the Episcopal Church to educate African-American teachers and clergy. Her experience at St. Augustine's began her lifetime membership in the Episcopal Church.

After forcing her way into a Greek class designed for male theology students, Anna Julia Haywood met the instructor, theology student George A.C. Cooper. The two were married in 1877, and George became the second African-American ordained to the Episcopal priesthood in North Carolina. The couple's happiness was short-lived; George A.C. Cooper died in 1879, two years and two months after their marriage.

After her husband's death, Anna Julia Haywood Cooper left St. Augustine's to seek additional training at Oberlin College, from which she received a B.A. in mathematics in 1884. She returned to St. Augustine's to teach on the college level in 1885 and eventually received a M.A. from Oberlin in 1887. Cooper continued her distinguished career in education as principal of the only African American high school in Washington D.C. Refused reappointment in 1906 because she refused to lower educational standards, Cooper moved to the Lincoln Institute in Missouri to teach languages.

Besides her work as an educator and advocate, Anna Julia Haywood Cooper was a leader in the African American women's movement of the late-nineteenth century. She assisted in organizing the Colored Women's League and the first Colored Settlement House in Washington, D.C. She wrote on issues of race and sex as women's editor of *Southland* magazine. Cooper also took an active role in national and international organizations founded to advance African Americans. She was a member of the Bethel Literary Society, she was the only women elected to the American Negro Academy, and she was a featured speaker at the historic Pan-African Conference in London in 1900.

Though Cooper matriculated for a doctorate at Columbia University, her life circumstances changed when she was called upon, at age fifty-five, to raise the five children of her nephew. She eventually transferred her credits to the Sorbonne and completed the Ph.D degree in 1925 at age sixty-five. Anna Julia Haywood Cooper was the fourth African American woman to be granted a Ph.D. degree. In 1930 she became president of Frelinghuysen University where she served until 1942. Cooper died peacefully at the age of 105 in her home in Washington, D.C.

Anna Julia Haywood Cooper's *A Voice from the South: By A Black Woman of the South,* is considered her most important work and is a compilation of her lectures, essays, and speeches. Throughout the book she makes a case for the important role of African American women, and of the importance of education to the future of all African Americans. Cooper accepted neither race nor gender as appropriate criteria for admittance to higher education, and argued that aptitude alone should be the determining factor. In the following document from *A Voice from the South,* Anna Julia Haywood Cooper challenges the Episcopal Church in regard to its lack of support for African American men and women.

NOTES

[1] Biographical information on Anna Julia Haywood Cooper found in Ann Allen Shockley, *Afro-American Women Writers*, 1746-1933 (New York: Penguin Books, 1988): 204-208

⧂

ANNA JULIA HAYWOOD COOPER
Excerpts from A Voice from the South

WOMANHOOD:
A VITAL ELEMENT IN THE REGENERATION AND PROGRESS OF A RACE (1886)[1]

[...]

Only the BLACK WOMAN can say "when and where I enter, in the quiet, undisputed dignity of my womanhood, without violence and without suing or special patronage, then and there the whole *Negro race enters with me*." Is it not evident then that as individual workers for this race we must address ourselves with no half-hearted zeal to this feature of our mission. The need is felt and must be recognized by all. There is a call for workers, for missionaries, for men and women with the double consecration of a fundamental love of humanity and a desire for its melioration through the Gospel; but superadded to this we demanded an intelligent and sympathetic comprehension of the interests and special needs of the Negro.

I see not why there should not be an organized effort for the protection and elevation of our girls such as the White Cross League in England. English women are strengthened and protected by more than twelve centuries of Christian influences, freedom and civilization; English girls are dispirited and crushed down by no such all-leveling prejudice as that supercilious caste spirit in America which cynically assumes "A

Negro woman cannot be a lady." English womanhood is beset by no such snares and traps as betray the unprotected, untrained colored girl of the South, whose only crime and dire destruction often is her unconscious and marvelous beauty. Surely then if English indignation is aroused and English manhood thrilled under the leadership of a Bishop of the English church to build up bulwarks around their wronged sisters, Negro sentiment cannot remain callous and Negro efforts nerveless in view of the imminent peril of the mothers of the next generation. *"I am my Sister's keeper!"* should be the hearty response of every man and woman of the race, and this conviction should purify and exalt the narrow, selfish, and petty personal aims of life into a noble and sacred purpose.

We need men who can let their interest and gallantry extend outside the circle of their aesthetic appreciation; men who can be a father, a brother, a friend to every weak, struggling unshielded girl. We need women who are so sure of their own social footing that they need not fear leaning to lend a hand to a fallen or falling sister. We need men and women who do not exhaust their genius splitting hairs on aristocratic distinctions and thanking God they are not as others; but earnest, unselfish souls, who can go into the highways and byways, lifting up and leading, advising and encouraging with the truly catholic benevolence of the Gospel of Christ.

As Church workers we must confess our path of duty is less obvious; or rather our ability to adapt our machinery to our conception of the peculiar exigencies of this work as taught by experience and our own consciousness of the needs of the Negro, is as yet not demonstrable. Flexibility and aggressiveness are not such strong characteristics of the Church today as in the Dark Ages.

As a Mission field for the Church the Southern Negro is in some aspects most promising; in others, perplexing. Aliens neither in language and customs, nor in associations and sympathies, naturally of deeply rooted religious instincts and taking most readily and kindly to the worship and teachings of the Church, surely the task of proselytizing the American Negro is infinitely less formidable than that which confronted the Church in the Barbarians of Europe. Besides, this people already look to the Church as the hope of their race. Thinking colored men almost uniformly admit that the Protestant Episcopal Church, with its quiet, chaste dignity and decorous solemnity, its instructive and elevating ritual, its bright chanting and joyous hymning, is eminently fitted to correct the peculiar faults of worship—the rank exuberance and often ludicrous demonstrativeness of their people. Yet, strange to say, the Church, claiming to be missionary and Catholic, urging that schism is sin and denominationalism inexcusable, has made in all these years almost no inroads upon this semi-civilized regionalism.

Harvests from this over-ripe field of home missions have been gathered in by Methodists, Baptists, and not least by Congregationalists, who were unknown to the Freedmen before their emancipation.

Our clergy numbers less than two dozen[2] priests of Negro blood and we have hardly more than one self-supporting colored congregation in the entire Southland. While the organization known as the A. M. E. Church[3] has 14,063 ministers, itinerant and local, 4,069 self-supporting churches, 4,275 Sunday-schools, with property valued at $7,772,284, raising yearly for church purposes $1,427,000.

Stranger and more significant than all, the leading men of this race (I do not mean demagogues and politicians, but men of intellect, heart, and race devotion, men to whom the elevation of their people means more than personal ambition and sordid gain—and the men of that stamp have not all died yet), the Christian workers for the race, of younger and more cultured growth, are noticeably drifting into sectarian churches, many of them declaring all the time that they acknowledge the historic claims of the Church, believe her apostolicity, and would experience greater personal comfort, spiritual and intellectual, in her revered communion. It is a fact which any one may verify for himself, that representative colored men, professing that in their heart of hearts they are Episcopalians, are actually working in Methodist and Baptist pulpits; while the ranks of the Episcopal clergy are left to be filled largely by men who certainly suggest the propriety of a *"perpetual Diaconate"* if they cannot be said to have created the necessity for it.

Now where is the trouble? Something must be wrong. What is it?

A certain Southern Bishop of our Church reviewing the situation, whether in Godly anxiety or in "Gothic antipathy" I know not, deprecates the fact that the colored people do not seem *drawn* to the Episcopal

Church, and comes to the sage conclusion that the Church is not adapted to the rude untutored minds of the Freedmen, and that they may be left to go to the Methodists and Baptists whither their racial proclivities undeniably tend. How the good Bishop can agree that all-foreseeing Wisdom, and Catholic Love would have framed his Church as typified in his seamless garment and unbroken body, and yet not leave it broad enough and deep enough and loving enough to seek and save and hold seven millions of God's poor, I cannot see.

But the doctors, while discussing their scientifically conclusive diagnosis of the disease, will perhaps not think it presumptuous in the patient if he dares to suggest where at least the pain is. If this be allowed, a *Black woman of the South* would beg to point out two possible oversights in this southern work which may indicate in part both a cause and a remedy for some failure. The first is *not calculating for the Black man's personality*; not having respect, if I may so express it, to his manhood or deferring at all to his conceptions of the needs of his people. When colored persons have been employed it was too often as machines or as manikins. There has been no disposition, generally, to get the black man's ideal or to let his individuality work by its own gravity, as it were. A conference of earnest Christian men have met at regular intervals for some years past to discuss the best methods of promoting the welfare and development of colored people in this country. Yet, strange as it may seem, they have never invited a colored man or even intimated that one would be welcome to take part in their deliberations. Their remedial contrivances are purely theoretical or empirical, therefore, and the whole machinery devoid of soul.

The second important oversight in my judgment is closely allied to this and probably grows out of it, and that is not developing Negro womanhood as an essential fundamental for the elevation of the race, and utilizing this agency in extending the work of the Church.

Of the first I have possibly already presumed to say too much since it does not strictly come within the province of my subject. However, Macaulay somewhere criticises the Church of England as not knowing how to use fanatics, and declares that had Ignatius Loyola been in the Anglican instead of the Roman communion, the Jesuits would have been schismatics instead of Catholics; and if the religious awakenings of the Wesleys had been in Rome, she would have shaven their heads, tied ropes around their waists, and sent them out under her own banner and blessing. Whether this be true or not, there is certainly a vast amount of force potential for Negro evangelization rendered latent, or worse, antagonistic by the halting, uncertain, I had almost said, *trimming* policy of the Church in the South. This may sound both presumptuous and ungrateful. It is mortifying, I know, to benevolent wisdom, after having spent itself in the execution of well-conned theories for the ideal development of a particular work, to hear perhaps the weakest and humblest element of that work asking "what doest thou?"

Yet so it will be in life. The "thus far and no further" pattern cannot be fitted to any growth in God's kingdom. The universal law of development is "onward and upward." It is God-given and inviolable. From the unfolding of the germ in the acorn to reach the sturdy oak, to the growth of a human soul into the full knowledge and likeness of its Creator, the breadth and scope of the movement in each and all are too grand, too mysterious, too like God himself, to be encompassed and locked down in human molds.

After all, the Southern slave owners were right: either the very alphabet of intellectual growth must be forbidden and the Negro dealt with absolutely as a chattel having neither rights nor sensibilities; or else the clamps and irons of mental and moral as well as civil compression must be riven asunder and the truly enfranchised soul led to the entrance of that boundless vista through which it is to toil upwards to its beckoning God as the buried seed germ to meet the sun.

A perpetual colored diaconate, carefully and kindly superintended by the white clergy; congregations of shiny faced peasants with their clean white aprons and sunbonnets catechised at regular intervals and taught to recite the creed, the Lord's prayer and the ten commandments—duty towards God and duty towards neighbor, surely such well tended sheep ought to be grateful to their shepherds and content in that station of life to which it pleased God to call them. True, like the old professor lecturing to his solitary student, we make no provisions here for irregularities. "Questions must be kept till after class," or dispensed with altogether. That some do ask questions and insist on answers, in class too, must be both impertinent and annoying. Let not our spiritual pastors and masters, however, be grieved at such self-assertion as merely signifies we have a destiny to fulfill and as men and women we must *be about our Father's business.*

It is a mistake to suppose that the Negro is prejudiced against a white ministry. Naturally there is not a more kindly and implicit follower of a white man's guidance than the average colored peasant. What would to others be an ordinary act of friendly or pastoral interest he would be more inclined to regard gratefully as a condescension. And he never forgets such kindness. Could the Negro be brought near to his white priest or bishop, he is not suspicious. He is not only willing but often longs to unburden his soul to this intelligent guide. There are no reservations when he is convinced that you are his friend. It is a saddening satire on American history and manners that it takes something to convince him.

That our people are not "drawn" to a church whose chief dignitaries they see only in the chancel, and whom they reverence as they would a painting or an angel, whose life never comes down to and touches theirs with the inspiration of an objective reality, may be "perplexing" truly (American caste and American Christianity both being facts) but it need not be surprising. There must be something of human nature in it, the same as that which brought about that "the Word was made flesh and dwelt among us" that He might "draw" us towards God.

Men are not "drawn" by abstractions. Only sympathy and love can draw, and until our Church in America realizes this and provides a clergy that can come in touch with our life and have a fellow feeling for our woes, without being imbedded and frozen up in their "Gothic antipathies," the good bishops are likely to continue "perplexed" by the sparsity of colored Episcopalians.

A colored priest of my acquaintance recently related to me, with tears in his eyes, how his reverend Father in God, the Bishop who had ordained him, had met him on the cars on his way to the diocesan convention and warned him, not unkindly, not to take a seat in the body of the convention with the white clergy. To avoid disturbance of their godly placidity he would of course please sit back and somewhat apart. I do not imagine that that clergyman had very much for the Christly (!) deliberations of the convention.

[...]

The institution of the Church in the South to which she mainly looks for the training of her colored clergy and for the help of the "Black Woman" and "Colored Girl" of the South, has graduated since the year 1868, when the school was founded, *five young women,*[4] and while yearly numerous young men have been kept and trained for the ministry by the charities of the Church, the number of indigent females who have here been supported, sheltered and trained is phenomenally small. Indeed, to my mind, the attitude of the Church toward this feature of her work is as if the solution of the problem of Negro missions depended solely on sending a quota of deacons and priests into the field, girls being a sort of *tertium quid* whose development may be promoted if they can pay their way and fall in with the plans mapped out for the training of the other sex. Now I would ask in all earnestness, does not this force potential deserve by education and stimulus to be made dynamic? Is it not a solemn duty incumbent on all colored churchmen to make it so? Will not the aid of the Church be given to prepare our girls in head, heart, and hand for the duties and responsibilities that await the intelligent wife, the Christian mother, the earnest, virtuous, helpful woman, at once both the lever and the fulcrum for uplifting the race.

As Negroes and churchmen we cannot be indifferent to these questions. They touch us most vitally on both sides. We believe in the Holy Catholic Church. We believe that however gigantic and apparently remote the consummation, the Church will go on conquering and to conquer till the kingdoms of this world, not excepting the black man and the black woman of the South, shall have become the kingdoms of the Lord and of his Christ...

---

[1] Quoted from Charles Lemert and Esme Bhan, eds., *The Voice of Anna Julia Cooper* (Lanham: Rowman & Littlefield, 1998), 66-70.

[2] The published report of [18]91 shows 26 priests for the entire country, including one not engaged in work and one a professor in a non-sectarian school, since made Dean of an Episcopal Annex to Howard University known as King Hall.

[3] African Methodist Episcopal Church.

[4] Five have been graduated since [18]86, two in [18]91, two in [18]92.

VIDA DUTTON SCUDDER

(1861-1954)

Vida Dutton Scudder (1861-1954),[1] educator and Christian Socialist, was born in 1861 in Madura, India, the only daughter of David Coit Scudder, a Congregationalist missionary, and Harriet Dutton Scudder. David Scudder died a year later and Harriet returned to her parents' home in Auburndale, Massachusetts with her daughter, originally named Julia Davida. The young Vida Scudder was described as a sensitive child, with intellectual gifts; she was in the first class of Girls' Latin School, Boston. Vida spent much of her childhood in Europe traveling with her mother, and from these experiences developed a deep love of art and literature. In the 1870s, both Vida Dutton Scudder and her mother Harriet were confirmed at Trinity Church, Boston, by Phillips Brooks.[2]

In 1880, Vida Scudder enrolled in Smith College—her first real separation from her mother. After graduating from Smith College, she studied Elizabethan literature for a year at Oxford University. Scudder received an M.A. from Smith in 1889. In 1887, she began her first teaching assignment as an instructor of English literature at Wellesley College; she became a full professor in 1910. Scudder taught at Wellesley, with occasional leaves of absence for health problems or to engage in activism, until her retirement in 1928.[3]

Though Vida Dutton Scudder had a long and distinguished teaching career, her love of art and literature was matched by a growing social conscience and a deepening spirituality. In 1887, she began the College Settlements Association, and two years later joined the Society of Christian Socialists. Shortly afterwards, Scudder began her lifetime association with the Companions of the Holy Cross. In 1893, Scudder took a leave of absence from Wellesley to work with Helena Stuart Dudley to found Denison House in Boston.

Vida Scudder experienced a breakdown in 1901 due to the stress of her teaching position and social activism. Neither her mother nor Wellesley College completely understood or appreciated Vida Scudder's radicalism. Vida retreated to Italy to recuperate for two years, where she became absorbed in medieval literature and the lives of Italian saints. She came back to Massachusetts renewed and became more active in church and socialist groups; she also started a group for Italian immigrants at Denison House and took an active part in organizing the Women's Trade Union League.

In 1911, Vida Scudder founded the Episcopal Church Socialist League, and formally joined the Socialist party. Her support of striking textile workers in the Lawrence, Massachuetts strike in 1912 drew a great deal of criticism and threatened her teaching position. A year later she was appointed to the new Joint Commission on Social Service for the Episcopal Church. Though she initially supported President Wilson's decision to enter World War I, by 1923 she had joined the Fellowship of Reconciliation. By the 1930s, Vida Dutton Scudder had become an absolute pacifist.[4]

After her retirement from Wellesley College in 1928, Scudder was able to donate more of her time to writing; she authored a total of sixteen books on a variety of religious and political subjects. She combined her intense activism with an equally vibrant and deep spirituality. Throughout Vida Dutton Scudder's life her deepest relationships and her primary support network were women. In 1919, Florence Converse and her mother moved into the household of Vida and the ailing Harriet Scudder, thus providing Vida Scudder with the family atmosphere she craved. Florence Converse was her closest companion for the remainder of her life.[5]

Vida Scudder's commitment to a disciplined life of prayer, silence, and retreat was nourished through her participation in the

Society of the Companions of the Holy Cross. Scudder served as Companion–in–Charge of probationers from 1909 to 1942. Throughout these years she was a mentor to women from a wide variety of backgrounds and vocations, nurturing them in a spiritual path that combined social justice with a disciplined life of intercessory prayer, retreat, and worship.[6]

The following documents are from Vida Scudder's autobiography, *On Journey*, published in 1937. In the first excerpt, Scudder discusses her breakdown and experiences in Italy; in the second she reflects on the life of prayer and various "names" for God.

NOTES

[1] For biographical sources, see Vida Dutton Scudder, *On Journey* (New York: E.P. Dutton & Co., 1937); Theresa Corcoran, *Vida Dutton Scudder* (Boston: Twayne Publishers, 1982).

[2] Scudder, On Journey, 15-76; Corcoran, *Vida Dutton Scudder*, 1-11.

[3] Scudder, 99-118.

[4] Scudder, 231-290.

[5] Corcoran, 108-10.

[6] Steele W. Martin, "Social Justice and Spirituality: Vida Scudder," *The Living Church* (October 3, 1999): 12.

VIDA DUTTON SCUDDER
Excerpts from On Journey*

I Meet The Saints

"The unexpected is always happening," wrote my mother to her friend, sister of Professor Palmer, in March. "*Vida* has broken down pretty completely, so she has had to give up her college work and our trip to Italy." This illness, which abruptly pulled me—I had almost said jerked me—away from all my activities, lasted with diminishing severity till 1904. It was unexpected. I knew I was tired, and had applied to the always generous college for leave of absence for the spring term. We were, as my mother said, planning for Italy, Florence Converse with us, and a dear young cousin. But on the train one evening, returning from college where I had been hostess to some distinguished guest, something crashed in my head. I was used to severe headaches; this was different. I staggered home, and for many weeks lay sleepless in a darkened room, with explosions of such pain as I didn't know possible going on inside my brain.

It was exasperating. I worried over my classes, dropped as if one were to drop a baby on the sidewalk. It was also, like any new experience, interesting. The doctors diagnosed no organic trouble, but deep exhaustion which would be slow to conquer; and, forced into this unknown sphere of passive suffering, I found myself not wholly unreconciled, when once adjustments involving other people had been made. I had a theory that suffering and failure were a surer road to reality than success and happiness; physical suffering was the simplest form of initiation into their realm. And I had more than physical pain to bear; that lessened within a few weeks, till I could endure light and people several hours a day; the harder thing as weeks and months dragged on was the sudden check to ambition or to fruitful living. Also, I dreaded causing anxiety, giving trouble, and being taken care of. The stern lesson that receiving is a more exacting spiritual attitude than giving was never easy for me to learn.

My rector, Mr. Brent, as he then was, came to me. I told him that now I was no longer driven by duties I wished to cultivate a life of prayer. Those night hours with pain in them were free, and long. I think he laughed. He discouraged me gently, told me not to whip myself into any activity, even spiritual; bade me sink as far as I could into non-existence. So he brought home to me a truth which has since meant much in my quest for reality: that surrender is more important than aspiration, to the seeking soul. I have tried to express this truth in a crucial chapter in one of my books, "Brother John." Surrender conditions not only the Unitive but the Illuminative way; it is especially incumbent on those who like myself were—and are—at the beginning of the way of Purgation.

I must here, however reluctantly, write a little about my religious life. It has been evident that I had never severed connection with the

Church; and I have not to this day. Some readers will shrug their shoulders, superior to my conventional attitude; but my attitude was not conventional. In the first place, it was with constant struggle through many years that I maintained my provisional loyalty; in the second place, even within the loyalty there was, to use the modern phrase, the tension of a constant dialectic. For to remain a member of an historic Church is not to achieve finality. A creed is not an imprisoning wall, it is a gate, opening on a limitless country which can be entered in no other way. I am within that country, Laus Deo, but I have only begun to explore it; I am finding it, now glorious in beauty, now arid and forbidding. Again and again the explorer hesitates in a maze of paths pointing in sundry directions. But he cannot stop; the religious life never suffers one to stand still. I will not say what happens, as he pauses, irresolute; but there are Guides.

Before I left college I had, as already indicated, become fully alive to negative forces. I shall not dwell on these, for I could not say anything fresh. Like Matthew Arnold, who swayed me a good deal, my difficulty was with the primary article of the Christian creed. What we Victorians used to call materialism never affected me much; I felt myself part of a living universe, and I was already claiming such faith as is found in "Adonais" and "Lines Above Tintern Abbey." Yet I could not go even so far as Arnold, in postulating "A Something Not Ourselves that makes for righteousness"; righteousness inheres in personality alone, and it was at Personality I balked. I suspect my perennial difficulty in realizing myself as an integrated unit, a Person, had something to do with this. Not many years later, I amused a friend, who flings the phrase back to me to this day, by describing myself as "a pantheistic mystic with a Christian terminology." For a long time, I did not get any further. How, then, can I say that I was inhabiting that country entered through the portals of the Christian creed? Von Hügel, who has been a chief guide of my later years, was once arguing eagerly in exposition of a theology far from orthodox; suddenly he paused, as he and his friend passed a little chapel. "I always spend a few moments at this hour in adoration before the Blessed Sacrament," said he; and entering, fell on his knees. The man who told me that story found it surprising; it seemed entirely natural, to me.

I remained an orthodox Christian, because I knew that faith was an adventure; and also that it was a growth, springing straight from life. Not from one's little private life so much as from the experience of the race, turned Godward. I am called a revolutionist, but I am also very much of an authoritarian—that is, I am humble enough to find tremendous force in testimony. Religion, says Whitehead, is what one does with his solitariness. I think this only partially true; my own approach is social, and the witness of other minds has great weight with me. Often I find this witness to faith where least expected. Urged by my students, I had published in '95 a little book called "The Witness of Denial,"—lectures from my course on Victorian prose on positive elements in the thought of some leading Victorian agnostics. "The movement of denial," wrote I, "has cast in its various phases shadows of assertion. Each phase of doubt has had its positive aspect, its effort to find in its very negations solace and stimulus for the soul." That book is probably worthless; I had not opened it for forty years or so till just now, when my eye was caught by this sentence; but the title is curiously characteristic of me. And if I found comfort in those who denied, far more was I impressed by the testimony of direct Christian experience; it was the witness of the saints that held me.

Also among my acquaintance, those to whom Christianity was vital were those who most surely, so I felt, "inhabited reality." I perceived that they moved in a light from Elsewhere. Helen Cone, in her poem, "The Glorious Company," said what I stumble in saying: -

> "Faces, faces, faces, of the streaming marching surge,
> Streaming on the weary road toward the awful steep,
> Whence your glow and glory as ye set to that sharp verge,
> Faces lit as sunlit stars, shining as ye sweep?
>
> 'Lo, the Light,' they answer: 'Oh the pure, the pulsing light,
> Beating like a heart of life, like a heart of Love,
> Soaring, searching, filling all the breadth and depth and height,
> Welling, whelming with its peace worlds below, above.'
>
> O my soul, how art thou to that living splendor blind,
> Sick with thy desire to see even as these men seep
> Yet to look upon them is to know that God hath shined:
> Faces lit as sunlit stars, be all my light to me!"

Supplementing this social approach came, of course, scrutiny as thorough as I could make it of the theistic and Christian schemes. Yearly my respect grew for Catholic theology. Every article in the historic creeds, with the exception of that postulating personal survival, held for me suggestion of something revealed not by thinking, but by life. I was no literalist; the Latin term for the creed, *Symbolum,* has always been a comfort to me; but the Christian "Symbol" reflected deeper as well as wider experience than any other of which I was cognizant. Ancient formulae may, of course, fall dead on the ear as cultures change; the language of the past seems alien to the unthinking. But I am cautious about rejecting such language lightly, for the reason that it brings report from a plane where neither need nor perception alters much from age to age. Religious formulae, far more than scientific, enshrine permanent, I dare to say eternal, values; and to refuse to use formulae at all in religion was not to be honest but to capitulate to the principle of isolation, which is death. I thought sadly at times that honesty was impossible to me; but neutrality is impossible in these matters; and I was inwardly assured that it would be less honest for me to range myself with those who denied than with those who affirmed.

That was about as far as I had gone in 1901. But at least I was "within the gates." No inner certitude was vouchsafed me. I read the mystics as much as I dared, but mystical experience has rarely if ever been granted my analytical mind. Often I have bitterly appropriated to myself the words in Newman's "Dream of Gerontius":

> "It is thy very energy of thought
> Which keeps thee from thy God."

Of the more personal aspects in my religious life, I do not care to speak. But I will tell a dream of mine, which has been an enduring support to me. I have had such dreams sometimes; one can always distinguish them from the usual type.

This came soon after I had begun to teach. During a transition at Wellesley, pending the appointment of our present finely equipped Bible department, some of us young teachers supposed to be fairly modern in our ideas were asked to teach the college "Bible courses" for a couple of years. Students had been restive under these courses, which by the irrevocable arrangements of Mr. Durant, were obligatory on all. I spent the preceding summer in Europe, and plunged eagerly into preparation, slight enough perforce, for work in this new field. I studied all the "higher criticism" of that date in German on which I could lay my hands—I was staying in Geneva—with a good teacher who could supplement my inadequate knowledge of the language, and I enjoyed the work immensely. The voyage home was stormy and I stayed much in my cabin. One morning, just before dawn—the hour when, witness Dante, such things happen—this dream came to me:

I was a monk, or recluse, living in far Northern Germanic forests; evidently Christianity was not many centuries old. The forest was vast and chilled. Moved to leave my refuge I made my way through great trees of secular growth, entangled in mists, to the coast, where gray waters tossed tumultuously, and I entered a little waiting boat. There was neither sail nor oar. I was borne swiftly over those waters in a general southerly direction, for many years,—or aeons; dreams occur in the Timeless. At last my boat paused at the edge of a small island; barren cliffs with a surface of smooth rock towered above me. I knew why I had been sent: I was to carve the Face of Christ on that cliff, for the solace of wayfarers. Sculptor's tools were in my hand, and mysteriously and perilously I climbed the cliff to the appointed spot, a narrow ledge high above the sea. Again time ceased; for years unnumbered I chipped and shaped, holding my post precariously, laboring in prayer and anguish at my great task. I had inner sight of what I wished to render; but terror increased. Was my vision true, or a fantasy of my own mind? Did there exist in the universe the authentic Image of the Lover? Was there a Lover? Ages passed, my task was finished; defeat overwhelmed me. I turned my eyes from my poor work to those wide waters, and they were no longer tossing angrily, they were silvery and calm; I see them yet. Over them, from the horizon's edge, One came walking. He approached. He raised His Face to mine. It was the Face that I had carved. I met His eyes.

[...]

Foundations

...Every definition of "God" that I have ever met is helpful to me. Sometimes in prayer I escape the convention of those three letters by changing the word. "Deus Meus et Omnia!" I cry with Francis. "Theos"—the Russian "Bog"—the Indian "Brahm"—"Allah illa Allah!": to one devoutly brooding, the Nameless One draws near; and I bow before Him Who says in the supreme words of revelation, "I Am That I Am." Only one approach is sadly unreal to me; I cannot with any personal comfort or sense of reality say "Our Father." I am very sorry about this. I think the trouble may be that I never knew, and never missed, my earthly father. I am shamed. But I do long for the child heart to be given me, and still hope to retrace my long journey, on Shelley's "boat of desire," voyaging past Age's icy caves, "and Manhood's dark and tossing waves," "beyond the glassy gulfs

> Of shadow peopled infancy,
> Through death and birth, to a diviner day,"

to that realm where the angels of little children forever behold the Father's Face.

---

* Vida Dutton Scudder, *On Journey* (New York: E.P. Dutton, 1937): 231-37; 363.

SUSAN TREVOR KNAPP

(1862-1941)

Susan Trevor Knapp (1862-1941)[1] was one of the most influential early deaconesses in the Episcopal Church and a guiding force behind the New York Training School for Deaconesses. Little is known about Knapp's childhood. She was born in 1862, the daughter of Edward Jarvis and Mathilda Knapp. Susan Knapp was an academically gifted woman; she had an extensive knowledge of history and literature and could read and write Greek.[2]

Though her first application in 1891 for admission to the New York Training School for Deaconesses was thwarted when her doctor refused to sign a health certificate due to a minor heath ailment, Knapp was undaunted. She found another physician, applied once again, and completed the two year course in 1894. After one year away from the New York Training School, Susan Trevor Knapp returned to teach church history and New Testament. She quickly proved to be a valuable asset to the school and assumed more responsibility while William Reed Huntington set the school's direction.[3]

Susan Trevor Knapp was set apart as a deaconess in 1899. In the same year, Knapp and another deaconess, Harriette Goodwin, traveled to England to study training programs there. While in England she met Bishop Randall Davidson and Mrs. Davidson, two of the founders of the English deaconess movement. (Randall Davidson later became archbishop of Canterbury.) The Davidsons had previously served in Rochester, one of the most innovative centers of the English deaconess movement. Unlike William Reed Huntington, who believed that deaconesses should be free to marry, Susan Trevor Knapp considered her vocation to be a lifetime commitment requiring a celibate lifestyle. Further, Knapp discovered that English deaconesses were much more self-governed than their American counterparts. In the English system, deaconesses still had clergy wardens, but they acted only in an advisory capacity. Here at last, Susan Knapp found what she needed to support her perspectives on the formation and vocation of deaconesses.[4]

Upon her return to New York, Susan Trevor Knapp quickly moved to institute her learning from England at the New York Training School of Deaconesses. In 1903, she was appointed dean. Knapp infused the school with a new level of vitality. She made the curriculum more academically rigorous, expanded the level of practical training, diversified the work placements, and recruited top students. She took seriously the need for missionary training. Further, Knapp revitalized the worship life of the New York Training School, encouraged students to develop their own prayer lives, and cultivated the schools' communal spirituality. During these interior changes to the New York Training School, she also moved the physical plant from Grace Church to the grounds of the Cathedral of St. John the Divine. After Dr. Huntington's death, Susan Trevor Knapp was essentially in charge of the New York Training School for Deaconesses.[5]

Knapp's work attracted international attention. She traveled, wrote, and lectured on the deaconess movement in the United States and abroad. Her last three years at the New York Training School for Deaconesses was characterized by power struggles with the board of trustees, some wanting to revert to Huntington's policies and some concerned with the school's overall financial management. Rather than accept a demotion to housemother, and the appointment of a priest whose specialty was Sunday School education as her successor, Susan Trevor Knapp resigned in 1916. She retired to Japan where for twenty-five years she tutored students in English and bible. She died in Los Angeles in 1941.[6]

Susan Trevor Knapp, along with Mary Kingsbury Simkovitch, an Episcopal social worker, were both appointed to the Episcopal

Commission on Social Service. They were the only two women on the committee. The following document is Susan Trevor Knapp's interpretation of "the Relation of Social Service to Christianity," delivered at the Thirty-first Church Congress in 1913.

NOTES

[1] The primary source of biographical information on Susan Trevor Knapp is Mary Sudman Donovan, "Paving the Way: Deaconess Susan Trevor Knapp," *Anglican and Episcopal History*, 69, no. 4 (1994): 491-502. Also see Donovan's book, *A Different Call: Women's Ministries in the Episcopal Church, 1850-1920* (Wilton: Morehouse-Barlow, 1986): 108-115; 118, 138, 150, 152, 155.

[2] Donovan, "Paving the Way," 491-92.

[3] Ibid.

[4] Ibid, 493-95.

[5] Ibid, 493-96.

[6] Ibid, 496-500.

◌ଛ

SUSAN TREVOR KNAPP
The Relation of Social Service to Christianity*

To those who believe the Incarnation of the Son of God to be the central fact of human history, faith in the Incarnate Son of God becomes the supreme duty, and the well spring of all right action. Social Service, considered in relation to this controlling truth, is soon discovered to be a part of the right action, and to be inseparably linked with the faith, which is its source and inspiration.

I would say here that there could be no question in the minds of the most devout or the most scrupulous regarding the relation of social service to the Christian Church, were it not that, in its practice, she has too often been unfaithful to her trust by dwarfing and crippling her ideal of that service, until she has made it seem an unholy thing.

In this brief paper, I cannot attempt to do more than *touch* upon the view of social service we gain from Holy Scripture, from the Law, The Prophets and the words and works of our Lord. I shall only be able to quote certain short passages, which stand out strongly because of their pre-eminent importance, and which are fresh in our minds as occurring in the Lenten lessons we have lately read.

The command found in the ancient law, "Thou shalt love Jehovah, thy God, with all thy heart and with all thy soul and with all thy might," which our Lord placed forever at the head of Social Service by coupling it with the second command, "Thou shalt love thy neighbour as thyself," gives us Social Service as dependent upon absolute devotion to God. Great as this service is, it stands *second*; it is also attached to a condition placed upon us, which logically leads us, just because we love our neighbor as ourselves, to bring him to the same state of absolute devotion to God, for, if loving one's neighbor as one's self is dependent upon loving one's God, then that love would, of necessity, concern itself first and before all else in bringing the two loved ones together. This is a fundamental social instinct,—and this is service.

In the great drama we have been reading during the mornings in Lent, the author teaches us *the second* great truth we need to emphasize today. Social Service can never make up, in the character of the one who is serving, for a lack of knowledge of God, as He has revealed Himself, and of ourselves in our relation to Him.

Job reviews the Social Service which he accomplished in his prosperous days thus: "I delivered the poor that cried, the fatherless also, that had none to help him. The blessing of him that was ready to perish came upon me; and I caused the widow's heart to sing for joy. I put on righteousness, and it clothed me; my justice was as a robe and a diadem. I was eyes to the blind, and feet was I to the lame. I was a father to the needy; and the cause of him that I knew not I searched out. And I brake the jaws of the unrighteous, and plucked the prey out of his teeth." (XXIX, 12–17.) A fair picture of a philanthropist! Most of us today would rest content were such a eulogy pronounced upon ourselves, but *that far-away author* leads his hero to deliverance through a very different portal than that of philanthropy. It is when Job says to

Jehovah, "I have uttered things which I understood not. I had heard of Thee by the hearing of the ear; but now mine eye seeth Thee; wherefore I loathe myself and repent in dust and ashes." It is then the author is prepared to close his volume. We note also that he adds in his conclusion, "Jehovah turned the captivity of Job when he prayed for his friends,"— a special bit of social service, which appealed to him as being of importance.

When we turn to our Lord Jesus Christ, we find *a wealth of material* in the forms, both of precept and example, upon which the statement that He was the great advocate of social service may rest, but we also find ourselves confronted at the outset of our study with spiritual truths, by which all such service must be tested. Our desire being to be imitators of Christ in His relations with His fellow-men, we seek naturally to have the mind of Christ while we imitate His work.

What was His point of view regarding the great problems of human life? We find that the problems of life and death, of good and evil, of riches and poverty, of blessedness and woe, were all of them weighed in the spiritual balances of eternity. The only *real life* is eternal life; the only *real good* is godliness; the only *real riches* are spiritual riches; the only *real poverty* is spiritual poverty; the only *real blessedness* is that which endures beyond the confines of earth, and the only *real woe* is eternal woe.

He warns the healed man of the danger of spiritual sickness; He congratulates the persecuted on the blessedness of their state; He speaks of the physically dead as being *asleep* and of the unawakened as being *dead while he liveth*. Immediate suffering was relieved by the tender heart of Jesus, but His gaze seemed ever to rest on a point beyond the immediate situation. He could work reform where reform was needed, but He was not a reformer.

Harnack tells us, "The Gospel is not one of social improvement, but of spiritual redemption." To feed the hungry and give drink to the thirsty, to welcome the stranger and clothe the naked, to visit the sick and befriend the prisoner,—this is not so much the Gospel of our Lord Jesus Christ as it is the natural response to all suffering which is made by the heart, which, through faith in the Gospel, has become wedded to its Lord. As we study deeper into the matchless life, we are as much impressed by the serene detachment as we are by the loving service.

Clearly the service of such a Christ is not to be accomplished by the mere healing of physical sickness, by the relieving of material adversity alone; no, nor by the building up of character by means of standards which lack definite spiritual foundation.

Granting, then, the claim of Holy Scripture that social service is dependent upon devotion to God, that social service will never be accepted in the place of devotion to God, and that our Lord requires of His followers warfare for the spiritual redemption of their fellows, we turn to the question as it presents itself to the Christian Church today and ask: Shall she send her sons and daughters to take their part in the great movements which are seeking the betterment of mankind? Yes, by all means,—only let her see to it that her sons and daughters are trained and equipped for that service.

If we follow the figure, and we have warrant for doing so in Holy Scripture, that the Church is the Mother, we find analogies in home-life at its best, and in the relations of the home to all which lies about it. It is clear that the household which exerts an uplifting influence in a community is that in which the Mother devotes herself, before all else, to the training of her own children, that their characters may conform to the ideal which is her pattern, and that they may be enlightened by the knowledge of the truths which have been her guide in life. The Church's duty towards Social Service, which is a very real one, will be fulfilled only as she creates in her own children a greater conformity to the Divine Pattern, and enlightens them with more intelligence concerning the truths for which she stands.

The proportion of communicants in our Church who can give in these days an intelligent reason for the faith that is in them is appallingly small. Until this believing ignorance is supplanted by an educated faith they are utterly unready to face the problems which arise in Social Service.

St. Paul tells us one needs the self-discipline of an athlete to win Christ for oneself, and the courage of a soldier in order to fight the battles of Christ. If the Church would require something of this self-discipline and courage in those who are so ready to stumble haphazard into Social Service, she would herself regain her birthright of leadership *in this holy war.*

I would add also, let the Church be sure that the sons and daughters she sends out are bound to *her* by a right loyal faith, and are not to be counted among those who, preferring destructive criticism to constructive help, desert her and wander in a kind of spiritual confusion, because she does not respond quickly to their new-found enthusiasm.

Added to this training in character, which is the Church's first duty, there is need for training in thoroughness and efficiency. The day has gone by forever when it could be considered a part of piety to fear scientific methods in Social Service. We *need* the scientific methods of the great philanthropic organizations, and we *need their thoroughness* also. They have much to offer the Christian Church, which they offer freely. The Christian Church has much to offer them, which she offers far too timidly, if she offers it at all.

The Church's touch upon the deep and tragic questions of the day is too superficial; it deals in most cases with the work of alleviation rather than with the sources of the evil. Who could say she is now resisting unto blood striving against sin? I fear we must acknowledge that, for the most part, she is not resisting unto serious personal inconvenience, and yet all about her are those whose lives are wretched while they might be happy, and sickly while they might be strong, and God's little ones, in well nigh unbelievable numbers, are being "caused to stumble," yes, and to fall out of sight and hearing into the abyss of evil. "It must be that offences come," our Lord tells us, "but woe to him through whom they come,"—through whom they come directly by evil act, or indirectly by evil failure to act.

While the Church could never fail to appreciate those rare souls, who realize they are the stewards and not the owners of their fortunes, and who, therefore, become fellow-workers with and not the patrons of their fellow men, she should discountenance forever the fantastic spectacle of the rich making intermittent and ill-regulated efforts to take part with the poor in times of crisis, when things have become dramatic. Believe me, to those for whom the drama is not a spectacle, but a rigorous experience, these would-be helpers seem like children running out of luxurious nurseries to play the game of poverty, who may be trusted to run back again at the first touch of hunger.

But what concerns us more, I suppose, than the Social Service done in the state or town into which the Christian Church may enter, is the work done in the diocese or parish. There is an extraordinary kind of Social Service practiced here and there today within the very household of faith, in which,—by a strange reversal of the order of things,—the children are saying that the Mother should be seen and not heard,—and she,—having been thus silenced, waits in the background, "mute and inglorious," until the children have had enough of their experiment.

A short while ago I was told a tale, (and I have verified the same), of a men's club of many hundred members, belonging to a parish in a northern city, a club which had been conducted for many years under the reversed conditions I have just described. This winter the vicar of the Chapel of the parish decided to hold a service *especially* for the club, and, after advertising it duly, it was held and was attended by two club members. If we test this incident by the most modest claim Social Service can ever make for its object,— that people may be lifted into a state of decency—I would ask in this connection, "Where was the decency?" The failure of this experiment, as of all kindred experiments, was due to the breaking of one of the primary laws of life.

Success is never won, where those who are working withhold from the enterprise the best they have to put into it. The ethical worker, who honestly confesses to an agnostic position, gives of his best and wins a real success. The Christian worker, eliminating all expression of his religion, rarely matches up to him for obvious reasons.

It has been well said that the ideal community of missionaries in a foreign field offers to the Christian Church the norm for Christian Social Service. We find within a well developed and well manned community of this sort every kind of activity. The Church is in the centre of the situation; the school and the hospital are there; the agricultural and other industries are there also; and everything is attended to by those who have been led into the community by one common motive, the desire to reveal our Lord Jesus Christ to those who have never known Him. Houses are built by these people, fields are tilled, horses are shod and flocks are tended; nothing is too secular to be an appropriate occupation.

"I am trying to find a volunteer to take back to India," said an English missionary to me, "to take care of our live stock. He will be assisted by natives, but it must be a missionary who carries the responsibility." Now it is in such a community as this, as I have said, that we find the norm of Christian Social Service. There is no shrinking from the necessity to engage in purely secular employment, when it presents itself, and the employment ceases to be secular in the doing. And the result?—*Incidentally,* perhaps, the natives become proficient in some industry which enables them to provide more adequately for those dependent upon them; *incidentally,* perhaps, they rise in the social scale, and their homes exhibit marks of real ethical advance, and these steps in advance are of great value. But ask the Bishops of China and Japan, the Bishop of the Philippine Islands if their goal is reached when these improvements are accomplished? They would pronounce their work a failure and worse than a failure if the work should stop here. No,—they are at work over the least as well as the greatest of their tasks for one end, that the Lord Jesus Christ should reign in the hearts of every unbeliever who crosses their path.

Are we not forced to acknowledge that the quest of many a social worker belonging to the Church in our so-called Christian land stops immeasureably below the requirement of the Gospel? We hear it urged that here the doors of the Church stand open and so our part is done. An open door may be a dreary thing; it is not the open door of the sheep-fold in the Highlands of Scotland which attracts the sheep; it is the shepherd who stands on the threshold, and who, with clear call and compelling gesture, gathers them into the fold.

---

* Susan Trevor Knapp, "The Relation of Social Service to Christianity," a paper delivered at the *Thirty-first Church Congress* (New York: Thomas Whittaker, Inc., 1913):26-33.

MARY KINGSBURY SIMKHOVITCH

(1867-1951)

Mary **Kingsbury Simkhovitch (1867-1951),**[1] settlement worker and founder of Greenwich House, was born in Chestnut Hill, Massachusetts, in 1867. She was descended from old New England families, and her parents attended the Congregational church in their town. Mary Kingsbury would attend Sunday Evensong at Grace Church, Newton, with her father to hear the choir. Mary grew to love the chant and the order of the Prayer Book Office. In her late teens, Mary would slip into Trinity Church, Boston, on Friday afternoons to listen to Phillips Brooks. Before college, she was confirmed in Trinity Church. At nearly the same time, her parents grew more comfortable in the Episcopal Church and were confirmed at the Church of the Redeemer in Chestnut Hill; her father eventually became senior warden.[2]

Mary Kingsbury chose to attend Boston University rather than to go away for college, and once there she continued her visits to Trinity Church, as well as trips to Beacon Hill to listen to the Cowley Fathers preach their mission on Bowdoin Street. Her association with the Cowley Fathers led her to St. Augustine's, an African American congregation where Kingbury played the organ, visited families, and ran a girls' club. It was her first substantive encounter with African Americans and the poor. She was shocked to learn that some of the miserable tenements which housed the families in the parish were owned by other Episcopalians.[3] Though she read theology ambitiously during these years, Mary Kingsbury admitted that it was the church people she encountered who most influenced her interest in reform. "During all these years, then, my religious life had been enriched, not through argument or reason so much as through association with persons whose impact upon my imagination and whose leadership, both spiritual and in the social field, had disclosed human values which I cherished and which gave me a sense of direction."[4]

Mary Kingsburg graduated from Boston University in 1890, Phi Beta Kappa. While at Boston University, Kingsbury also met Helena Stuart Dudley of Boston's Denison House, who influenced her interests in the settlement house movement. In 1899 she married Columbia professor Vladimir Simkhovitch, who shared her interests in social reform. The couple had two children.

In 1902 Mary Kingsbury Simkhovitch and several others founded Greenwich House, in Greenwich Village, New York City. She was director of Greenwich House from 1902-1946; the settlement was known for it social services, neighborhood theater, music, and crafts. Simkhovitch's major reform interest was the improvement of public housing and she served as vice chairman of the New York Housing Authority for a time before her death at Greenwich House in 1951. Mary Kingsbury Simkhovitch believed the role of a settlement house was to be a catalyst for community development and the empowerment of indigenous leadership.

The following document, *The Red Festival*, was written by Mary Kingsbury Simkhovitch in 1934 for the *New Tracts for New Times* series. In the essay, Simkhovitch discusses the emerging social consciousness of the era from the perspective of the feast of Pentecost.

NOTES

[1] The standard biographical sources are Mary Kingsbury Simkhovitch, *Here Is God's Plenty: Reflections on American Social Advance* (New York: Harper & Brother, 1949), and her *Neighborhood: My Story of Greenwich House* (New York: Norton, 1938.).

[2] Simkhovitch, *Here Is God's Plenty*, 154-61.

[3] Ibid, 163-65.

[4] Ibid, 164-65.

MARY KINGSBURY SIMKHOVICH
The Red Festival[1]

Different aspects of truth have their special times for appropriation by men. May we not say that Pentecost is the great festival of today? For the Holy Spirit neglected by us in our thought of God takes this special time to remind us that He does not neglect us.

What characterizes this period of history? In the first place the shrinkage of the world. Radio, the telegraph, mass production, banks, exchange of news, books, art, and ideas all bring us close together. No nationalism can destroy this welding process. This world shrinkage has in it the fundamental excitement that comes from a growing understanding, one of another. Brotherhood is forced upon us. There is the growing knowledge that we are all of one blood, all the children of God. This knowledge comes to us as a revelation. It is borne in on us, as we say. To us, as Christians, we cannot doubt this knowledge comes from the Spirit of God, who acts as the unifier of our experience, giving it meaning. For there is no meaning in facts by themselves. They have to be organized to be significant. All organization speaks of an Organizer. Just as art is the organization of materials, so the Spirit organizes history.

Another characteristic of this period is the antithesis of this world shrinkage. It is nationalism. The evils of nationalism are easily apparent, the selfish desire to exist at the expense of others, the reliance on force, and the persecution of enemies. But there is a living element in nationalism one cannot discount, and that is the bringing about of common purposes. The industrialist can no longer go it alone without considering the fate of the agriculturist. The farmer is obliged to understand the city man. Labor and capital cannot disregard the consumer. The whole question of a balanced economy comes to light. The prosperity of no one group can be accepted if it destroys another.

There may indeed be—in fact there is sure to be at first—a hodgepodge of conflicting interests, of hypocrisy, of chiseling, of travesty. But at bottom there is growing the conviction that we are all in the same boat, and in order to be saved we must pull together.

The Christian cannot doubt but that the Spirit of God is at work in nations, ploughing deep into the subsoil and bringing to light fresh energies and new attitudes.

Another mark of our time is intellectual courtesy—a listening attitude is growing. With the toppling down of old beliefs, prejudices, and standards each man can do no other than listen to the point of view of someone else. The stiff lines of social usage, the solidified convictions of generations have cracked, and out of all the wreckage is beginning to bloom a listening and respectful attitude on the part of men ready to see what is good and what is useful for new times. This fact is not negatived by the equally obvious fact that new convictions are arising as intolerant as the old. The distrust of religion may be as strong as a narrowly held religious belief. And communism is as dogmatic as democracy or capitalism. But taking into account all the passions and violences of modern thought and action, it still seems fair to say that on the whole there is a more active and world-wide discussion of our fate, spiritual and temporal, than has ever taken place before. There is a breeze blowing all over the world. As Christians, we believe that Breeze to be the Holy Spirit, breaking up the hardness, the sloth, the sensuality, the indifference of man to man that has made the planet what it is today.

For the most marked characteristic of our time is the concern of man for man. Whatever may be the weaknesses of communism (and no economic system of fallible humanity will work 100%) no observer of Russia can fail to see that its greatness rests on the practical application of a faith in the possibilities of the downmost man. That faith is stupendous. It is without cynicism, without sophistication. The civilized modern man may smile at such faith. He is certain to deplore the lack of special rewards that ought, as he thinks, to come to the most able. He thinks it naif to suppose any economic system can command allegiance unless it can secure personal liberty of speech and action. But at the same time, he cannot fail to see that a great common purpose and program has done away with those psychoses of fear, of world weariness, and lack of love of life, which infest the youth of many other countries. Every man is to have his chance in Russia to share the social product. Everyone is heir to the family fortune which, though it may be small today, is probably destined under modern skill to be plentiful tomorrow.

Can we as Christians fail to see that this faith in humanity is an integral part of our religion, no matter how loudly communism may trik against religion, as we understand it?

Indeed it is not possible to instance any country of the world where old forms of life are not breaking up and where new attitudes and forces and hopes are not evident. We are in a world that is alive as never before. All is called in question. Ages of faith in the past could affect only a limited number. For transportation was difficult and the means of communication few and laborious. Today the voices of the Pope, of Hitler, of Mussolini, of Franklin Roosevelt, of Stalin, of Ramsay Mac-Donald are heard around the world. Today every community and every newspaper, every theatre, every forum gives at least partial glimpses of opposing or contrasting plans and programs for mankind.

It is not clear what sort of a planet we shall have. The Holy Spirit who fosters brotherhood and joint effort, security, peace, and love, who is heard today more loudly and widely than ever before, may be shut out by violence and refused by the social sin of acquisitiveness and the power of men over men. Or it may be that the consciousness of God's participation in human affairs and His desire to dwell in humanity as He dwelt in Jesus may be welcomed by men of goodwill who in new forms and ways will build a new society and with it a new, if ever the same, Church.

For Pentecost did not determine the forms in which the religion of Jesus should appear from age to age. He broke bread and at His Table His followers meet and recognize one another as His disciples. That sacred rite makes every human family's meal a matter of concern. For what about those families for whom today there is no bread? The Bread of Heaven must have its counterpart on earth.

For the Church there is always the Holy Table, the fellowship of the faithful, and repentance for sin. But at Pentecost there was no Gothic architecture, fine vestments, national council, prayer books, or Bible. There was just the Holy Spirit and the faithful who listened to Him.

History has disclosed His presence in the Church and Society. For we are taught[2] that the fruits of the Spirit are love, joy, peace, long suffering, gentleness, goodness, faith, meekness, and temperance. Wherever these have existed the Spirit has been at work.

It is, then, the fresh revelations of the Spirit in our life that we would do well to note. Reverence is needed as we get glimpses of these revelations. Instead of fear of the new in the sense of anxiety and distrust, we must approach these new revelations of the Spirit with a reverent welcome.

Wherever wages are so low that men cannot feed their children, one must recognize the Spirit of God in those who call these facts to our attention. It will not do to fail to listen to these facts. For so we are not listening to the Living God. Wherever little children have to assume the work which belongs to people, there the Spirit has not been listened to. Wherever any branch of the human race may not claim fellowship in the affairs of men, there Pentecost has failed to register.

Sensitiveness to social sin is more widely felt in these days when, as we may well believe, the Holy Spirit is recognized as closer to mankind than ever in the past.

The awakening of the social conscience is in proportion to the growth of understanding which is far deeper than toleration. We are not asked by the Spirit to tolerate one another, but rather to understand one another, and when we understand we love, just as where we truly love we come to understand. Group life tends to produce understanding, and our modern world is made up of groups. Labor is organized, the professions are organized. Functional activities of all sorts have developed. Common action provokes common thought. Groups become richer as they incorporate various attitudes of their members.

Understanding develops in group experience of all sorts, but sometimes ends with its own boundaries. As Christians, we are asked to extend this understanding beyond all our special group experiences, beyond our membership in families, in neighborhoods, in unions, in professional societies, in national life, to an understanding of all men as the children of God. And we are asked to make the Church coextensive with all men, for the Church is just that—the followers of Jesus and sharers in the life of His spirit. No individual or group is then alien to the workings of the Spirit. All must be redeemed, the family, the nation, and all the processes of production and distribution. Nothing human can be kept free of God and His Spirit.

The Church exists to carry on the Spirit's work. But we cannot confine that work to the Church. We run across the Spirit whenever we have eyes to see and ears with which to hear. An artist's portraiture, a symphony of Beethoven, a group of children in a nursery school, a crowd of workmen in a city square may all reveal the living Spirit of God calling upon the children of men to live, not as those who perish, but as sharers of Eternal Life.

We cannot keep the Spirit of God from entering the world and penetrating its every relationship. But we can refuse to recognize and welcome new models of His entry into the world. We can be blind to brotherhood that comes in an alien guise. We can turn our backs on His appearance in the lives of those who, perhaps without knowledge of whom it is they serve, are bringing in changes in society that open the way for His coming. We can prevent His filling our own hearts with Pentecostal zeal for a new world. Or we can recognize the fruits of the Spirit listed in the Epistle to the Galatians wherever we find them, and so find new signs about us in strange places, perhaps in the byways and hedges.

The Spirit bloweth where it listeth. We must watch where He appears and adore Him there in every cradle and on every cross.

---

[1] Mary Kingsbury Simkhovitch, *The Red Festival*, New Tracts for New Times, (Milwaukee: Morehouse Publishing, 1934).

[2] Galatians 5:22.

EMILY MALBONE MORGAN

(1872-1937)

Emily Malbone Morgan (1872-1937)[1], founder of the Society of the Companions of the Holy Cross, was born in 1862, the youngest child of a New England family. Her parents were Henry Kirke Morgan, a wealthy merchant, and Emily Malbone Brinley. In Emily's childhood, the family attended Trinity Church, Hartford. Emily Malbone Morgan had little formal education, but was exceedingly well-traveled and read voraciously from her uncle George's library. Her mother was a very devout Episcopalian and maintained a correspondence with some of the leaders of the Oxford Movement. At the age of nine Emily Morgan was taken to England to hear Edward Bouverie Pusey, among others, preach. Though she was deeply influenced by Anglo-Catholicism and appreciated "well-ordered ritual," Emily Malbone Morgan resisted the ideal of "church parties" and strove to recognize the strengths in the varieties of churchmanship.[2]

Emily Malbone Morgan began the religious society that was to become the Society of the Companions of the Holy Cross in 1884 with eight of her friends in Hartford, in response to a request for prayers from a friend, Adelyn Howard, who struggled with an incurable bone disease. Morgan and a friend decided to form a religious society with communal intercessory prayer at its center. Though they desired a religious society with the devotional intensity of a religious order, they remained equally committed to a structure flexible enough to accommodate women whose vocations were lived in the world. Members of the society were to meet for retreat in the summers. The members adopted the name, the Society of the Companions of the Holy Cross, and an official prayer. Chapters extended nation-wide very soon; presently, there are approximately 800 "Compan-ions" throughout the world. Then, as now, the society requires a period of discernment before admission, lifetime vows, observing a "Holy Routine" during retreats, an official prayer, a vocational state-ment, a cross membership emblem, and a daily discipline of inter-cessory prayer. [3]

Beginning in 1889, Emily Malbone Morgan financed summer hospitality for women mill workers and their children. Gifted with a keen business mind, she earned the funds for her philanthropy by giving lectures on the arts and publishing travel stories in a Sunday school paper. Morgan continued this ministry of hospitality until her death in Boston in 1937.[4] The Society of the Companions of the Holy Cross also met in these hospitality houses during the early years of the order. In 1914, Adelynrood, in Byfield, Massachusetts, was dedicated as the retreat house of the Society of the Order of the Holy Cross. In order to make this dream a reality, the Companions purchased the property and designed and built the house, which remains a retreat center to the present day.

Many women religious leaders and activists in the Episcopal Church have been associated with the Society of the Companions of the Holy Cross throughout its history. Emily Malbone Morgan served as Companion-in-Charge from the society's inception until her death in 1937. The following excerpts from *Letters To Her Companions* give a glimpse of Morgan's reflections on the society's common life.

NOTES

[1] Biographical sources for Morgan include her *Letters To Her Companions* (Adelynrood: the society of the Companions of the Holy Cross, 1944. Also, biographical information and information on documents for this collection provided by Joanna Bowen Gillespie.

[2] Morgan, *Letters To Her Companions*, 18-19.

[3] Joanna Bowen Gillespie, notes on Emily Malbone Morgan, August 2001.

[4] Morgan, *Letters To Her Companions*, 8-11.

EMILY MALBONE MORGAN
Excerpts from Letters To Her Companions, 1897, 1904*

...We are an order of women living in the world with a desire for the stronger development of the spiritual life in ourselves and others, and we must develop that life along the lines of the world in which we live and with a sympathetic sense of the needs of the nineteenth century. Any pseudo-nunlike life would be at best but a weak imitation of those who possess a sacred vocation to which most of us have not been called. What we must try to understand by our association together is our own vocation as that of women living in the world and having individual influence, social or otherwise, banded together to meet the serious religious, educational, and social problems of our age, first by prayer and then by battle. We are distinctly called to understand intelligently the great yearning needs of the century so nearly gone and the century just dawning. Emphasis should be laid therefore on the intellectual as well as on the spiritual life of such a house, by a study of great movements, of Church history, of social problems and conditions. We might elaborate indefinitely on the possibilities of such a house, and on that which might grow into a larger work than just the summer months of association together, to interpret the life of the Church to a larger number of people and to grow in that power which makes for righteousness. It is always far better, however, to leave God and the future to settle our plans and the details of them...

[...]

...We offered daily thanksgivings for Companions all over the country, for the Church, and for the world. We listened to strong words which will abide with us, we prayed that that week in the hill country might become to us a Mount of Transfiguration, a mount at which we might sit at our Lord's feet and again listen to the Beatitudes, a mount on which by meditation on the sorrow of Calvary we again rededicated ourselves to His service, and from which we went forth strengthened with the fortitude of that Cross which shall yet conquer the world. What left the deepest impression on my mind was our early service of thanksgiving on Sunday morning, which was, after subjects of personal thanksgiving were offered, simply the deepest ascription of praise. It was not the great Eucharistic service which is usually our privilege on Sunday mornings, and God forbid any suggestion should be made that anything could ever take its place. Perhaps it was the supreme effort everyone had to make to supply a lack of priest and altar and sacrifice that made us appreciate more than ever before what thanksgiving was, what the Eucharist in its fullness might mean. Therefore the one great lack of our conference taught its deepest lesson and helped us to realize that where intercession binds us still to earth, praise may admit us to the highest Heaven.

In closing, I can only share with you some of the thoughts that came to me as a result of our week together in the hills, and what I believe may be gained slowly but surely by mutual intercession and thanksgiving. It is the tendency of the heart as we grow older to contract rather than to expand in its sympathies, and this is just what the life of specific intercession and thanksgiving may counteract. There must sooner or later come to every life that crisis when ideals die at the first strong touch of the real, when we reach that time when life's dream is passed and we do not yet realize that life's purpose stays. Perhaps this is a more critical crisis than when we stand in early maidenhood "with reluctant feet, where the brook and river meet." An evanescent enthusiasm no longer buoys us up—the heart fails under hurt of any kind. We would have loved mankind with a mighty love, yet mankind not only does not return our love, but in a measure it rejects it, as it rejected the love of the Master. It is then when love is turned back on itself that our testing time has come, and we must see that if in our loss of hope our hearts must break, they break not like a flint but like a coconut, to give out sweet milk of consolation and human kindness to a yearning world.

[...]

There was one aid to simplicity not touched upon in the conference, perhaps because too deep for utterance—the influence of sorrow. Yet if death is the great equalizer, surely sorrow is the great simplifier of all human things. I do not mean so much the sorrow which brings in its train the kindly expression of legitimate sympathy as that which is part of the daily struggle and the daily care. How the craving for material comfort vanishes before a great and growing secret anxiety! How luxury seems as nothing beside the interior comfort of a few hours' freedom from friction and strain! Are there not many to whom life offers outwardly everything who would have looked forward during the past two months with a sense of relief and joy to two hours by a country wayside, where the stillness of an autumn landscape bathed in purple haze was broken only by the sound of falling leaves, and who for recreation find the most rest in those simple things which are the heritage of all—a growing plant, a playful animal, a sunset behind the exquisite etched outline of November trees? There is no greater cultivator of simplicity, or anything which so reduces needs to their least proportion, as sorrow does. Given a bed, a little sleep—if possible to wakeful eyes—enough to eat, enough fresh air, a chance of healthful exercise, and we have everything really to satisfy physical well-being and to keep us well. "Enough is as good as a feast." More means repletion. We do not realize this perhaps until our hearts are clutched by a pain that makes life different; then we know, and henceforth, to some, life holds but one simple problem—how to meet the needs of those who have never had enough...

Much that I know of simplicity I have learned by long association with working people. They are direct in their thoughts, almost curt in their speech, and don't keep you waiting long in the vestibule of their opinions. Once I was elaborating a beautiful theory of rest and how to put one's self to sleep which I had read in a book and never put into practice, and a girl spoke up suddenly and brightly and said: "Bless me! I have no time for all that, I just make the sign of the cross on my pillow and then lie down in the arms of God." You see in one short sentence she went directly to the great heart of all things and left nothing to be said about rest...

On Monday evening we had one of the loveliest of birthday parties, given for a Companion who said she had not had one since she was nine years old. We followed our ordinary occupations during the day, but assembled just before dinner about our new trellised porch. Our birthday lady was asked to plant the first vines. We then went in to dinner, where many gifts were piled about her plate. Our Companion is one who engages in gentle and matter-of-fact ministries while others talk, and during the conference she constituted herself water-carrier for the dormitory. It was a not uncommon sight to look across the campus and see her during those days in short skirt and shirt sleeves up, making her way to and from the spring. It seemed therefore appropriate to secure her can and drink her health in pure spring water, while at the command of the toastmistress we each arose in turn and read our rhymes commemorative of the occasion, lame in the feet, but warm in affection to celebrate the day. Afterward some of our neighbors joined us and we went into the Common Room and had parlor fireworks until the dining-room floor was cleared for dancing, when each one did her own particular specialty before the dances were called off, the door being left open into the kitchen and the kitchen family sharing our good time. We ended off with ice cream and cake and the lady of the occasion getting up on a chair and thanking us while we responded with three cheers. We had compline at half-past ten, with a special birthday prayer, and the atmosphere of the whole evening was filled with love and goodwill on the part of all. I had to take an early train next morning, but to me it seemed the most charming ending of my two weeks there, and as if the prayers of the summer had passed into loving action as they must always do to make them real—until we become disembodied spirits.

As many of you know, one of my greatest interests has always been the study of recreation and vocations and rest for self-supporting people who are overtaxed. I have been told by some that this is a somewhat material interest, this helping other people to laugh who have forgotten how, even if it be to help them to laugh at the right things. Many grave-minded people say that the great work of life is to save souls for a future state of enjoyment. Anyone who has done much work of this kind knows how frequently one has to meet with the argument on the part of very religious people that it is useless to ameliorate conditions here, and to add largely to the sum of others' enjoyment, for these are all worthless in comparison with the joys of eternity. In a study of the Gospels one would seem to glean, however, that one way to make our own eternity bright is to render life a little less burdensome to others; otherwise it seems strange that a reward should be promised for the giving of a cup of cold water or that our Lord should lay stress in his parable of the

Last Judgment on the clothing of the naked, the visiting of the prisoner, the feeding of the hungry, the welcoming of the stranger. Not long since, my attention was called in a sermon to the study of how much our Lord's life was involved in social acts. He said of Himself that He "came eating and drinking." He hallowed by His Presence the wedding at Cana and many other feasts. He saw a multitude approach and His first thought was the buying of bread that they might eat. He pictured the joys of the world to come under the figure of a banquet, and assembles our deepest and most sacred associations with His Real Presence here on earth in the breaking of bread and the partaking of wine, so that the Lord's Table and the Lord's Supper are familiar terms among all Christians.

Indeed the breaking of bread at the ordinary meal is one of the loveliest symbols of human fellowship. I can remember some years ago at one of my houses when twenty of us sat down at table and nine different nationalities were represented. At my right hand was one of great promise who I feel will do much for her race, the African race in the United States, and on the left hand sat one of the simplest of human souls, yet from a world's point of view rich beyond the dreams of avarice. The feeling came to me so naturally and delightfully as I sat there that we represented a fragment of the Kingdom of Heaven when we shall all sit down together at the Heavenly banquet. It cannot come all at once, because we are shortsighted and very human and particular, and condemn even a woman's soul because she eats with her knife, and think others strange because they prefer chopsticks to knives and forks. These funny little human shibboleths that prevent us so often from looking into the real faces of each other and make us cheat ourselves of real friendships because we are so proper and other people are so queer!

I think during the past four years at Adelynrood we have laid the right accent on our life in relation to our hospitality toward others, but I am hoping each year our prayers may pass into more and more loving actions of social graciousness that shall give them a living reality. St. John the Baptist in preparation for the mission of a great prophet must stand as the type of the ascetic, the recluse, the dweller in solitude, the type of monasticism. We learned during the Retreat that it is only the exceptional person who is called to the special mission of prophet-reformer or religious, and that the calling of most of us is to the highest living out of life under ordinary circumstances and to follow Christ in all the varied social relations of life; therefore, that the cultivation of all social gifts on our part lies in the line of ordinary duty...

---

* Emily Malbone Morgan, *Letters To Her Companions* (Adelynrood: The Society of the Companions of the Holy Cross, 1944). 45-47; 70-73. Used with permission of The Society of the Companions of the Holy Cross. Readers who wish to copy the excerpts should request permission from the Society: Companion-in-Charge, SCOHC, Adelynrood, South Byfield, MA.

HARRIET M. BEDELL

(1875-1969)

Harriet M. Bedell (1875-1969), deaconess and missionary among indigenous peoples, was born in Buffalo, New York in 1875. She graduated from the State Normal School and taught history and English in Buffalo Public schools, also teaching Sunday School on the Seneca Reservation. When she was thirty, Bedell experienced a call to missionary service after hearing a lecture by an Episcopal missionary to China. Her family was unsupportive of her desire to go to China, though she eventually studied at the New York Training School for Deaconesses, and was appointed as a missionary among the Cheyenne at Whirlwind Mission, Oklahoma. Bedell remained in Oklahoma for ten years, 1907-1917, where she taught Christian education and provided medical care.

From the time of her arrival in Oklahoma until a few years before her death in 1969—long past her official retirement—Bedell worked tirelessly among American Indian and Alaskan people. After the federal government relocated the Oklahoma tribes in 1916, she was transferred to Alaska and taught at a boarding school in Nenana. After requesting a transfer to a more remote site closer to native people, Bedell was sent to Stevens Village on the Yukon, approximately 40 miles south of the Arctic Circle, where she traveled by dogsled as the only missionary teacher and nurse for an entire community. Bedell was set apart as a deaconess in 1922 during the General Convention in St. Mark's Church, Portland. During her last years in Alaska, Harriet Bedell opened a boarding school in Tanana that was eventually closed due to a lack of funds.

In 1932, Deaconess Bedell discovered the plight of the Seminoles in Florida after giving a series of lectures for the Florida Chain of Missions. Using her own meager salary, Bedell reopened a mission among the Mikasuki Indians. Though forced to retire "officially" at age 63, she continued her ministry of health care, education, and economic empowerment among the American Indians of the Everglades until Hurricane Donna wiped out the mission in 1960. Active into her 80s, Bedell drove twenty thousand miles a year during the course of her ministry. The diocese of Southwest Florida celebrates Harriet Bedell Day on January 8, the anniversary of her death.

Deaconess Bedell was one of the most popular writers in the national Episcopal mission periodical, *The Spirit of Missions.* She won the respect of indigenous peoples through her compassion and her respect for their way of life and beliefs. The following document was written in 1910 while she was active in ministry among the Cheyenne who eventually adopted her into the tribe and gave her the name of "Bird Woman."[1]

NOTES

[1] There are various sources for information on Harriet M. Bedell. See, Owanah Anderson, *400 Years: Anglican/Episcopal Mission Among American Indians* (Cincinnati: Forward Movement, 1997): 42, 160-163; 271-272; 307-308. Also, William B. Hartley, *A Woman Set Apart* (New York: Dodd Mead, 1963). A folder of Bedell's papers are located in the Schlesinger Library, Radcliffe College. Also see the website www.marcoeagle.com.

Harriet M. Bedell
Among the Indians of Oklahoma*

We live in an Indian camp, and come in very close contact with the people. There is a Church day-school of thirty-nine pupils, ranging from five to seventeen years, and all our work goes hand in hand with work in the homes. The Indians live in *tipis*, in a most primitive way. Beds are of covered dry grass, and the cooking is done on a fire made in a hole in the ground. Around each *tipi* is a kind of stockade made of the tall weeds which grow so plentifully here. The Indians eat any kind of animal flesh, even dog, preserved by cutting very thin and hanging in the sun to dry.

Their manners, customs, language and dress are just as strange as though found in any foreign land; in fact, I sometimes wonder if I am really in our own country. Only when Uncle Sam brings my mail do I realize that I still live under the Stars and Stripes.

Among the older people many of the old-time customs still prevail, such as wailing at funerals, burying all belongings with the dead, the cries of the medicine man, calls for feasts from the hills, and the old kettle-drum ceremony, lasting all night.

Both men and women wear their hair long, in two braids over the shoulders, the men's only differing in having a third very small braid from the middle of the back of the head in memory of the old "scalp lock." The women wear a short, loose gown with flowing sleeves, belted in at the waist, with fancy metal belts or twisted colored scarfs. The men wear white man's dress, except for their moccasins of buckskin, heavily beaded in beautiful Indian designs. Many still paint their faces, and during their festive times still like to wear feathers and highly ornamented costumes. The school pupils wear clothing which we provide–when our friends help us to secure it.

The English meaning of their names is most interesting. *Wenhaya* means "Sage Woman"; *Vicrehia*, "Bird Woman"; then we have "Big Nose," "Blind Bull," "Crooked Nose," "Turkey Legs," "Short Neck," "Antelope Skin," etc. When the little children come to school I must give them names. The son of "Chicken Hawk" I call "Paul Chicken

Hawk." I have "Sarah Little Man," "James Tall Meat," "Ruth Howling Crane." It is said (though I am not sure of this) that the child is named from the first thing the mother thinks about or sees after the child is born. There are a few pretty names, like "Annie Red Cloud," "Tall Chief," "White Bird," but some are very suggesting, as "Slow-as-Smoke," "Lying-on-a-Side," and "Walking Woman," etc.

It is the idea of the government and all interested in the Indians to encourage them to live on their own allotments, to have one spot which they may call home; but they will camp together in spite of all that is being done. For this reason our mission camp is approved by the government on account of the uplifting influence not only among the children but in the homes.

"What is the Church doing?" perhaps you are beginning to ask. The Church was established at Darlington by the Rev. J. W. Wicks. Its origin was as follows: In 1875, Oakerhater, a young Cheyenne leader, was sent with some seventy others to Fort San Marco, Fla. They were prisoners of war and among the worst of their tribes. They remained at the fort three years, then the older ones were allowed to return to their homes, while twenty-two young men remained in the East for education. Among these were three who had been visited during their imprisonment and taught by an earnest Churchwoman and officer of the Woman's Auxiliary of Central New York. Through her interest and efforts Oakerhater, and Oksteher, another young Cheyenne, were placed in charge of the Rev. J. W. Wicks, who was then rector of St. Paul's Church, Paris Hill, N.Y. They were baptized and confirmed in the fall of 1880. Oksteher died soon after, but Oakerhater continued his studies until the spring of 1881, when he was ordained deacon by Bishop Huntington at Syracuse. He went immediately to his tribe, where he began work under the Rev. J. H. Wicks, who was at this time in charge. The work continued with some changes, and through the influence of Mrs. Whirlwind—an old chief's wife, who was a devout communicant of the mission—was transferred to the Whirlwind allotment, where a government day-school had been conducted, which had been closed some time, much to the disappointment of the Indians; for they love their children as well as white parents do, and it was very hard to have them taken to schools far away for five years or more. So a Church day-school was established, which was hailed with joy by the Indians, and which has continued to grow, the only drawback being the lack of funds to carry it on; but even with financial discouragements the work continues to prosper. This school and the industrial work have always been considered but means to the great end—the spreading of Christ's Kingdom. It is slow work, and often discouraging, but the Indian can accept Christ as his Saviour and still wear his hair in braids, cook his food on an open fire, and live in a *tipi*.

The Indian is thought to be unresponsive. So he is—to outsiders, but I will tell one or two of my experiences with him. With our Indian deacon, David Oakerhater, I attended the funeral of a young Christian Indian whom I had visited while he was very sick with tuberculosis in a camp about seven miles away. After the service at the grave I tried, with David's help, to comfort the parents (not Christians), saying that their son was not in that hole, but that he had gone to a beautiful place where all is peace and happiness, and where there is no sickness, and that if they would follow in his footsteps they would see him again. I apparently made no impression, and left feeling that I had given little comfort. As the Indian never returns to live on the site where loved ones have died, these Indians came to Whirlwind. They sent for me the next morning, and through an interpreter told me how I had comforted their hearts, and that they would try to do as I said. Let us pray that they, too, may soon come into the Fold.

The other day an Indian (Robe Red Wolf) came in. I said, *"Ha na tze hu hile?"* ("What can I do for you?"). He replied, "I just came in to talk." They he said something like this: "I'm glad I'm Christian. I'm happy now different way. It's hard for Indian to be Christian, and hard to give up old ways; but when we become Christian, then we glad. I am glad missionaries are here. They teach us good way. My wife no Christian. You make her Christian." Is it worth while? Every day brings experiences similar to these.

I am often asked why, upon leaving boarding-school, the educated Indian so soon falls back into the old ways. It is quite clear to me. The girl in boarding-school learns many useful things under proper conditions and with beautiful equipments—cooking by electricity, using stationary tubs and mangles in a well-furnished laundry. She returns to her home. How different everything is! A hole in the ground instead of a stove, dried grass for beds, no chairs, no tables. How can she put into practice what she has learned? Her mother, too, is in charge of the home, and will not allow the daughter to make changes. Our own mothers would not. Then is all this education wasted? I think not. The homes of the next generation are sure to be on a higher plane.

We believe our methods are the solution of the problem. We being with conditions as we find them, working up to higher ideals. The older schoolgirls and some of the young married women in the camp come to the mission-house each day in turn to do the work which each day brings. The boys of the mission care for the horses, help on washday, work in the garden, and learn to be useful generally. We feel quite encouraged. A few have bought stoves; some home-made tables may now be seen; beds are raised from the ground; and in many of the homes washing and bathing are regularly done.

We have short Evening Prayer every night at seven o'clock, and the pupils come as regularly as they come to school. We seldom have an absence, and so are always sure of a congregation. Many of the older Indians come too. The instruction is varied: On Monday we have the Catechism, and the scholars do well; a few of the older ones, I am sure, can say it through without a mistake; on Tuesday there is Bible drill in finding places and memorizing; Wednesday and Friday nights are specially for the older ones, though they come every night; the service is nearly all in Cheyenne, and we have a five-minute meditation. On Thursday we have Prayer Book drill in finding places and reading of rubrics. You would be pleased to see how readily even those who understand little English can find their places. On Sunday we have services both morning and evening, nearly all in Cheyenne; Sunday-school in the afternoon, and once a month a devotional meeting for the communicants. There are now twenty-five of these, and a more devout group of people it would be hard to find. A clergyman comes on a weekday to administer the holy Communion once a month. Nearly all in the school are baptized. The older people are slow in accepting Christianity, but when they do, their faith is beautiful—so simple and trustful; I get many a lesson from them. The Indian is naturally religious, and unless the Church carries to him the true Gospel of Christ he does many strange things in the name of worship.

We have just opened a reading-room by which we hope to reach young people not in school. Though poorly equipped it has proved a success, but the room is far too small. We hope soon to have a chapel; then we can take the large room, which we are now using solely for services, for a reading-room. Some will come to the reading-room who do not now come to chapel. We have pictures for those who cannot read. Those of the life of Christ have aroused much interest, and when we told the story of each picture it was evident that some had never heard it before, though they had heard of Christianity. Quiet games are also allowed, and with very simple reading-matter, highly illustrated, we hope to have something for all who come. The room is open every night after chapel until nine o'clock.

Is it worthwhile? I ask again; and I say "Yes," most emphatically. But the inwrought traits of character must be considered in dealing with the Indian. With the same advantages for the same length of time, he might have stood side by side with the white man in civilization. He may not now reach the same height as his European brother, but he does approach it. Then why not help him?—for he can become a Christian long before he reaches that high plane which it has taken centuries of civilization to attain.

---

* Harriett Bedell, "Among the Indians of Oklahoma," *The Spirit of Missions*, 85, no 4 (April 1910); 271-74.

FRANCES PERKINS

(1880-1965)

Frances Perkins (1880-1965)[1], Secretary of Labor and the first woman to hold a Cabinet post in the United States, was born Fannie Coralie Perkins in Boston, Massachusetts, in 1880. She legally changed her name to Frances Perkins in 1905. As a social reformer, Perkins advocated a variety of liberal causes in the interest of workers, including social security, unemployment compensation, minimum wage and maximum hours, and child welfare legislation. She was on the New York State Industrial Board from 1923 to 1929 and was its chairperson from 1926 to 1929. In 1929, Franklin Delano Roosevelt, then governor of New York, appointed her state industrial commissioner. Later, after her appointment as Roosevelt's Secretary of Labor in 1933, Frances Perkins became one of the most important architects of the New Deal program, as well as the 1935 Social Security Act. After President Roosevelt's death, she served on the U.S. Civil Service Commission until 1953.[2]

Frances Perkins was raised in Worcester, Massachusetts in a comfortable Republican household. She graduated from Mount Holyoke College in 1902, and began a series of part-time teaching and volunteer positions. As a science teacher at Ferry Hall School in Lake Forest, Illinois, Perkins became familiar with Hull House and spent her free time at the settlement in Chicago. At Hull House, Perkins received her first exposure to labor unions, as well as the conditions of the working poor.

After 1907, Frances Perkins served in a variety of labor organizations in Pennsylvania and New York. While in New York, in 1911, she witnessed the Triangle Shirtwaist fire. After the tragedy, she took a position with the Committee of Safety of the City of New York, which monitored the health and safety of workers. She also pursued graduate studies and received an M.A. in economics and sociology from Columbia University in 1910.[3]

In 1913, Frances Perkins married Paul Caldwell Wilson, an economist. Perkins insisted on keeping her maiden name at the time of her marriage. The couple had one surviving daughter, Susanna Winslow Perkins Wilson in 1916. During the 1920s, Paul Wilson experienced increasing bouts of depression for which he received treatment until his death at home in Washington, D.C. in 1952. Perkins remained devoted to her husband throughout his lifetime, visiting him frequently even when she was Secretary of Labor.[4]

Frances Perkins was sustained throughout her life by her deep religious faith that strengthened her resolve to fight for better conditions for working people. Perkins had joined the relatively new congregation, Church of the Holy Spirit, Lake Forest, Illinois, and was confirmed there. Frances Perkins was drawn to the Episcopal Church by its aesthetics, the liturgy, and the rhythm of the liturgical calendar. She also was nourished by a disciplined prayer life, and became a regular retreatant at the All Saints Convent in Catonsville, Maryland. "I have discovered the rule of silence is one of the many beautiful things in the world," she once wrote.[5] At the convent— where she registered as "Mrs. Wilson"—Frances Perkins would sometimes discuss her work with the mother superior, but mainly went there for spiritual refreshment. She was aware of the tendency for humanitarians to get discouraged in the struggle. However, Frances Perkins believed that the religious basis of her work was integral to her longevity. She did what she did "for Jesus' sake" and not simply as a "humanitarian urge."[6]

In 1948, shortly after she resigned as Secretary of Labor, Frances Perkins presented the St. Bede Lectures, at St. Thomas Episcopal Church in New York City under the topic of "The Christian in the World." Throughout the lectures, Perkins revealed a theology that was deeply incarnational. For Frances Perkins, God becoming human in Jesus was the organizing principal for her sense of the role of humankind in a Christian society. Further, she saw a Christian society as one that expresses social cooperation through legal, economic, and social relationships.[7] The following excerpt is from Frances Perkins' lecture on "The Vocation of the Laity."

NOTES

[1] The most comprehensive work on Frances Perkins is George Martin's *Madam Secretary: Frances Perkins* (Boston: Houghton Mifflin, 1976). Biographical information also provided by Susanna W. Coggeshall.

[2] Martin, parts I & II.

[3] Ibid. part II & IV.

[4] Ibid, part III.

[5] Quoted in Martin, *Madame Secretary*, 281.

[6] Ibid, 280-81.

[7] Frances Perkins, "St. Bede's Lectures," 1948, 1:24; 3:36. The St. Bede's Lectures are located in the Rare Book and Manuscript Library, Columbia University Library. The texts for these lectures were loaned by Donn Morgan, along with his invaluable insights on the religious life of Frances Perkins.

FRANCES PERKINS
Excerpts from The Vocation of The Laity*

..Now, we are all familiar – none of us who are churchmen, can fail to be familiar – with the function of the laity in the liturgical life and order of the church. We know that the order of the eucharist is designed for the participation of the people in the offering of the sacrifice, and we say here – we offer ourselves, our souls and bodies to be a living sacrifice. This has become a part of our understanding; that no liturgical action is complete without the participation of the laity. This has been one of the great elements of knowledge which our church, I think, has handed on to her children everywhere; that they have no[t] only a function, but that they have a duty to the ecclesiastical life of the church.

But in particular, as we discuss the Christian in the world, and the problems connected with the Christian life in the world as it is today, we must examine in some detail the special vocation of the laity to conduct and carry on the worldly and secular affairs of modern society. For this is a duty which has been particularly laid upon the Christian laity, laid, as a matter of fact, upon all mankind; for we must remind ourselves of what we already know of the doctrine of man: That God made all men, all mankind, the race of man, and that to the race of man is committed the earth and the fruits thereof; and that man must manage that earth, that land, that production of food, that maintaining of his physical life by the labors which he performs with the land and with the natural resources that God has given him. So that to all mankind there comes a vocation, there comes the obligation to conduct the affairs of the world, and to maintain in health and decency the people who live in the world. But peculiarly there is what we call, not a function, not an obligation, but a true vocation for Christian laymen to conduct the affairs of the world, conduct the secular affairs of life in a Christian way, and according to the laws of God and the Christian principles which we are taught by the church to recognize, to analyze, to imitate, and with God's help, to apply. We must apply them in every function and every activity which fall to laymen naturally.

We can never overlook, of course, the fact that man's nature has to be considered in considering how Christian laymen shall exercise their vocation to conduct the secular material affairs of the world in order that all men may be maintained in health and decency; that the earth may produce her fruits; that they may be distributed; that men may come together for the production of greater and more comfortable dwellings and covering and shelter against the storm. In considering these activities we must consider them not as important in themselves, but as important in view of what we know about the nature of men.

[...]

...Now, to men and women, therefore, to laymen, is entrusted by God this special function of managing the material and secular life of the country and of the world.

We discussed, of course – if I may run over the items – the concept that the Incarnation was the principle, the great and mighty principle upon which we rely for our understanding of man's function in a Christian society, and of what a Christian society ought to be. We rely on that and we have had revealed to us through that Incarnation some knowledge of man as man, and his relation to God; and the opportunity to develop a life fit for the children of God, a world, a society fit for the children of God to live in, comes to us as we meditate on, and come more and more to understand that great and mighty principle which is presented to us in the Incarnation. It becomes in this one world, this one world that we talk about, of course, the realization that in Christ we have the great, the mighty, the overwhelming principle of God and man made one; of God and man reconciled to each other, and through that, of course, of man's possibility to be reconciled to himself; that is, to comprehend himself, and to go on living with this Divine aid which comes to him through the Incarnation.

It is the reason for man's effort, it is the cause of man's effort to build a Christian society. This knowledge of the Incarnation, this fact of the Incarnation, gives to man the capacity with God to love his fellow creatures, and to work, and to cooperate with God for the establishment of a Christian order of society. A kind of holy society which we conceive to be the will of God who made man, and taking upon himself our nature, made possible for us to understand what are the almost limitless possibilities for the development of the nature of man.

[...]

Now, politics, of course, used to be regarded as something that had no part in religion. There used to be a saying, "Keep politics and religion apart!" You are supposed to never discuss them at the dinner table. I often wonder what they did discuss. What is there so interesting as politics and religion – the two most interesting and most compelling, most important subjects, really, with which man is concerned? For all men are concerned with politics. Aristotle and Aquinas, even William Temple, Archbishop of Canterbury, and Kane and Demant, to bring it up to date with recent books, all say the same thing about politics: That it is an essential and permanent function of man; that man will always have politics. It is essential to his nature as man, and for the ordering of his society, of his relationships, each to the other. Not all Christians apparently will always believe that. There has been a lot of heresy, I am told. Pelagius, of course, with his perfectionism, was the great, attractive heretic. Almost everybody in the Anglo Saxon world really was greatly intrigued by his heresies. There was so much of it that we would love to believe. Man is almost perfect and is about to become perfect is the way it works out, and people would like to believe it.

[...]

So within the exercise of the political functions is a duty of Christian people to take part in politics. I feel that more sincerely than I can possibly say. The withdrawal of Christian people of high purpose and nobility of mind and heart, the withdrawal of people like that from political life, has been a terrible loss not only to the world, but particularly to our form and organization of government and society. For a democracy is harder to operate than, we'll say, a benevolent monarchy, much harder. It was a hard way of doing things that our ancestors chose when they wrote the Declaration of Independence. The writers and those who drew it up anticipated, certainly, that good Christian men (not women, of course, at that time) would be the first to take their full part in the development of the political activities and in the establishment and maintenance and operation of the state as the political function and exercise of man in the protection of his order of society.

[...]

But I think that we always have to remember what economics and politics are. They were always treated of in the old books as part of moral theology. Economics was defined as that department of moral theology which deals with the way men earn their living; and politics as that department of moral theology which deals with the way men order society. It is, I think, in recognition of these two great activities, great functions of man as part of a moral theology, that we will begin to realize how the law of God can be determined and how it can operate in those fields.

---

* Frances Perkins; 'The Vocation Of The Laity," St. Bede Lectures, St. Thomas Church, New York, New York, (February 2, 1948): 1-3; 4-5; 18-19; 2124-25 Access to the photocopy generously provided by Donn Morgan. Original from the Columbia University Library, Rare Book and Manuscript Division. Permission to reprint here by Susanna Coggeshall.

LUCY RANDOLPH MASON

(1882-1959)

Lucy Randolph Mason (1882-1959)[1] labor activist and reformer, was born at Clarens, Virginia, on Seminary Hill near Alexandria, and was raised in Richmond. Her father, Landon Randolph Mason, was an Episcopal priest, and her mother, Lucy Ambler Mason, was the daughter of an Episcopal priest. Though Lucy Randolph Mason was from the prominent heritage of the First Families of Virginia, the family's finances were limited. The Mason's were strong advocates for marginalized persons throughout the South and they raised Lucy and their other children with a strong sense of Christian service and social responsibility.[2]

Unable to attend college for economic reasons, Lucy Randolph Mason trained herself to work in an office, and spent the ten years after she finished her formal education as a stenographer. In 1914, she was appointed industrial sectary of the Richmond YWCA, where she worked on protective labor legislation for women and children. She resigned in 1918 to care for her aging father, yet continued to work as a volunteer in a number of agencies and reform organizations, including the Union Label League, the Richmond Equal Suffrage League, and the Committee on Women in Industry of the National Advisory Council on Labor. She returned to the YWCA in 1923 as general secretary in Richmond and raised the visibility of the organization in labor and social reform, especially in the African American community.[3]

Throughout the 1930s, Lucy Randolph Mason continued to advocate for better working conditions for women and children, minimum wage laws, and social security legislation. In 1932 she became executive secretary of the National Consumers League. The president of the Congress of Industrial Organizations (CIO) invited Lucy Randolph Mason to join the Textile Workers Organizing Committee in 1937, and to return to the South to promote the need for unions. As public relations representative for the CIO, she traveled extensively and worked with religious and community leaders and the media in supporting the interests of labor. In addition, she publicized civil rights violations and lectured widely in colleges and university. At a time when southern community leaders easily associated labor unions with communism, "Miss Lucy" was successful in advocating for the needs of workers.[4]

In the 1940s and 1950s, Lucy Mason Randolph traveled less extensively, yet continued to work for the marginalized, particularly African Americans, through local religious and community organizations. In 1952 Lucy Randolph Mason published her autobiography, *To Win These Rights: A Personal Story of the CIO in the South*. In the same year, she received the Social Justice Award of the National Religion and Labor Foundation. She died in Atlanta in 1959.

The following excerpt from *To Win These Rights* documents Lucy Randolph Mason's early years as a labor and social activist.

NOTES

[1] The primary source for biographical information is Lucy Randolph Mason, *To Win These Rights: A Personal Story of the CIO in the South* (New York: Harper & Brothers, 1952).

[2] Ibid, 1-18.

[3] Ibid.

[4] Ibid, 19-32.

LUCY RANDOLPH MASON
Excerpts from To Win These Rights:
A Personal Story of the CIO in the South*

Clarens, where I was born on July 26, 1882, is a long, two-story white house on the Episcopal Seminary Hill, near Alexandria, Virginia. It was then the home of my great-aunt Miss Virginia Mason and her sister Ida.

At that time our family was living in Shepherdstown, West Virginia, where my father, Reverend Landon Randolph Mason, was the Episcopal minister. Mother was Lucy Ambler before her marriage, and her father was Reverend John Cary Ambler, an Episcopal missionary to the mountains of West Virginia, whose visits when we were young were occasions of great joy to all of us. When I was six weeks old, Mother returned to Shepherdstown with the new baby.

Father's first parish had been at Drakes Branch, in the southern part of Virginia. He had two or three country "missions" as part of his Drakes Branch Parish. Mother used to say that the salary was $500 a year, paid mostly in black-eyed peas and bacon.

Sometimes in my CIO work I have heard it said that I could not appreciate the needs of working people because I "was born with a silver spoon in my mouth." To dispel any illusions as to the financial status of the family, here are other bits in our history. In Shepherdstown, father's second parish, the salary was $900. We moved to Marietta, Georgia, when I was eight years old. The salary there was $1500. We stayed less than a year because father thought the available schools unsatisfactory for the education of the children. He accepted a call to Richmond with a top salary there of $2600. A modest rectory was supplied in all of these places.

My mother had to be a remarkable financier to make the money cover the needs of the family and help the boys attend the University of Virginia. My brothers used to get jobs in summer vacations, by which they contributed to the cost of going to college.

[...]

"UNTO THE LEAST OF THESE"

Both mother and father had a strong sense of social responsibility. It was part of their religious conviction. Their deep concern for human welfare led them into many unusual contacts. Father would respond to calls for help from poverty stricken families who had no connection with our congregation. I remember his carrying a bushel of coal on his back, from a store to the home of a destitute family, one winter day when an eighteen inch snow had stopped all traffic. That was typical of his way of answering calls for help. In times of epidemics such as scarlet fever, he went wherever he was needed, often sitting up all night with some ill or dying person.

One night a group of men were together at the Commonwealth Club in Richmond, talking about father and his life of self-denial and service. One of the men said,

"Mr. Mason is the most beloved man in Richmond—it is time somebody was doing something for him."

Another man said, "Let's give him a trip to England this summer."

A quick canvass was made and the men in the club that evening raised $500, enough for a modest trip abroad in those distant years, and appointed a committee to take it father.

Being a frugal young woman I had saved enough to take some one to England with father. I wanted mother to go, but she had many reasons for not undertaking such a trip and insisted that I should go. So I had my first trip to England at the age of twenty-six and never regretted spending my savings that way.

Mother had a Bible class Sunday afternoons in the State Penitentiary, located in Richmond. Many of the men she met there came to our house when they were released. Some of them stayed with us while looking for work. They used the third-floor bedroom next to mine, but none of us ever had any fear of their doing harm. Through these contacts, mother discovered the atrocious cruelties that were perpetrated within the prison walls. She and her friend Mrs. Whitehead, and Dr. Carrington, a private medical practitioner who gave part of his time to serving the penitentiary inmates on a salary basis, decided to tell what they knew of the barbarities in that institution. Another friend of mother's, Mr. Charles Baughman, who was in the printing and stationery business, donated the cost of printing leaflets that were distributed throughout the state.

The public was shocked by these revelations. The penitentiary authorities proclaimed that owing to a smallpox scare in Norfolk, one hundred miles away, the prison must be closed to all visitors. They kept a quarantine on the penitentiary for a year or more. But the revelations made by mother led to some immediate reforms and doubtless contributed to the sweeping changes that took place some years after her death.

One morning Mother received through the mail a newspaper clipping about a young girl who had killed her baby and tried to kill herself. She had been committed to jail. Mother never knew who eased his conscience by mailing her that clipping, but she went immediately to the jail and was permitted to see the girl, who was in a desperate state of mind. We knew where Mother had gone and were not surprised when a phone call came from her at supper time saying she must spend the night in the cell with the girl, who still threatened to kill herself.

Mother and Father practiced what Jesus said when he described the final test that made men fit to inherit the Kingdom of God. They took in and fed the stranger; they refreshed the spirit of the thirsty; they gave clothes to those who lacked them; they visited the sick; and they went to those in prison. They knew they served God as they cared for His children, remembering the Command "Love thy neighbor as thyself." Indirectly, Mother served the lepers of the world since she raised money for the Leper Mission that housed, fed, and clothed them. The Mission also helped promote the cures for leprosy that have brought many formerly afflicted people back to health. Somewhere in India there is a cottage in a leper colony which bears her name.

[...]

COOPERATING WITH LABOR UNIONS

When I first became "union conscious" I do not know. I suppose it grew out of my concern because of the industrial accidents that happened to so many of the working people I knew, the long work days in Richmond's factories, laundries, stores, and everywhere else. These ten- and eleven-hour days were not only bad for the people who worked them, but disrupted normal family life. They burned my conscience and during my long life I have spent a lot of time laboring to shorten hours of work for both men and women.

[…]

It early became apparent that the best paid workers were union members, and they had an eight-hour day, with half of Saturday off. So it seemed natural that my sympathies and hopes should turn toward the unions. I remember that when I was still a stenographer there was a street railway drivers' strike and I avoided riding on street cars for the duration of the strike. There was a lot of snow and sleep that winter, and traveling on foot was not easy.

Early in life I joined the Union Label League. The label was used on garments made in factories whose workers were union members. The label meant better working conditions and wages. I searched diligently for clothing with labels, but rarely found any in Richmond stores. At least we League members asked questions and showed our interest in union-made goods. Frequently, I spoke to union meetings on this and other subjects. (Years later, in New York, I became a member of the International Ladies Garment Workers Union Label Committee, whose purpose was to win public support for clothes bearing this label.)

During the governorship of Westmoreland Davis we had strong support from him and his splendid secretary, Col. LeRoy Hodges. Those two worked together in accomplishing man reforms. Virginia owed them a special debt of gratitude for bringing about the complete reformation of the State Penitentiary and making it a place in which human beings might live.

At that time, the only organized body of men who stood by our women's organizations in fighting for progressive and humane legislative measures were the Virginia and Richmond Federations of Labor. During World War I, Samuel Gompers, president of the American Federation of Labor, appointed me "Virginia Chairman of the Committee on Women in Industry, of the National Advisory Committee on Labor." Usually such a point went to a union member or representative. This was my first union appointment.

[…]

In the early winter of 1931 a group of church women from six southern states invited me to spend two months traveling in the South trying to create public opinion for better child labor laws and shorter hours of work for women.

I accepted and had an illuminating time. I met governors, legislators, newspaper editors, ministers, college professors, labor representatives, social workers, civil leaders—and manufacturers. This was the only period in which industrialists, or some of them, were glad to see someone who advocated both state and federal legislation to curtail hours of work. For 1931 was the bottom of the Great Depression, millions of men and women formed an enormous pool of unemployed who would work under any conditions and for any wages, however low. The South's leading industry—cotton textiles—was in a terribly depressed condition. Over-production and full warehouses had resulted in a glutted market and depressed prices. In a frantic endeavor to meet competition by continually lowering costs, textile manufacturers had lengthened hours of work, resorted to almost general night work, and cut wages until seven or eight dollars a week was common pay...

* Lucy Randolph Mason, *To Win These Rights: A Personal Story of the CIO in the South*, (New York: Harper and Brothers, 1952): 1-6; 8-9.

ANNA "ELEANOR" ROOSEVELT

(1884-1962)

Anna "Eleanor" Roosevelt (1884-1962)[1], reformer, diplomat, humanitarian, was born in New York City in 1884, the first child of Elliott Roosevelt and Anna Hall Roosevelt, and the niece of President Theodore Roosevelt. She attended school in England; upon her return home at age seventeen she became involved in settlement work and the National Consumer's League. Biographers have linked her later activism with this early involvement in social reform.

During the early years of her marriage, Eleanor Roosevelt raised five children and supported Franklin Delano Roosevelt's political career. After 1921, on the advice of her husband's physician, she began to take an active interest in national and international affairs in order to renew his interest in politics. During her husband's presidency, Eleanor Roosevelt was an advocate for a wide range of New Deal and reform causes, including child welfare, equal rights, and labor. She was an indefatigable traveler, a popular speaker, and wrote a syndicated newspaper column. During World War II she toured military bases throughout the United States, Great Britain, and the South Pacific.

After her husband's death, Eleanor Roosevelt was appointed by President Harry Truman as a delegate to the United Nations, where she was chair of the UN Commission on Human Rights. She played an integral role in the adoption of the Universal Declaration of Human Rights in 1948.

Eleanor Roosevelt was a lifelong Episcopalian. She was baptized in Calvary Episcopal Church, Gramercy Park, New York City, near the home of Theodore Roosevelt. After she returned from school in England, she was confirmed at the Church of the Incarnation, also in Manhattan in 1903. Her marriage in 1905 to her distant cousin, Franklin Delano Roosevelt, was recorded in the parish register, through the actual event took place at a cousin's home on East Sixty-Seventh Street. During the early years of their marriage, the Roosevelts attended the Church of the Incarnation, as well as St. James Episcopal Church in Hyde Park, New York. Eleanor Roosevelt maintained an association with St. James Episcopal Church for the rest of her life.[2]

After Franklin Delano Roosevelt was appointed assistant secretary of the navy in 1913, Eleanor Roosevelt moved with her husband to Washington, D.C., where the family attended St. Thomas Church, and where the children attended Sunday School. The Roosevelts maintained their ties with the parish during his presidency, 1933-1945, though the president preferred holding services at the White House. After leaving Washington, Eleanor Roosevelt set up her primary residence in Hyde Park, and continued at the parish there until the final weeks of her life. Eleanor Roosevelt did not like attending church on her own, and often attended with her grandchildren, relatives, or even visiting dignitaries, such as Queen Juliana of the Netherlands.[3]

Eleanor Roosevelt was not one to dwell on theological abstractions or debate doctrine. Instead, she enacted her faith through relationships and causes. Eleanor Roosevelt's spiritual formation throughout childhood was nurtured through worship, Sunday school, family prayer, and bible reading. Eleanor Roosevelt's early religious faith conformed to conventional patterns. However, her mature faith reflected her belief in the inter-relatedness of all humankind and the importance of service to the global community.[4] While remaining a Christian, she developed an interfaith perspective through her work and travels. "The vital thing which must be alive in each human consciousness is the religious teaching that we cannot live for ourselves alone, and that as long as we are here on this earth we are all of us brother, regardless of race, creed, or color," said Eleanor Roosevelt.[5]

The following document, *Christmas: A Story*, was published in 1940 and is written in a format for children and adults. The story takes place in the Netherlands during the Nazi occupation, and is the story of a young girl's faith and refusal to be defeated by evil. Eleanor Roosevelt's friendships with the reigning monarchs of the Netherlands helped reinforce the United States wartime and postwar alliance in Europe.

NOTES

[1] There are many biographical sources for Eleanor Roosevelt. For an overview, see Eleanor Roosevelt, *The Autobiography of Eleanor Roosevelt* (New York: Da Capo Press, 2000; rpt. 1961); and Blanche Weisen Cook, *Eleanor Roosevelt*. 2 Vols. (New York: Penguin, 1998, 2000).

[2] Maurine Beasely, et al., *The Eleanor Roosevelt Encylopedia* (Westport: Greenwood Press, 2001): 435

[3] Beasely, 436.

[4] Beasely, *The Eleanor Roosevelt Encylopedia*, 437-440.

[5] Quoted in Beasley, 436-37.

ELEANOR ROOSEVELT
Christmas: A Story*

ST. NICHOLAS'S EVE, 1940, was cold and the snow was falling. On the hearth in Marta's home there was a fire burning, and she had been hugging that fire all day, asking her mother to tell her stories, telling them afterwards to her doll.

This was not like St. Nicholas's Eve of last year. Then her father had come home. Seven-year-old Marta asked her mother to tell her the story over and over again, so her mother, whose fingers were never idle now that she was alone and had to feed and clothe herself and Marta, sat and knit long woolen stockings and talked of the past which would never come again, and of St. Nicholas's Eve 1939.

The war was going on in Europe in 1939, but Jon was only mobilized. He was just guarding the border, and was allowed to come home for the holiday. Marta's mother said:

"On Monday I got the letter and on Tuesday, St. Nicholas's Eve, he came. I got up early in the morning and started cleaning the house. I wanted everything to shine while your father was home. Soon I called you, and when you were dressed and had had your breakfast, you took your place in the window watching for him to come. Every time you saw a speck way down the road, you would call out to me, but I had time to get much of the holiday cooking prepared and the house in good order before you finally cried: 'Here he is,' and a cart stopped by our gate. You threw open the door and ran down the path. I saw him pick you up in his arms, but he was in such a hurry that he carried you right on in with him and met me as I was running half-way down the path."

Her mother always sighed and Marta wondered why her eyes looked so bright, then she would go on and tell of Jon's coming into the house and insisting on saying: "*Vroolijk Kerstfeest*," meaning "Merry Christmas," all over again to her and to Marta, just as though he had not greeted them both outside.

Marta's mother had been busy making cakes, "*bankletters*" and "*speculuas*," just a few since that year none of the family or friends could come to spend St. Nicholas's Eve with them, for no one could spend money to travel in such anxious times. She and Marta had saved and saved to get the food for the feast, and now that was in the larder waiting to be cooked.

They both felt sorry that the two grandmothers and the two grandfathers could not come that year, for Jon and big Marta had lived near enough to their parents so that they could often spend the holidays together. Little Marta loved to think about her grandfathers. One grandfather could tell her so much about the animals and the birds and make them seem just like people, and her mother's father could tell her stories, long, long stories, about things that happened in cities, about processions and having seen the Queen, and so many wonderful things that she could dream about after the visit was over.

Besides, it meant that both her grandmothers helped her mother, and that gave her mother more time to go out with her, so it really was a disappointment when the grandparents could not be with them for this St. Nicholas's Eve. Little Marta did not know it, but to her father's parents it was more than a disappointment. They had wanted so much to see their son again. Like all mothers, his mother feared the worst where her own boy was concerned. Perhaps she had had a premonition of what the future held, but, as with all peasants, the hard facts of life are there to be counted, and the money saved for the trip would keep food in the larder if the winter was going to be as hard as everything indicated, so they did not travel.

Marta's mother had told her that perhaps St. Nicholas, on his white horse with his black servant, Peter, would not bring any presents that year to fill her wooden shoes, but Marta would not believe it. Her first question to her father was: "Will St. Nicholas forget us?"

"No, little Marta," said her father. "The good Saint, who loves little children, will come tonight if you go to bed like a good girl and go quickly to sleep."

Marta put her little shoes down by the big fireplace, and her mother took her into the bedroom and tucked her away behind the curtains which shielded her bunk along the wall on the cold winter night.

Then there had been a long quiet time when Jon and Marta's mother sat together and talked a little, Jon telling what life was like for the army on the frontier and then lapsing into that complete silence which can only come to two people who are very fond of each other. After a while Jon opened up his knapsack and took out the things he had managed to bring to fill those little wooden shoes, and the package which held the last present from her husband that Marta's mother was ever to receive. With it was the usual rhyme:

> *To a busy little housewife*
> *From one who thinks of her through strife,*
> *To keep her safe from all alarm*
> *And never let her come to harm,*
> *Is all he dreams of night and day*
> *And now forever "Peace" would say.*

Needless to say, she guessed the giver before they went to bed.

On Christmas morning Marta woke and ran to look for her wooden shoes. "St. Nicholas has been here," she cried, "and he's given me many sweets, a doll, and bright red mittens just like the stockings mother made me as a Christmas gift." Then the whole family went skating on the river and there were many other little girls with their fathers and mothers. Everyone glided about and the babies were pushed or dragged in their little sleds. The boys and girls chased one another, sometimes long lines took hands and, after skating away, gathered in a circle, going faster and faster until they broke up because they could not hold on any longer.

Then at last they went home to dinner. On the table [sat] a fat chicken and a good soup.

At first they ate silently and then as the edge of their hunger wore off, they began to talk.

"Marta," said her father, "have you learned to read in school yet? Can you count how many days there are in a month?"

"Oh, yes," replied Marta, "and Mother makes me mark off every day that you are gone, and when we are together we always say: 'I wonder if Father remembers what we are doing now,' and we try to do just the things we do when you are home so you can really know just where we are and can almost see us all the time."

Her father smiled rather sadly and then her mother said:

"Jon, perhaps it is good for us all that we have to be apart for a while, because we appreciate so much more this chance of being together. There is no time for cross words when you know how few minutes there are left. It should make us all realize what it would be like if we lived with the thought of how quickly life runs away before us. But you are so busy, Jon, you do not have time to think about us much in the army, do you?"

A curious look came into his eyes and Jon thought for a moment with anguish of what he might have to do some day to other homes and other children, or what might happen to his, and then he pulled himself together and you could almost hear him say: "This at least is going to be a happy memory," and turning to Marta, he began to tease her about her fair hair, which stuck out in two little pigtails from the cap which she wore on her head. Seizing one of them he said:

"I can drive you just like an old horse. I will pull this pigtail and you will turn this way. I will pull the other one and you go that way."

Peals of laughter came from Marta, and before they knew it, the meal was over and the dishes washed and she had demanded that they play a make-believe game with her new doll, where she was a grown-up mother and they had come to see her child.

Such a jolly, happy time, and then as the dusk fell, Marta's father put on his uniform again, kissed her mother, took Marta in his arms, and hugged her tightly, saying: "Take good care of Moeder until I come back."

Then he was gone and they were alone again. The year seemed to travel heavily. First letters came from Jon, and then one day a telegram, and her mother cried and told Marta that her father would never come back, but her mother never stopped working, for now there was no one to look after them except God and He was far away in His heaven. Marta talked to Him sometimes because mother said He was everyone's Father, but it never seemed quite true. Marta could believe, however, that the Christ Child in the Virgin's arms in the painting in the church was a real child and she often talked to Him.

Strange things Marta told the Christ Child. She confided in Him that she never had liked that uniform which her father went away in. It must have had something to do with his staying away. He had never gone away in the clothes he wore every day and not come back. She liked him best in his everyday clothes, not his Sunday ones, which made him look rather stiff, but his nice comfortable, baggy trousers and blouse. She was never afraid of him then, and he had a nice homey smell; something of the cows and horses came into the house with him, and like a good little country girl Marta liked that smell. She told the Christ Child that her mother had no time to play with her any more. She had to work all the time, she looked different, and sometimes tears fell on her work and she could not answer Marta's questions.

There was no school any more for her to go to and on the road she met children who talked a strange language and they made fun of her and said now this country was theirs. It was all very hard to understand and she wondered if the Christ Child really did know what was happening to little children down here on earth. Sometimes there was nothing to eat in the house, and then both she and her mother went hungry to bed and she woke in the morning to find her mother gone and it would be considerably later before her mother returned with something for breakfast.

Thinking of all these things as her mother told the story again, on this St. Nicholas's Eve, 1940, Marta took off her wooden shoes and put them down beside the open fire. Sadly her mother said: "St. Nicholas will not come tonight," and he did not. Marta had an idea of her own, however, which she thought about until Christmas Eve came. Then she said to her mother: "There is one candle in the cupboard left from last year's feast. May I light it in the house so the light will shine out for the Christ Child to see His way? Perhaps He will come to us since St. Nicholas forgot us."

Marta's mother shook her head, but smiled, and Marta took out the candle and carefully placed it in a copper candlestick which had always held a lighted candle on Christmas Eve.

Marta wanted to see how far the light would shine out into the night, so she slipped into her wooden shoes again, put her shawl over her head, opened the door, and slipped out into the night. The wind was blowing around her and she could hardly stand up. She took two or three steps and looked back at the window. She could see the twinkling flame of the candle, and while she stood watching it, she was conscious of a tall figure in a dark cloak standing beside her.

Just at first she hoped the tall figure might be her father, but he would not have stood there watching her without coming out into the candlelight and picking her up and running into the house to greet her mother. She was not exactly afraid of this stranger, for she was a brave little girl, but she felt a sense of chill creeping through her, for there was something awe-inspiring and rather repellent about this personage who simply stood in the gloom watching her.

Finally he spoke:

"What are you doing here, little girl?"

Very much in awe, Marta responded: "I came out to make sure that the Christ Child's candle would shine out to guide His footsteps to our house."

"You must not believe in any such legend," remonstrated the tall, dark man. "There is no Christ Child. That is a story which is told for the weak. It is ridiculous to believe that a little child could lead the people of the world, a foolish idea claiming strength through love and sacrifice. You must grow up and acknowledge only one superior, he who dominates the rest of the world through fear and strength."

This was not very convincing to Marta. No one could tell her that what she had believed in since babyhood was not true. Why, she talked to the Christ Child herself. But she had been taught to be respectful and to listen to her elders and so silence reigned while she wondered who this man was who said such strange and curious things. Was he a bad man? Did he have something to do with her father's going away and not coming back? Or with her mother's worrying so much and working so hard? What was he doing near her house anyway? What was a bad man like? She had never known one.

He had done her no harm—at least, no bodily harm—and yet down inside her something was hurt. Things could be taken away from people. They had had to give up many of their chickens and cows because the government wanted them. That had been hard because they loved their animals and they had cared for them and it meant also that they would have little to eat and much less money when they lost them, but that was different from the way this man made her feel. He was taking away a hope, a hope that someone could do more even than her mother could do, could perhaps make true the dream, that story she told herself every night, both awake and asleep, of the day when her father would come home, the day when hand in hand they would walk down the road again together. When he would put her on his shoulder and they would go skating on the canal. Somehow this man hurt that dream and it was worse than not having St. Nicholas come. It seemed to pull down a curtain over the world.

Marta was beginning to feel very cold and very much afraid, but all her life she had been told to be polite to her elders and ask for permission to do anything she wished to do. She said: "I am hoping the Christ Child will come. May I go in now and will you not come into my house?"

The man seemed to hesitate a minute, but perhaps he decided it would be interesting to see the inside of such a humble home where there was so much simple faith. In any case, he wanted to impress upon this child and upon her mother that foolish legends were not the right preparation for living in a world where he, the power, dominated, so he followed Marta into the house without knocking. Marta's mother, who had been sitting by the fire knitting when Marta went out, was still there, yes, but in her arms was a baby and around the baby a curious light shone and Marta knew that the Christ Child had come. The man in the door did not know, he thought it was an ordinary room with an ordinary baby in a woman's arms.

Striding in, he said: "Madam, you have taught this child a foolish legend. Why is this child burning a candle in the hope that the Christ Child will come?"

The woman answered in a very low voice: "To those of us who suffer, that is a hope we may cherish. Under your power, there is fear, and you have created a strength before which people tremble. But on Christmas Eve strange things happen and new powers are sometimes born."

Marta was not interested any more in the tall figure in the cloak. The Christ Child was there in her mother's lap. She could tell Him all her troubles and He would understand why she prayed above everything else for the return of her father. St. Nicholas would never again leave them without the Christmas dinner and she could have the new doll, and the sweets which she longed to taste again. Perhaps if only she went to sleep like a good little girl, there would be a miracle and her father would be there. Off she trotted to the second room, slipped off her shoes, and climbed behind the curtain.

Marta could not go to sleep at once, because though there was no sound from the other room, she still could not free herself from the thought of that menacing figure. She wondered if he was responsible for the tears of the little girl up the road whose father had not come home last year and who had not been visited either by St. Nicholas.

Then before her eyes she suddenly saw a vision of the Christ Child. He was smiling and seemed to say that the little girl up the road had her father this year and that all was well with her. Marta was happy—fathers are so very nice. Perhaps if she prayed again to the Christ Child, when she woke up He would have her father there too, and so she said first the prayer she had always been taught to say and then just for herself she added: "Dear Christ Child, I know you will understand that though God is the father of all of us, He is very, very far away and the fathers we have down here are so much closer. Please bring mine back so that we can have the cows, the pigs, and the chickens again and all we want to eat and the tears will not be in my mother's eyes." The murmur of her prayer died away as she fell asleep.

A long time the power stood and watched Marta's mother, and finally there came over him a wave of strange feeling. Would anyone ever turn eyes on him as lovingly as this woman's eyes turned on that baby? Bowing low before her, he said: "Madam, I offer you ease and comfort, fine raiment, delicious food. Will you come with me where these things are supplied, but where you cannot keep to your beliefs?"

Marta's mother shook her head and looked down at the baby lying in her lap. She said: "Where you are, there is power and hate and fear among people, one of another. Here there are none of the things which you offer, but there is the Christ Child. The Christ Child taught love. He drove the money-changers out of the temple, to be sure, but that was because He hated the system which they represented. He loved His family, the poor, the sinners, and He tried to bring out in each one the love for Him and for each other which would mean a Christlike spirit in the world. I will stay here with my child, who could trust the legend and therefore brought with her into this house the Christ Child spirit which makes us live forever. You will go out into the night again, the cold night, to die as all must die who are not born again through Him at Christmas time."

The man turned and went out, and as he opened the door, he seemed to be engulfed in the dark and troubled world without. The snow was falling and the wind was howling, the sky was gloomy overhead. All that he looked upon was fierce and evil. These evil forces of nature were ruling also in men's hearts and they brought sorrow and misery to many human beings. Greed, personal ambition, and fear all were strong in the world fed by constant hate. In the howling of the wind he heard these evil spirits about him, and they seemed to run wild, unleashed with no control.

This has happened, of course, many times in the world before, but must it go on happening forever? Suddenly he turned to look back at the house from which he had come. Still from the window shone the little child's candle and within he could see framed the figure of the mother and the Baby. Perhaps that was a symbol of the one salvation there was in the world, the heart of faith, the one hope of peace. The hope he had taken away from Marta for the moment shone out increasingly into the terrible world even though it was only the little Christ Child's candle.

With a shrug of his shoulders, he turned away to return to the luxury of power. He was able to make people suffer. He was able to make people do his will, but his strength was shaken and it always will be. The light in the window must be the dream which holds us all until we ultimately win back to the things for which Jon died and for which Marta and her mother were living.

---

* Eleanor Roosevelt. *Christmas: A Story*. New York: Knopf, 1940. Permision to reprint here from Nancy Roosevelt Ireland.

ELLA CARA DELORIA

(1889-1971)

Ella Cara Deloria (1889-1971), anthropologist and linguist, was born in 1889 at White Swan on the Yankton Sioux Reservation in southeastern South Dakota. Her parents gave her the Dakota name *Anpetu Waste*, Beautiful Day.[1] Her father, Philip Deloria, was a convert to Christianity and an ordained deacon at the time of Ella's birth. Philip Deloria and his wife, Mary Swan Bordeaux, had their new daughter baptized at White Swan's St. Philip the Deacon Chapel on Sexagesima Sunday.

Ella Cara Deloria was born into a large, loving, extended family. Both parents had children from previous marriages; the couple had two more children after Ella's birth. Ella's mother Mary, of biracial ancestry, was raised as a traditional Dakota. Dakota was the primary language of the Deloria home. Historian Vine Deloria Jr., Ella Cara Deloria's nephew, tells the story that at the time of her birth, her father Philip Deloria looked at his household of five daughters and began to doubt that he would fulfill the prophesy of the medicine man Saswe that spoke of four generations of sons in the family. It was Ella, then, who became the inheritor of her father's stories and the family traditions. (After the birth of another daughter, Susan, the Deloria's did have a son, Vine, who eventually became an archdeacon.)[2] Both traditional Sioux values and Christian values, as expressed in the Episcopal Church, were dominant themes in Ella Cara Deloria's life and work.[3]

The Deloria family was prominent on the reservation, and provided leadership for the Episcopal Church. Ella's grandfather, Chief Frank Deloria, requested the establishment of an Episcopal mission among the Yankton people in 1869. Ella Cara Deloria's father, Philip, was assigned to St. Elizabeth's Church at Wakpula, South Dakota on the Standing Rock Reservation in 1890 and ordained a priest shortly thereafter.[4] Ella Deloria attended St. Elizabeth's mission school there; in 1902 she transferred to All Saints boarding school in Sioux Falls, South Dakota. She attended Oberlin College and later received a B.S. from Columbia Teachers College in 1915.

After college, Ella Deloria returned to All Saints as a teacher, until 1919. Her next position, with the YWCA, allowed her to travel throughout the West and gain a familiarity with many American Indian schools and reservations. In 1923 she was hired by the Haskell Indian School in Lawrence, Kansas, to teach physical education and dance.

In 1928, Deloria began to work with the prominent anthropologist Franz Boas, first as a translator and later as a field researcher, on Dakota language and culture. Her collaboration with Boas—and later with his student Ruth Benedict—continued until the late 1940s. Though the collaboration never brought Deloria a secure income, it did allow her to complete a variety of projects related to Dakota-language and culture and to gain national recognition as a scholar and the leading authority on the Sioux.[5]

Ella Cara Deloria continued her research, writing and lectures well into her later years. In 1955-1958, she returned home to direct her old school at St. Elizabeth's mission. In the 1960s she worked on Sioux dialects through the University of South Dakota and was active on the board of St. Mary's School for Indian Girls, the last church mission of the Episcopal Church. She died in 1971 after a series of ailments and was buried with her family in South Dakota.[6] Her acclaimed last work, the novel *Waterlily,* was published posthumously in 1988.

The excerpt here is taken from her book *Speaking of Indians,* published in 1944. The book is an ethnological examination of Dakota society at the end of World War II. Though recent commentators may find her comments regarding Christianity among the Sioux optimistic, the book is appreciated for Deloria's positive approach to old Sioux culture.

Notes

[1] Ella Cara Deloria, *Waterlily* (Lincoln: University of Nebraska Press, 1988): 229.

[2] Ella Cara Deloria, *Speaking of Indians* (Lincoln: University of Nebraska Press, 1944): ix-xi.

[3] Ibid, 229-230.

[4] For additional info on the Deloria family, see Owanah Anderson, *400 years: Anglican/Episcopal Mission Among American Indians* (Cincinnati: Forward Movement, 1997): 112-14.

[5] Deloria, *Speaking of Indians*, xiv-xv.

[6] Ibid, xviii-xix.

ଓ

Ella Cara Deloria
Excerpts from Speaking of Indians*

Where no records exist there can be no final and absolute treatment of a phase of Indian life as it flourished well over a hundred years ago. The Dakota people of the past were not asked to analyze for posterity their beliefs about God. We cannot really know, therefore, in so many words by them uttered, exactly what they believed and how they expressed that belief. We can only get it from stories that have come down. Even the oldest informant today is far too young.

Personally, I have never had a chance to question any but Christian Dakotas, except for one man who, though baptized, preferred to practise his religion in the pagan manner—meaning pagan as the opposite of Christian and without any derogatory overtones. Yet even he had been born into a society already influenced, undeniably, by Christianity and he was not hostile to the church. Perhaps he was eighty, he thought he was, yet he was amazingly keen and alert, and he was physically youthful in his lightness, speed, and agility. He was an Indian ascetic, if I ever saw one, lean and clear-eyed. He made a most reliable informant about the ancient religious practices of his people.

As for the others, they were all men mature in their Christianity, men of integrity, known to all the people as leaders of thought, and influential in personal example. Two of them were clergymen. Completely at home and active in their church life, they yearned for no outgrown and ancient way. Even so, without exception they talked about the belief of their forefathers with a tender reverence that was beautiful. Obviously it was not for them; yet neither was it therefore something to treat lightly, to be amused at, or to conceal with shame. Quite simply they discussed their subject without questioning even those things about it that are incredible today, because it was their grandfathers who once believed it and told them so. There are some things you do not try to rationalize; you just accept with bowed head: the Wisemen following a Star; the Shepherds who heard the *Gloria in Excelsis;* the Resurrection and Glorious Ascension. These informants talked about the religion of their ancestors in that spirit. So shall we look at it here. Who am I to question what was once very real and solemn to others?

[...]

In the fullness of time, just when the Teton-Dakotas needed a friend, the church came to them, as, approximately thirty years earlier, under remarkably similar circumstances it had come to the Santees, their fellow Dakotas in Minnesota.

I have tried to show how white civilization had hit Teton-Dakota life with cruel impact and thrown it into wild confusion. But now all was still once more—with the stillness of defeat. It was as though, after being sucked without warning into a remorseless whirlpool and helplessly lashed and bruised by the wreckage pounding around them, the people had at last been thrown far off to one side and were sitting there, naked and forspent, dully watching their broken life being borne along, and lacking both the strength and the will to retrieve any of it. And what good was it now anyway, in pieces? The sun dance—without its sacrificial core; festive war dances—without fresh war deeds to celebrate;

the Hunka rite of blessing little children—without the tender Ring of Relatives to give it meaning —who would want such empty leavings? No, it was better just to get along somehow without.

But it left them lonely, with an ache in the heart and an emptiness of soul. And then the church came and filled that emptiness to overflowing. When next you hear anyone question the depth of Dakota Christianity, implying it is only a veneer, a convenient exterior, don't you believe it! It is their very life. I know, because it was already going strong when I was old enough to remember, and I grew up watching its working all about me.

It may be different or similar with the various other tribes; that is for those who know other situations to tell. I have to get very personal here and tell you what I myself know. The mission that I know best happens to be that of the Episcopal church; but the situation is doubtless much the same with the work of the Congregational and the Presbyterian churches as well as the Roman Catholic, for those were the Christian bodies that came to the Dakotas and faithfully stayed by them throughout the years. I do not concentrate on the work of my own church for any other reason than that by doing so I can give you first-hand glimpses of what happened there. I am mindful of and grateful for all the good that has been accomplished by all Christian missions everywhere.

The masses of people accepted the church eagerly. But certain ones, like Chief Gall who lived a mile from the mission, took a long time to study out the gospel message with care and to appraise it critically. I am told that at the beginning Gall always came to church painted up as for a war council, looking austere and a little frightening. The young clergyman knew he was on trial, he and his message. Gall would sit by the door with his weapons—he never came without them—and would watch every move the minister made in the chancel and take in every word he uttered, with a grimly searching look that was disconcerting. At any minute if the missionary had said something that seemed off key, Gall might just as well have finished him off then and there in the interest of his people. (Who is this mere boy, all dressed up in white and talking to deceive us? I will get rid of him!) But in the end, he made a great feast with the clergyman as his honor guest. When all had eaten and smoked the pipe together, he spoke to him in a public oration, calling him *misun,* "my younger brother"—a social kinship term, certainly, since Gall was a Teton of the Tetons, while the clergyman was a prince of the Yanktons, another dialect division.

[...]

And so Gall was baptized and confirmed; and all his days he received special instruction from time to time, calling the missionary in to have things clarified ever and again. He was not just grabbing at externals. He was a student of Christ's teachings. A man of tremendous influence, he inspired many. When he died he was buried in consecrated ground, and a stone in the mission cemetery marks his grave to this day.

[...]

Through trouble and tears, pleasure and laughter, the church has stood by the people, and it must be said that in their devotion they have stood by it, too. It has meaning for them; it functions even in their social life. Never is there a meal but grace is said first in all reverence. Never a feast or an hour of games or even a political meeting but a church service precedes it. That is habit; it has been from the beginning. Only the other day, I heard of a woman who came late to work at a mission in western South Dakota and explained the reason.

"I was so sleepy. Lawrence was going off to war on the early train. So we got up at three in the morning and ate breakfast. Then his father had prayers, and then we started for town."

I know that father. He is a very ordinary layman, and he never made any pretensions as a religious leader among his people. Yet, quite as a matter of course, he reads prayers before he sends his boy off to war. What a way to do! If all fathers did that, would it not be something for the boys to think back on as they face the enemy? Nor is that an isolated case. It is the kind of thing they do without stopping to debate the matter.

Among Episcopalians the church year is very definitely ordered, with its sequence of feasts and observances starting from Advent. The people were already familiar, before my day, with the Dakota translations for the seasonal names, used them freely, and understood what they represented. They followed through with the proper collects, epistle, and gospel selections and read their teaching very carefully, for many had by this time learned to read. They sang appropriate hymns of the church seasons, some of which their own religious leaders had composed. Notably there is one hymn whose author was the first Dakota priest back in the early seventies. Its theme runs, "Kinship is a good thing; God devised it; let us all remember to live according to it." It identifies Christian brotherhood with the old Dakota kinship system and its laws of interpersonal responsibility and loving kindness, which of course is right. To me, that is the most typical of all Dakota-made Christian hymns.

Missionary work was not neglected either. The Santees in Minnesota, first to become Christians, sent missionaries westward to the Yanktons. The Yanktons in turn sent missionaries westward to the Tetons. And now the Tetons who had heard the gospel were sending lay missionaries to other Tetons who as yet had not heard it. Whenever there was an election of officers, there were several chosen "to take good news." These Christians, at their own expense, enthusiastically made regular journeys to the outlands, where they held meetings and passed on to the people what they knew. The people, in true Dakota style, feasted them royally first and then heard their message.

Even before they could read and write, the people elected the officers of their general church organizations and woman's auxiliary according to parliamentary procedure, Dakota brand. This was something that did not come out of their former life. It was a new thing, yet they took to it readily. They nominated, one at a time, seconded the nomination, then voted, for and then against. If those for were more than those against, the nominee won. Otherwise he was out, and the next name was put up. It took a long time, but there was lots of time.

In all earnestness, and with a genuine desire to help others, the people worked to raise money by making things to sell and in other ways. It is significant, however, that, until very lately, food sales were not resorted to. They clashed too badly with Dakota hospitality. The fund grew throughout the year. Then there came the day of apportioning it, before going to annual convocation to report. They had a meeting in which their clergyman read off to them the various projects they regularly helped and the special emergency calls for that particular year.

[...]

Those Dakotas are very devout. They do not talk foolishly, or even just sociably, within the church proper. Their veneration of the sacred mysteries and the outward symbols of them is a truly beautiful thing, satisfying in its absoluteness. Nor is that a new trait. From far in the past they were used to stepping lightly where solemn rites went on, to sense at once what was holy ground, and quickly "take off their shoes."

Here then is one picture of the transfer from the old religion to the new. You will see that it was no problem, that instinctively the people themselves dropped whatever was in conflict with it and retained those fine elements from the past that were fundamentally right as a firm foundation for the Christian life. If you could watch a Christian die, as I have, calm and full of faith and trust, you could never say, without being grossly unfair to Dakota Christianity, that it is only a veneer.

---

* Ella Deloria, *Speaking of Indians*(Lincoln: University of Nebraska Press, 1944): 49-51; 98-101; 105-107; 108-109.

SARAH LOUISE "SADIE" DELANY

(1890-1999)

Sarah Louise "Sadie" Delany (1890-1999),[1] educator, was the daughter of Henry Beard Delany and Martha Logan Delany, both educators at St. Augustine's College in Raleigh, North Carolina. Henry Beard Delany was a St. Augustine's graduate, teacher, and vice-president before his ordination to the priesthood. In 1918 he was consecrated as suffragan bishop of North Carolina. Martha Logan Delany taught domestic science at St. Augustine's and was matron of the school.

Sadie Delany followed in her parents' footsteps as an educator. In 1930 she became the first African American teacher of domestic science in the New York City Public school system. After her brother moved to New York, Sadie Delany followed in 1917 with her younger sister Bessie to pursue her education. Both women taught school for years in the South in order to save money to finance their educations. Sadie Delany studied at the Pratt Institute and graduated from Columbia Teachers College in 1920. Her first teaching job was at PS 119 in Harlem. Sadie Delany eventually received a Masters Degree in education from Columbia University in 1925. She retired from teaching in 1960 at the age of seventy-one.

Along with her sister Bessie, Sadie Delany maintained the highest professional standards while overcoming significant racism and sexism. Both sisters associated with many of the famous African

Americans of the Harlem Renaissance, including Langston Hughes, W.E.B DuBois, and Paul Robeson. While they lived in Harlem, Sadie and Bessie Delany attended St. Martin's Episcopal Church. Both sisters remained committed to the Episcopal Church, and the strong values and discipline they inherited from the Delany family, throughout their lifetimes.

Sarah Louise Delany, the last surviving child of Bishop Henry Beard Delany, died at the age of 109. The following excerpt from her last book *On My Own at 107*, recounts her feelings and struggles after the death of her sister Bessie.

NOTES

[1] Sarah L. Delany with Amy Hill Hearth, *On My Own at 107: Reflections on Life Without Bessie* (San Francisco: HarperSanFrancisco, 1989).

SARAH LOUISE "SADIE" DELANY
Excerpt from On My Own at 107[*]

I sure miss you, old gal.

The Lord left me here, and took you. He took my little sister. More than 104 years by my side, and now you're gone.

I just keep telling myself, you're up there with Mama and Papa, and all our brothers and sisters. You've gone to Glory. You're in a better place.

I have to tell you the truth. This being alone is *hard*. For the first time in my life, I don't have you by my side. I'm 107 years old now and it's like I'm just learning how to walk.

I still get up early in the morning and say my prayers, just as we always did. I do my yoga exercises. I eat my breakfast. I read my mail. But you're not there to do these things with me.

Letting go of you was the hardest thing I've ever done. The day of the funeral was the longest day of my life. I made sure the funeral was done right. I wanted to be sure my sister had a proper send-off! We had a big funeral, with all the dignitaries, at the Cathedral of Saint John the Divine in New York City. Oh, it was a big affair. You'd have been tickled by it.

Bessie, I wanted to walk into that old church myself, up those steps and down that long aisle, but they wouldn't let me. I went in a wheelchair, so I wouldn't get tired.

Two things stand out in my mind from that day. One was a group of schoolchildren from Harlem. They were kind of shy, but they came up to me at the church with these beautiful handmade cards. You would have liked that. The other thing I remember was that the bishop permitted me, as a special honor, to sprinkle holy water on the casket. I tried all day to be strong hut that's when I broke down crying.

I asked our nephew Lemuel Jr. to handle everything, since he's an undertaker. After the service, he drove straight down to North Carolina in the hearse. He took you home. Left New York City and drove straight on down there. I knew you were in good hands, little sister.

Now you may think this is crazy, but I went down to Raleigh for the burial. I flew down there in an airplane, yes indeed! I had to see it for myself. I had to see my sister buried.

We had another service in Raleigh. This was the first time I'd been back to the campus of Saint Augustine's since you and I went to visit about twenty years ago. Oh, Bessie, things have changed. Most of the old buildings are gone. But the chapel's still standing that Papa built with his own hands, a hundred years ago.

I did everything just as we had planned. I left that space for me in the family plot between you and Mama, just like you wanted. I remember how you used to say that I should have the space next to Mama since I was the Mama's child. I always thought that was awful sweet of you.

When you live this long, you sure bury a lot of people. Now I feel like I've outlived everybody! Mama and Papa are long gone; all of our brothers and sisters are gone. I'm the only one left.

I'm trying real hard not to indulge in self-pity. It just makes me feel worse if I do. Only one time since you left us, dear little sister, did I allow myself to feel sorry for myself. It was about two weeks after you left us. I felt despair that you were gone and frustrated because I can't do everything I want anymore. *What good am I?* I thought.

One of our young friends stopped by while I was feeling like that and I told her what I'd been thinking.

"Well, *I* need you," she said. "Don't you go leaving me." And we laughed.

Afterwards, I felt ashamed. I kind of laughed at myself. Why, I have been so blessed in my life!

[...]

Folks ask me why I've lived such a long and happy life and I always say the Lord deserves the credit. Another factor, I'm sure, is that it runs in the family Why, Mama lived to be ninety-five years old with no medical intervention whatsoever.

Another reason is the way we live—exercise, eating lots of fruits and vegetables, no smoking, things like that. Plenty of folks want to know what makes us tick, don't they, Bessie? I remember how doctors suggested that we leave our bodies to science so they could try to figure us out, but you were absolutely opposed to it, ever since that one doctor tracked us down a few years back.

The doctor got right to the point. She said she was in charge of some kind of "brain project" and wanted our brains after we died!

I guess it was the way she asked that annoyed you so much, Bessie. You said, "Honey, you're crazy You say you want my brain? I've got news for you. I came into the world with it. And I'll be taking it with me when I go!"

Now, I think a lot of credit for our longevity should go to Mama and Papa for the way they raised us. We didn't have any money as a family; growing up, but we lived a godly life. And we learned good habits, how to take care of ourselves properly. We ate well because there was a farm on the campus of Saint Aug's.

What we didn't have at Saint Aug's, Papa would get for us one way or another. I remember Papa going off to the market in Raleigh at the end of the day and buying wagonloads of fruit that hadn't sold that day The farmers were anxious to get rid of it, so Papa bought it cheap. A whole wagonload of watermelons, for a *dime*.

To think that we used to share one scrawny little chicken among ten children and two adults—and that was a Sunday treat! Somehow, we were happy with that. We thought we were doing pretty good.

Another thing about Mama and Papa is that they had high expectations of us. They expected as much from the girls as the boys. Remember how Papa encouraged us to take Greek and Latin along with the boys?

I've been thinking a lot lately about Mama and Papa. Ever since you left us, Bessie, it seems like Mama and Papa are on my mind day and night.

I was wondering where they got some of their ideas from. I guess it was from their college days at Saint Augustine's back in the 1880s. Mama and Papa always looked up to the people they met at Saint Aug's, like Dr. Anna J. Cooper. It makes me sad that most folks today don't know who Dr. Cooper was. There was a time when she was nationally famous for her work as an educator. She pushed for educational opportunities for Negro girls at a time when no one cared about that.

I just remembered something that brings a big smile to my face. I know someone who never forgot Dr. Cooper all these years. As a matter of fact, someone's been quietly sending money to make sure Dr. Cooper's grave, down in Raleigh, has been kept up real nice, and even paid for a special plaque to remind the world of Dr. Cooper's contributions.

That anonymous person was you, little sister.

You always did live up to what Mama and Papa expected of us. You always worried that you didn't, but there's some proof.

I don't think parents have the same expectations of children that were placed on us. We worked so hard, helping Mama and Papa. We helped raise all our younger brothers and sisters. We had to do well in school and do our best; there was no other option.

Someone asked me the other day if it was all work and no play when we were growing up. Did we ever go on vacations? Did we ever go on special outings?

"Well," I told 'em, "there really was no such thing as a vacation. Folks went to see their kinfolk when they could, but you didn't go off to the beach or the mountains the way folks do today."

Bessie, they looked at me like I was crazy! They were horrified!

Then I told 'em how once a year everyone would drop what they were doing all over Wake County when the word got out that the circus was coming.

"What was it like? How many elephants were there? How many clowns?" That was what they wanted to know.

I said, "Why, there was one elephant."

They thought that was funny. "One elephant? That's all?"

I tried to explain that it was an awfully big deal at the time, but they just didn't understand.

I said, "Look. We didn't have TV, and we only knew what an elephant looked like from books. It was very exotic!"

It made me feel lonely for you, Bessie. I remember distinctly how exciting it was, and I know you never forgot either.

I remember how some of our homefolks would visit us in New York City, back in the '20s, and they would try to act nonchalant. They were country folks but they were hiding the fact that they were in awe about the tall buildings and the fancy stores.

You were so impressed with the subway, Bessie, and wanted to show it off. And those kinfolk from down South, why, they tried to pretend they weren't impressed. You came home and you were so annoyed.

You said, "Sadie, our homefolks acted like they'd been riding on a subway their *whole lives*." I laughed and I said, "Well, Bessie, they're country people and they're afraid that people will laugh at them."

And you said, "Well, I'm a country person, too, but I'm not afraid of what other people think."

Yes, that was my sister Bessie. Proud, forthright—a tribute to your parents and your upbringing. That's something I really admired about you, Bessie: you never forgot where you came from.

---

* Sarah L. Delany and Amy Hill Hearth, *On My Own at 107:Reflections on Life Without Bessie* (San Francisco: HarperSanFrancisco, 1989): 6-9; 52-57.

KING YOAK WON WU

(1890-1982)

King Yoak Won Wu (1890-1982), clergy spouse and leader of the True Sunshine Parish in San Francisco, was born in 1890. Her grandparents were from the province of Toi San in China; her father came to the United States during the California gold rush to help build the railroad. After her father's death, King and her sisters helped support the family through needlework. A very beautiful woman, King was known as "the beauty of Chinatown" in her day.[1]

In 1913, King married Daniel Wu, the first Chinese-American Episcopal priest and a 1912 graduate of the Church Divinity School of the Pacific, in Grace Cathedral, San Francisco. The couple had four children; their daughter Betty also married an Episcopal priest. A committed member of the church and partner in ministry with her husband, King Yoak Won Wu dedicated her considerable energies to the community of the True Sunshine Parish. Given her expertise in needlework, King made vestments, taught sewing and embroidery to parishioners, and ran the parish altar guild. She also made many visits to parishioners' homes and taught Sunday School. She died in 1982.

The following document is taken from an Oral History interview in which King Yoak Won Wu recounts her childhood, marriage, and years in parish ministry with her husband.[2]

NOTES

[1] The primary source for information on King Yoak Won Wu is her Oral History interview, conducted by the Rev. Fran Toy in October 1981. The transcript here was translated from the original tapes by the Rev. Diane Wong in June 2001. Biographical information and her "mother's voice" also provided by Betty Wu Ko, King Yoak Won Wu's daughter.

[2] The Oral History interview was conducted by the Rev. Fran Toy, October 27, 1981. Translation from the Cantonese by Diane Wong, June 27, 2001.

❦

KING YOAK WON WU
An Excerpt from the Oral History of King Yoak Won Wu*

I was born in San Francisco, California and I am now 91 years old. My maiden name was Won and my given name, King Yoak means Beautiful Jade in English. My grandfather was a farmer in China. My father came to the United States during the gold rush in California to work on the railway. He was married to my mother in China, but he came to the United States alone. After ten years, he returned to China to bring my mother over. I am the fifth child of eight siblings. The eldest child was a boy, and the rest of us were girls.

We lived in San Francisco's Chinatown, and we very seldom have contact with people of other groups. One day, my mother fell on a hilly street and was unable to get up. An American lady helped my mother up, brushed the dirt off her and helped her to come home. This was our first encounter with an American. She was very kind and she told us that she was a Christian. That was the first time we knew about Christianity. I also remember the big earthquake and fire of San Francisco, and to this day, I am very nervous and scared of earthquakes.

My father died when I was 7 years old, and all of us had to help support the family. All the girls in the family did needlework to help supplement the income. I started to do embroidery and sew when I was very young.

We all, my brother and sisters attended Chinese school. With studies and needlework, we did not have too much free time, especially when our needlework was the main source of income. We would get up early in the morning, eat our rice and vegetables for breakfast, did more needlework until 9 o'clock when we would go to school. We would come home for a small lunch, did more needlework and go back to school by 2 o'clock. After school, we returned home to do more needlework. We all took turns preparing dinner, then more needlework until bedtime. The pay for the needlework was very low, and in order to survive, we had to take in a large quantity of work. In spite of all this hardship, my mother always prepared a special meal with chicken and special Chinese cakes for our birthdays.

When I was a teenager, an American lady from the Baptist Church taught us English. One day, she told us that a young Chinese seminarian by the name of Daniel Gee Ching Wu was going to give a talk at the church and invited all of us to go. So after hurrying with the needlework, we all went to listen to the talk by Mr. Wu. Then he was invited by the Congregational Church, and we all went to listen to him too. At that time, all the Chinese ministers were from China, and Mr. Wu was invited by the churches in Chinatown to speak. It was the first time for a young seminarian to be among the Chinese Christians in Chinatown. At the Congregational Church where he delivered a sermon, we met the minister and his wife. The pastor and his wife were very nice to us and we became regular churchgoers. Eventually we were all baptized at the church, the whole family including mother. We also attented the Episcopal Church as we knew that Mr. Wu was helping with the services there. So we had many opportunities to meet with him too. Mr. Wu and I were formally introduced at a reception at the Congregational Church by the pastor and his wife.

Daniel Gee Ching Wu (Daniel was his Baptismal name, Gee Ching his Chinese name, Gee means wisdom and Ching means purity in English) and I began our friendship. We would visit Golden Gate Park and we were always chaperoned by the whole family. Mr. Wu was still studying at the seminary at that time. The day of his graduation from the Church Divinity School of the Pacific was also my birthday. Our whole family attended his graduation, a very joyous day. When he was ordained a priest a year later (1913) it was also on my birthday. It was a blessing. He was also the first Chinese Episcopal priest in the United States. After his ordination, we were married, the first Asian couple to be married at Grace Cathedral, and my two younger sisters were my bridesmaids. I made my own wedding gown, Chinese style with mandarin collar and of Chinese brocaded silk, I was one of the first Chinese brides to wear white, (Chinese brides wear red) and I chose white because we were Christians, Rev. Wu wore a tuxedo with his clerical collar. I also made the wedding gown for Fran Toy's mother, and when Fran's mother was married, I helped her get dressed and I did her hair. That was around fifty years ago.

A year after I was married my first child was born. She was born on Easter morning right after I received Holy Communion from my husband. We named her Mary. A year later, my son Thomas was born. We named him after the Rev. Thomas Williams, a deacon, who was helping my husband. A few years later, my daughter, Lilla was born and three years after that, my daughter, Elizabeth was born. Lilla was named after the benefactress who supported my husband through seminary, and Elizabeth was named for St. Elizabeth Church in Honolulu where my husband was baptized and confirmed. Except for my daughter Mary who was born at home, all the other children were born at St. Luke's Hospital. At the hospital, the chaplains came to visit me and would also bring me Communion. Many times they would leave my door open so I can hear the hymn singing in the Chapel. At the hospital, I was able have a much needed rest. When Lilla was six months old, my mother-in-law came from China to help me with the children.

Due to the fact that the Episcopal Chinese ministry was so young, I had to help in the church a lot. I attended all the fellowship gatherings, visited the women and invite them to church, and took care of the altar every week. I bought and fixed all the altar flowers, sewed and washed all the altar linens, besides keeping the church clean. I made all of my husband's vestments, and even made a purple cassock for Bishop Block. When the children were older they all helped by cleaning the church. We also had a day school for children to learn the Chinese language and culture, and an evening school for men to learn English. That means that every day, we all helped in arranging the smaller desks for day school, and rearranged the larger desks for evening school, and of course arranging the chairs and kneelers for Sunday services.

My husband and I helped many members when they were sick in visiting doctors or to go to the hospital, I remember one time a young girl came and asked me to visit her little brother who was sick. I went to their home, but when I saw how sick the boy was, I went and got a Chinese doctor to examine him and to write a prescription for him. By midnight, the little boy grew worse, and I was asked to go get the doctor again. I walked all the way to the doctor's office, but he refused to go see the little boy, but gave me some medicine for him. I walked back to the boy's home, prepared the Chinese medicine tea for him, and when I saw that he had improved, I called my husband to have him wait for me outside the front door. It was very late and I was scared, and I ran all the way home. There was another family at church whose daughter had some infection. I went to visit her, but I was afraid that what she had was contagious, and I did not want to expose my children to this illness. When I arrived at the church, I went straight to the bathroom, changed my clothes, rinsed my mouth, washed and scrubbed my arms and hands before I dared to go upstairs to the vicarage where the children were waiting for me with hugs and kisses. The daughter of another family died. I went with the family to the mortuary to see if everything was all right, but everything was very unsatisfactory, and the morticians did not do a good job with the body. I had to fix her hair and put on her make-up. The girl's fiance had given her a necklace, and I had to put that on her. But the necklace had a short chain, and her body was very heavy, and I had a hard time putting on her necklace. When I got home, my arms were still very cold and sore. The membership of the church grew and we had many more members, so that means that my husband and I had to make many visits to parishioner's homes. Because many of the members were poor, they got sick easily. I had to go to the doctor's often for checkups to make sure that I was still all right. It was really God's blessing that I remained healthy. Many times I had to accompany members to hospitals for surgeries, as they were very frightened. God gave me the courage to minister to people when they were sick or when they die. I know that because of this ministry, God blessed me with a long life. Most of the time my husband would go with me to visit our members, but he had to go back to the church after praying with the family and visiting with them as he either had to teach the evening school or prepare for a service. I always had to stay with the family longer. My own children were taken care of by their grandmother, and I am so blessed that the children were all very well behaved and loved and enjoyed helping to do tasks in the church.

My husband's salary was small and his $40.00 a month barely had enough for the family. But he did not like to ask the diocese or the church for more money, as his focus was on doing God's work. Eventually his salary was raised to $50.00 a month , but that was because the diocese realized that a church in Hawaii invited him to be their vicar and would pay him $50.00.

My husband worked under three bishops. Bishop Nichols liked my husband very much and was very proud that the first Chinese Episcopal minister in the United States was under him. He knew my husband worked very hard and brought in many new members to the church. Mrs. Nichols was always very kind to me. Bishop Parsons was a wonderful Bishop and was very good to my husband. At diocesan gatherings, Mrs. Parsons always sat with me and would explain many things to me. Bishop Block loved my husband and my family very much. He even had Church of Our Saviour in Oakland built in tribute to him.

I loved being a clergy wife and I loved and enjoyed doing God's work. My family, my children and grandchildren give me the most happiness. Being able to go to church and worship God is a great joy for me. Even though I cannot hear and see well now, I feel so blessed that God has been so good to me. I thank God everyday for all the blessings He had given to my husband, my children and to me.

---

* The Oral History interview was conducted by the Rev. Fran Toy, October 27, 1981. Translation from the Cantonese by the Rev. Diane Wong, June 27, 2001. Additions provided by Betty Wu Ko.

ANNIE ELIZABETH "BESSIE" DELANY

(1891-1995)

Annie Elizabeth "Bessie" Delany (1891-1995)[1], dentist, was a 1923 graduate from the School of Dental and Oral History at Columbia University and the second black woman to practice dentistry in New York State. She was the daughter of Bishop Henry Beard Delany, born enslaved, the second African-American bishop in the Episcopal Church, and Martha Logan Delany, a biracial free woman. Both parents supported their ten children in achieving high educational goals and were teachers at St. Augustine's College in Raleigh, North Carolina.

In recent years, Bessie and her older sister, Sarah "Sadie" Delany, have become the subjects of many articles, several books, a play, and a film, beginning with book *Having Our Say: The Delany Sisters First 100 Years*. The book was published in 1993 when Bessie Delany was 102 and her sister Sadie was 104.

Bessie Delany never married, choosing instead to pursue her independence through her profession and a busy home and social life. She moved to Harlem with her sister Sadie in 1917, and entered Columbia Dental School two years later. Delany graduated from dental school in 1925 and was known as "Dr. Bessie," she remained in practice until her retirement in 1950. She died at age 104 in her sleep at the home she shared with her sister. In the following excerpt from *Having Our Say*, Bessie Delany recounts her struggles in dental school.

NOTES

[1] Centenarian Sisters Bessie (1891-1995) & Sadie (1890-1999) Delany, *Women's Stories*, www.writetools.com; Emily Mann, "Having Our Say," *Charlotte Repertory Theatre Newsletter*, March 21-April 1, 2001.

ભ્ર

ANNIE ELIZABETH "BESSIE" DELANEY
An Excerpt from Having Our Say*

I had always dreamed I would become a medical doctor, but I ran out of time and money. I was in my late twenties already and I would have needed a few more credits to get into medical school. I was worried that by the time I earned the money and took those classes, I'd be too old.

So I picked up some science courses at Shaw University in Raleigh with the intention of being ready to enroll in a dental degree program in New York. My brother Harry was a dentist, and he was going to see if I could enroll at New York University, where he had graduated. But this was in 1918, and New York University would not take women in its dentistry program.

Instead, I enrolled at Columbia University. This was in the fall of 1919. There were eleven women out of a class of about 170. There were about six colored men. And then there was me. I was the only colored woman!

Columbia was intimidating, but so was everything else. The city was exciting and terrifying at the same time. I couldn't understand why the high-rise buildings didn't fall down, and the subway, well, that about worried me to death! A classmate of mine at Columbia said, "Let's try that old subway." And I said, "I don't think so." And he said, "What, are you afraid?" And I said, "Of course not! If you're willing to try it, so will I!" So we went and everything worked out OK, though once we were on it, I remember whispering to him, "You sure you know how we can get off this thing?"

Most of the students at the dental school were self-assured city folk, and their families were paying their tuition. I never had the luxury of focusing completely on my studies. I always had money on my mind. I needed more, honey! I had saved money from my teaching years in the South, but it wasn't enough. I remember that I always wore an old brown sweater to my classes, because I couldn't even afford a coat. One day, my brother Harry surprised me. He bought me a beautiful coat, with a small fur collar! When I put that coat on, honey, I looked sensational. I looked as good as Mrs. Astor's pet mule. And the first time I wore it to class, the students stood up and applauded. In a way, it was mean, because they were sort of making fun of me. It was like, "Oh, that Bessie Delany finally has something decent to wear." But I didn't care, no, sir!

My brothers were having the same difficulty with money, so they all worked their way through college as Pullman porters, which was one of the few jobs a Negro man could get. Hubert used to joke that he had earned an MBC degree—"master's of baggage carrying."

It was always harder for a Negro to get work than a white person. Even the street merchants in Harlem, in those days, were mostly white. There were certain companies that were nicer to colored people than others. For instance, everybody knew that Nestlé's would hire Negroes, but Hershey's wouldn't. Once I had encountered that, I used to walk through Harlem and scold any Negro eating a Hershey bar. Usually, they would stop eating it but sometimes they thought I was crazy. Well, honey, I do not allow Hershey candy in my home to this day.

As a woman, you couldn't be a Pullman porter, and I refused to work as a maid for white folks. So in the summer, I would go with my little sister Julia, who had come up from Raleigh to study at Julliard, to look for factory jobs. And you know what? They would want to hire Julia, because she was lighter than me. But we made it clear it was both of us or neither of us, and sometimes we'd get the job.

Once, we had an assembly-line job where they made sewing needles, and our job was to package them in these little batches, so they were ready for sale. Then for a while, we worked as ushers at a movie house. The pay was $12 a week, and we saw all these wonderful movies. My favorite movie star was Bing Crosby. Lord, we had fun. But I was always treated worse than Julia, and it was made clear that it was because I was darker-skinned. Julia was quite light—more like Sadie—and I guess she might even have passed for white if she had tried.

One time, we were waiting on line to get factory work and this white man tried to give me a break. It was always a white guy who was in charge, of course. He said, "Oh, I see. You are Spanish." This was supposed to be my cue to nod my head, since they'd hire you if you were "Spanish." But this made me furious. I said, "No, I am not Spanish. I am an *American Negro!*" I turned and walked out of there and Julia followed me.

Today I know they have this thing called Affirmative Action. I can see why they need it. There are some places where colored folks would *never,* not in a thousand years, get a job. But you know what? I really am philosophically against it. I say: "Let the best person get the job, period." Everybody's better off in the long run.

It was probably a good thing that I was a little older, mature, and so determined or I never would have made it through dental school. I had a few girlfriends, but I never told any of them that I was about ten years older. I never talked about where I came from, my teaching years, or any of that. I was always a big talker, but at dental school I was a private person. There was one girl in particular who used to bug me. She would say, "Bessie, how old are you?" or "Bessie, were you a teacher before you came to dental school?" But I didn't tell her anything.

The reason I was so secretive is that I wanted to be taken seriously. Most of the women were not taken seriously. Truth is, it was just after World War I and a lot of men were still overseas, or killed, so those girls were just looking for husbands. But not me. The boys, well, I stayed away from them. The white boys looked down on me and the colored boys were too busy trying to goose my behind! I had no interest in their shenanigans. I was a good-looking gal, and that always got me in trouble. But I was there to learn!

Before I enrolled in dental school I had a long talk with my Mama. She said, "You must decide whether you want to get married someday, or have a career. Don't go putting all that time and effort into your education and career if you think you want to get married."

It didn't occur to anyone that you could be married *and* have a career. Well, I set my sights on the career. I thought, what does any man really have to offer me? I've already raised half the world, so I don't feel the desire to have babies! And why would I want to give up my freedom and independence to take care of some man? In those days, a man expected you to be in charge of a perfect household, to look after his every need. Honey, I wasn't interested! I wasn't going to be bossed around by some man! So the men at college learned to leave me alone, after a while. There was no foolin' with me! In my yearbook, under the picture, they wrote: "Bessie Delany, the Perfect Lady." And that was the truth.

[...]

There are plenty of white folks who say, "Why haven't Negroes gotten further than they have?" They say about Negroes, "What's wrong with them?" To those white people, I have this to say: *Are you kidding?*

Let me tell you something. Even on my graduation day at Columbia, I ran into prejudice. It was the sixth of June, 1923. There I was, getting my Doctor of Dental Surgery Degree, and I was on top of the world. But you know what? The class selected me as the marshall, and I thought it was an honor. And then I found out—I heard them talking—it was because no one wanted to march beside me in front of their parents. It was a way to get rid of me. The class marshall carried the flag and marched out front, alone.

I suppose I should be grateful to Columbia, that at that time they let in colored people. Well, I'm not. They let me in but they beat me down for being there! I don't know how I got through that place, except when I was young nothing could hold me back. No, sir! I thought I could change the world. It took me a hundred years to figure out I *can't* change the world. I can only change Bessie. And, honey, that ain't easy, either.

---

* Sarah L. Delany and A. Elizabeth Delany with Amy Hill Hearth, *Having Our Say: The Delany Sisters' First 100 Years* (New York: Delta, 1993): 124-28; 131-32.

RUTH ELAINE YOUNGER [MOTHER RUTH, CHS]

(1897-1986)

Ruth Elaine Younger [Mother Ruth, CHS] (1897-1986)[1], religious, educator, and founder of the Community of the Holy Spirit, was born in New York City in 1897. Though her parents were Presbyterian, Ruth was eventually baptized and confirmed in St. Philip's Church in New York City. Before she was fifteen, Ruth Younger experienced a call to the religious life. However, she dealt with racism in the application process due to her biracial background—her father was black and her mother was white—and was refused admission in the United States. Father Hughson, then superior of the Order of the Holy Cross, petitioned on her behalf to the Sisterhood of St. John the Divine in Toronto and she was admitted as a postulant.[2]

Despite this painful experience—Ruth Younger likely experienced a great deal of racism in her life—or maybe because of it, she developed as part of her religious vocation a passionate concern to bring together people from diverse backgrounds in the Spirit of Christ.[3] This concern was reflected in the religious order and educational institutions Ruth Younger founded which were designed to serve persons of all racial and class backgrounds. Similarly, her interest in ecumenism was a natural outgrowth of this "vision of the power of Christian love."[4]

During her novitiate, Ruth Younger graduated from St. Hilda's College at the University of Toronto, and the Ontario College of

Education. When she was twenty-five she was professed as a sister and clothed in the habit of the order. Until 1949, Sister Ruth taught in schools and missions in Canada, and served for a brief time at St. Cyprian's Church in Detroit. In the same year, she was granted a leave of absence to begin a new ministry in New York City with Sister Edith Margaret . The following year the sisters opened a school in Morningside Heights and admitted eight preschool children.[5]

Sister Ruth believed she could work more effectively within the American Church. She and Sister Edith Margaret, with the assistance of Bishop Horace Donegan of New York, established the Community of the Holy Spirit in 1952. Ruth was named Reverend Mother, and served as the new community's superior until 1976. She earned a doctorate in education from Columbia University in the same year. By 1967, St. Hilda's and St. Hugh's School was moved into a new building, serving children from nursery through twelfth grade.[6] Mother Ruth was the head of St. Hilda's and St. Hugh's school until her retirement in 1985. She died peacefully in New York City in 1986, having lived the religious life for nearly sixty-four years.[7]

Mother Ruth was a woman of enormous energy and vitality. She was a keen business woman and a gifted teacher. She traveled widely and wrote voluminous correspondence. Mother Ruth was a popular retreat leader and a mentor to many. She possessed an indomitable spirit and had a forceful personally. Though Mother Ruth could be challenging to others, she was most challenging to herself. At the end of her life her sense of idealism had dulled and she felt that her accomplishments stopped short of her early vision.[8] However, she left behind a lasting legacy and vision for the Community of the Holy Spirit and for the entire church.

The following document was published about the same time as the opening of St. Hilda's and St. Hugh's School and captures much of Mother Ruth's original vision.

NOTES

[1] Biographical information on Mother Ruth came from a variety of sources, most especially through the assistance of Sister Mary Elizabeth, CHS. Print resources included an article by Sister Mary Elizabeth, CHS, "Re-former of Religious Life: the Rev. Mother Ruth," *The Living Church* (July 11, 1999): 12; one earlier article by Esther Burgess. "Mother Ruth, CHS, Educator and Founder," *Linkage 8* (September 1987), 7; and an obituary, "CHS Founder Dies," *The Living Church* (February 1, 1987): 7.

[2] Burgess, 7.

[3] Sister Mary Elizabeth, CHS, February 18, 2002.

[4] Sister Mary Elizabeth, *The Loving Church*, 12.

[5] Obituary, 7.

[6] Burgess, 7.

[7] Obituary, 7.

[8] Ibid.

03

RUTH ELAINE YOUNGER
[MOTHER RUTH, CHS]
St. Hilda's and St. Hugh's School:
Its Philosophy and Ideals*

St. Hilda's and St. Hugh's and happiness! St. Hilda's and St. Hugh's and wholesomeness. These are among the adjectives associated with the school by those who know it from the outside. Today the Community of the Holy Spirit—the religious order for women in the Episcopal Church which has built the School and directs it and teaches in it—has a fairly clear picture of what God's intentions were when he motivated the sending of two sisters down from Canada. But to these Anglican sisters arriving that fall day in 1949 in New York City, perhaps the vision was not quite so vivid.

Sent by their religious order, the Sisterhood of St. John the Divine, they were to undertake social service work of whatever kind might "open up". Patiently the Holy Spirit seemed to abide his time as they sought to make something of this assignment. Soon he intervened. After receiving permission from their superiors, the sisters set aside their own ideas of what they had been called to do, and followed his leadings.

This ability to change direction and to put themselves directly into the hands of the one whom they could truly trust, giving up preconceived plans and ideas, and launching into the adventure of new ways, has always been one of the fundamental principles behind St. Hilda's and St. Hugh's School. Yet by no means is the school a so-called "Progressive" school, nor is it a "permissive" school. As a body it can meet new challenges, new needs, new calls, because it is a thoroughly disciplined School. There is discipline, yes; but there is no regimentation nor authoritarianism. The School teaches its pupils to make choices, decisions carefully considered, to weigh and test results of action, to be responsible for their actions. Through this inner self-discipline he finds his freedom to be his true self.

This principle so deeply imbedded in the school is surely an outgrowth of the disciplined life of the sisters, the freely chosen discipline through which they find freedom, security, and the sense of their own uniqueness and worth. It is the hope of the school that each of its graduates has so achieved these values through the school's program. Discipline of mind, body, heart—even the youngest children at St. Hilda's and St. Hugh's soon come to reflect the happiness of the security they find in living in this atmosphere.

SCHOOL AT THE CROSSROADS

This happy response of the children was evident from the very beginning of the school, when in February, 1950, eight little children gathered together in a room of the rented house used as a convent by the two sisters. This first beginning was made on Morningside Heights only a block away from the present school. Here again, the direction the school was to take seemed directed by the Holy Spirit. This foundation was to be among the people, in the midst of bulging population; in the center of life with all its meanings, its abundancies of all kinds, its extremes, its poverty and lacks, its wealth of potentialities; its faiths and want of faith. The school was set at the crossroads. It was to serve all kinds of people, and no one particular kind of people. It was not to be a "melting pot"; rather it could be thought of as a refiner's vessel in which all that was most unique in each individual soul was to be nurtured and brought to flower. This school was to "educate"—to lead out, to bind and tie the pupil to the love of truth in all its aspects — to set for him ever higher visions and goals. Sound teaching was necessary, and this was to be crowned with further work at college level. The school was soon aware that its genius was to educate those who would be leaders in the world of tomorrow, and that this required a certain kind of direction.

As the Holy Spirit brought the school into being, he was at the same time forming a new family to care for it, so that through yearning prayer as well as hard work, its permanency would be secured, with the blessing of the Anglican sisterhood from which the two founding sisters came, its bishop, as well as the bishop of the diocese of New York. The new American religious order, the Community of the Holy Spirit was founded on August 27th, 1952. Young women came to offer themselves for whatever his Church and body needed. Further education was necessary for many of them, and this was provided. These women also caught the vision; as sisters they continued to create the kind of milieu in which this education was possible.

Perhaps in those early days they could not have expressed the uniqueness of this call into words; but they put it into action. Again this seems to be an expressive factor in the school; little time and energy is spent on words, on talking-about-things; rather the energy flows out through a corporate dynamic action that is actually in itself not achievable by a mere group of women; perhaps it is achieved through the unity of spirit and the yearning prayer of the sisters. This same spirit pervades the school; at least that is the hope and desire and intention of its founders.

WORKING IN THIS WORLD

As it developed and formed, the school's philosophy began to reflect certain characteristics. It had the ability to change, to adapt, to move out for further reaches under the promptings of the Holy Spirit; it seemed to find its purpose through prayer and dialogue; it strove to build in the solid disciplines of learning, and to foster loving concern and respect for each member.

The numbers of the children grew; no longer were they largely those of the faculty and staff of the great Morningside Heights institutions. The vision was coming into closer focus — revealing a school singing with the colors of many different races; surging with the vitalities of emerging nationalities; striving, with the intensity and drive of great cultures. There were no economic distinctions; children in the simple school uniform betrayed no hint of poverty or comfortable security; they are all loved alike, yet each for himself. And the child knows this. The sisters, vowed to poverty, have to earn their own living; the school consequently had to pay its way. This too was part of the plan and philosophy, for it was to be a part of the needs, hungers, drives, labors of common man. The heart of the school was to be a yearning heart, yearning through work, sacrifice, and prayer, for each other. It was truly to reflect the body of Christ working this world.

The sisters have found that there is always "enough", but never any surplus. There seems never to be any luxury of time or space. Apparently nothing could be tolerated which was not at once turned back for the good of the children. Always there have been needs, and always these needs have been filled, with abundance, generosity, graciousness—the lavishness of the giving of the Holy Spirit. This concept seems to have fired the heart-stream of the staff, students, and sisters; all rejoice in giving, to the fullest. And this challenge is continually carried to the child—that he spend himself in learning, loving, being; yet there is no forcing. Again the Holy Spirit is the teacher, as he abides the fullness of time.

LEAP FORWARD INTO GRACE

Yes, there is the patient waiting as the child grows in his own right and individual way; but there is another aspect of "time" which is very obvious to those who witness the school in action. There is the quickened pulse—the urgency of this moment; the knowledge that there may be only "today" wherein to experience together with the children the adventure and joy of the good news of the Christ. The Holy Spirit keeps pressuring; there is no moment to lose, there is no space to waste, all must be filled, must be brought to fulfilment. Perhaps there is only "today" in which to inspire these young souls to seek the good, the true, the beautiful: perhaps today, if they are to have it, they must experience the joy of creating a loving social community in their classrooms, where care and concern for each other is the accepted pattern. Together, at St. Hilda's and St. Hugh's, all share joy and wonder and awe as God thrusts upon them the privilege of this leap forward into grace.

Yes, most of these boys and girls find life a leap forward into grace even as they find the mid-twentieth century offering new channels for the living under grace. The members of the school are aware of the tremendous acceleration of time. They find graces come faster than ever before, and that they cannot be clung to, but must be shared within this new pattern of time. Today's child is not like the child of even a decade ago. This acceleration is a reality which already "colors" us psychologically, mentally, in the nerves, and in the emotions. The grasp of knowledge of most children is broad and surprising; he seems to know so very much intuitively. This must be fortified with knowledge, understanding, and compassion. His need for security is greater than ever before; there is the daily struggle against anonymity. The school attempts to provide these, even as it opens his horizons wider and wider, exposing him to even more insecurity. He finds his roots plunging deeper and deeper into the past, even as he in body as well as in spirit soars a freer being in space. Truly he is finding himself set in dominion over the earth.

As the boy or girl at St. Hilda's and St Hugh's finds himself transcending time as well as space, he also senses a "newness" covering the face of the earth. Surely, holy fear is the gift awaiting him, the gift he most needs. Should not the school provide every means to foster this new life in her children?

The school believes it must be ever alert and awake to the action of God in history right now, and it must find ways to confirm his actions. St. Hilda's and St. Hugh's is truly a new foundation, giving itself over into the hands of the Holy Spirit to be one more witness to the truth of the Resurrection Body, and to bring that life to the children God has entrusted to its care.

---

* Mother Ruth, CHS, "St Hilda's and St Hugh's School: Its Philsophy and Its Ideals," *The Witness* (January 26, 1967): 3-6.

MARGARET MEAD

(1901-1978)

Margaret Mead (1901-1978),[1] anthropologist, was born in Philadelphia, Pennsylvania in 1901. She graduated from Barnard College in 1924, and remained there for graduate study with eminent anthropologists Franz Boaz and Ruth Benedict. She was granted an M.A. in 1924 and a Ph.D in 1929. It was during one of her many field trips while a graduate student at Columbia that she wrote her classic work, *Coming of Age in Samoa* (1928).

Margaret Mead was the author of twenty-three books during the course of her career. Though others have questioned her cultural determinism and some of the conclusions that she drew from her data, Margaret Mead was nonetheless was a pioneer in the study of the effects of cultural conditioning and cultural change. She was also an outspoken commentator on many issues of the twentieth century, including sexual ethics, women's rights, child rearing, nuclear prolif-eration, race relations, drug abuse, and world hunger. She was posthumously awarded the Presidential Medal of Freedom in 1979—the highest civilian honor in the United States.

Margaret Mead held a variety of teaching and research posi-tions over her career, but was best known for her long association with the American Museum of Natural History. Her contributions to science were honored—she was elected to the presidency of the American Association for the Advancement of Science. Mead made many field trips to Oceania, and is perhaps best known for her studies of peoples there. Mead and her third husband, Gregory Bateson, had one daughter, Mary Catherine Bateson.

What is less well-known about Margaret Mead is that she was a devout Anglo-Catholic, regular churchgoer, and religious leader on a variety of church committees and organizations. Though Mead's parents were agnostic, a friendship she had with a clergy-man's daughter resulted in Margaret's baptism a few days before her eleventh birthday. The decision was not popular with Margaret's parents, who had no idea "how to deal with a child who insisted on fasting during Lent."[2] Margaret Mead was drawn to the Episcopal Church through its ritual, which she believed was what she needed to counterbalance the cognitive faith of her mother. "What I wanted was a form of religion that gave expression to an already existing faith."[3] Margaret Mead was baptized, first married, and ultimately buried at Trinity Church, Buckingham, Pennsylvania. She later advised, "Agnostic parents who wish their children to share in the wholeness of the human experience, including religious experience, should find ways of helping them...."[4]

It has been suggested that one the reasons Margaret Mead made little comment on her faith, though it and the Episcopal Church were very important to her, was due to her three divorces. Though she did not feel sinful about her divorces, she did not feel it was appropriate to publicize them, either. When she was asked to represent the Episcopal Church on the Committee for Assembly for the World Council of Churches, she did not agree until she was sure the committee knew she had been divorced.[5]

Margaret Mead was also a member of the Subcommittee for the Revision of the Book of Common Prayer. A faithful member of the committee, Mead was also effective; she could see religion as both a conservative force, as well as a force for change.[6] She was conservative about language and ritual, and appreciated the King James Bible, yet she saw the church more in terms of its social mission than as a mystic. Margaret Mead originally opposed the ordination of women to the priesthood, however, she later believed that "men have so damaged the priesthood that women are needed to repair it."[7]

In her many years on Episcopal and ecumenical committees she rarely missed a chance to worship. For her the church and the sacraments were a glimpse into the transcendent. She was not overly fond of preaching, largely because of the congregation's inability to respond.[8] Margaret Mead was active in local parishes in New York City, St. Luke-in-the-Fields and St. Matthew's and St. Timothy's, in particular. She attended the parish of St. Mary the Virgin, New York City, whenever it was possible on Good Friday.

The following document is an article on ritual that Margaret Mead wrote in 1966. It was published in a collection of her works on religion under the title, *Twentieth Century Faith: Hope and Survival* as well as an issue of *Worship* (February 1966).

NOTES

[1] A few of the sources on Margaret Mead that detail her religious life are the following: Jane Howard, *Margaret Mead: A Life* (New York: Simon and Schuster, 1948); Rhoda Metraux, *Margaret Mead: Some Personal Views* (New York: Walker and Company, 1979); James B. Simpson, "To Cherish the Life of the World": Margaret Mead, *The Living Church* (August 22, 1999): 10,

[2] Howard, *Margaret Mead*, 31-32; 35.

[3] Ibid, 32.

[4] Metraux, *Margaret Mead*, 177.

[5] Howard, 342-43.

[6] Howard, 347-48.

[7] Howard, 353; Simpson; *To Cherish the Life of the World*," 10.

[8] Howard, 343, 353.

MARGARET MEAD
Ritual Expression of the Cosmic Sense*

Is it possible to work out a formulation—of the kind anthropologists try for when we are studying a culture—that would describe the liturgical movement? The problem, it seems to me, is how to bring together within one context the desire to break down all barriers—the barriers separating bishops and other people, those separating the races of men, and those separating the laity (although one hears about lay men and lay women, nothing is said about lay children; I presume that sooner or later they will be included)—the desire to go back into the past and push forward into the future, and the desire to include the disreputable. In another period we would have said "the humble and lowly"; today, I think "disreputable" is one aspect of the more inclusive attempt to reach out to all those whose feet have been unwashed through the ages (and whenever the feet of some new group are washed, this shocks some people); it is part of the attempt to include all those who are denigrated and lost, as well as the dispossessed of our slums, urban and rural, and, beyond our own country, all the peoples of the earth.

At this moment in history the desire to reach out toward all men is entirely consistent with our new exploration, with the efforts we are making to probe the depths of the sea, to move out into outer space, and to consider whether the inhabitants of earth (one no longer says "this earth" or "the earth" but just "earth") are the only sentient creatures in the universe. From an age-long concentration on our world we are moving out to include the solar system, the galaxy, and we do not yet know how far beyond.

One other thing should also be included in the context of what we desire to bring together in a new whole. This is the beauty of liturgy. The use of precious metals, beautiful fabrics, and rich colors are all part of this. I think it is important to bear this in mind, for while we may feel it is wrong to spend money on precious vestments as long as there are hungry people, our attempt to respond to hunger and poverty should not bar out the development of every kind of beauty in the liturgy.

And now, if I were to describe the liturgical movement, I would say that it is an extraordinary breaking of bounds—a breaking of the boundaries that people feel have separated one part of our lives from another part. As the eucharist is carried into the simplest home, that home is broadened into a cathedral; and at the same time, behavior within cathedrals seems to be moving back and forth in an utterly unpredictable way. Ritual is an exceedingly important part of all culture, all the cultures we now know about and, hopefully, all the cultures we shall know about in the future.

I could, of course, discuss the way fire and water, darkness and light, earth and living things, are used the world over as symbols of new life. I could describe the many forms of ritual that break or purify man's tie to the earthly part of his nature, all those beliefs and acts that bind together rituals in every part of the world and create a resonance between the rituals of Christianity and the rituals of other peoples and other religions. Instead, I prefer to discuss what we know as scientists, as anthropologists, who study the different kinds of men inhabiting the earth and who now know that all men belong to one species. This is a biological affirmation of the idea of the Brotherhood of Man which the Church has always stood for but which many of its clergy and their congregations have found—and sometimes still find—difficult. But we now have a scientific basis for our belief in the brotherhood of man, something that is very helpful to modern clergy. We know that the tiniest Pygmy and the most isolated Australian aborigine are members of the same species to which we belong, and we know that all men share the same human characteristics as well as the characteristics that bind all of us equally to the rest of the natural world.

In the latter part of the nineteenth century and the beginning of the twentieth century scientists were fascinated, perhaps even obsessed, with the problem of how man is like the primates, the birds, and other living creatures; their studies emphasized what has so felicitously been called our creatureliness. But scientists working in the second half of the twentieth century have begun, and I think will continue, to explore those things that are unique to man. For although we eat and drink and sleep and care for our young as many other living creatures do, man also has certain characteristics, identifiable by ordinary scientific methods of research, that are unique to his species.

One of these peculiarly human characteristics is man's search for meaning in the universe. This search for meaning has been called the *cosmic sense* or, sometimes, the cosmological sense, but I prefer the simpler term. Slowly, as we have begun to identify many more than the traditional "five senses," we have also come to realize that there are many more ways in which man senses the universe. By the cosmic sense we mean man's need, a need found in every child and expressed in every culture, to relate to and understand the universe, so that individual life takes on meaning. Our knowledge of the cosmic sense comes, on the one hand, from the study of children and, on the other, from comparative studies of many different living cultures. On the basis of this knowledge it is possible to say that the need to find meaning in the universe is as real as the need for trust and for love, for relations with other human beings. It has been demonstrated that infants who are deprived of care by identifiable persons—infants in orphan asylums and foundling homes, who are well fed and medically cared for, but who have no single person to whom they can attach themselves—will die. It is a basic characteristic of human beings that, in infancy, they must have some close relationship to another human being in order to become human. So, equally, the need to have some relationship to the universe, to attach meaning to life, to perceive the outer world, to take it in and give something out, can be described as a basic human characteristic. And, of course, it is this need to which the whole liturgy of the Church gives particular expression.

In fact, speaking in tongues fits in exceedingly well with what I want to say. Think for a moment of the most expressive, gifted, and artistic person you have ever known, someone with the creative capacity to embody the deepest vision in a painting, in music, or in a ritual dance. Clearly, this creative ability is very rare and very imperfectly distributed among men. And now, for a moment, think of the deepest religious experience you have ever known, or, if you do not think your own religious experience has ever been equal to that of the saints, think about the deepest religious experience you have ever read about or encountered in another person. Clearly, the capacity for religious experience also is very imperfectly distributed among men. Moreover, these two capacities are very differently distributed among human beings.

This was true even among the very simplest people I ever studied, a mountain people in New Guinea.

Only a very few people have the capacity for a transcendental experience of the world in depth and with strength. Now, if those with this capacity were also those who are gifted with creative capacities for expression in speech, in painting, or in immediate flowing prayer, we might perhaps not have the same need for ritual. For experience would immediately be matched by expression of that experience, and in some form it would be there to be shared by those who lack both the capacity for experience and the power of expression. But because they are differently distributed, we find an extreme contrast. At one end of the scale there are the elaborate, beautiful, formal rituals that have been worked on by aesthetically gifted individuals through the ages. And at the other end of the scale there are people, lacking any of these special gifts, whose religious experience breaks through all expression. I think the individual speaks in tongues when his capacity to give structure to experience breaks down, and at certain moments in history it happens that those who have strong, immediate feelings have no words, no acts, no symbols that will appropriately contain what they have experienced, and so they temporarily abandon the structure of speech.

Some societies, as a whole, are extraordinarily impoverished, in the sense that their ritual is very slight, their artistic forms are very slight, and, very often, their experience also is very thin. It is on ritual forms that the imagination of each generation feeds. Children have the need to seek for meaning in the world around them—in the natural world—and to seek for transcendence in that world. If the forms are there, polished through many generations by the imagination and gift of many people, children's imagination can be caught, invigorated, and illuminated by the forms that are there, ready for new expression. In a thin, poor, ritually impoverished environment this cannot happen.

Certain societies have elaborated to an extraordinary extent the human capacity for expression in music, art, and ritual. Bali is one of these. In Bali today, those who are concerned with the liturgical reform movement of the Roman Catholic Church are having a delightful time. The language has a resonance like the clanging of bells. The Balinese are so imaginative that they can produce a miracle play at a moment's notice. And they are such gifted carvers and painters that one has only to present them with a large blank wall and in no time at all they will produce the most magnificent gargoyles. The Balinese are, in fact, a people with an enormously informed imagination. For this reason, also, they are ready to take into their hands and their voices the outlines of the Christian tradition and to give Christian ritual a new and delightful form that reaches deep into their own symbolism.

In contrast, there are people who have almost no developed capacity for ritual expression. I have worked with a people whose major ritual act is to spit betel nut juice. The juice is rusty red. The betel nut itself is a beautiful bright green and has a spherical shape. The lime chewed with the nuts is white. If in a sermon one wants to make a spherical point, the shape of the betel nut can provide the necessary simile. But on the whole this is a meager assemblage, and the ceremony is a meager one to build on.

Comparing different cultures, the same cultures at different periods, and the several parts of a single tradition, we can find many contrasts of this kind. Within the Christian tradition we have had a lamentable tendency to go to extremes in separating out fragments of the whole. When such a fragmentation has occurred, those who have grasped at one fragment sometimes have thought of it not as a different expression of the whole, but instead as a rather willful version of the whole. Comparing many of these versions, we can see that there has been tremendous variation in the capacity of different groups to build rituals that are enduring and have the continuity necessary to make them available to all the people born within a society.

This is, as I understand it, what the liturgical movement is trying to do with the traditional ritual of the Church—to use the old symbols, but to use them with a lively, fresh insight that will free both the rituals and ourselves from the rigidity of forms that cannot contain new vision. This can happen to languages as well. We speak of a language as going through a period of great productivity and then sometimes as settling into a kind of rigidity that fossilizes and destroys the thought of a whole period.

Ritual must carry the continuity that makes a tradition available to all who live within it. But this is not its only function. Ritual also gives people access to intensity of feeling at times when responsiveness is muted. This is especially striking in the ceremonies of second mourning that occur in many parts of the world. Many peoples have such a ritual of second mourning, which usually serves to free the mourners from the obligatory observances of mourning. It may take place when the bones are dug up, when the head is taken and put somewhere else, when the widow or the parents are relieved of isolation, and so on. In different cultures any one of a whole series of acts may be the signal for the ceremony of second mourning. And then, at the critical time, the mourners are expected once more to mourn intensely. But as the ritual may take place a year or more after the bereavement, the mourners will no longer feel so desperately sad as they did when the death occurred. One of the peoples I studied in New Guinea have a way of jerking their heads to induce the feeling. On such an occasion the women sit and jerk their heads until at last they get into a state in which they can mourn as convincingly as on the day the person died. Their mourning has all the physiological qualities of the first expression of grief, and for the moment the original grief is reinstated and made vivid.

This, then, is a second function of ritual—to lift people above the dullness that inevitably follows on moments of high feeling and to reinstate the high ecstasy that is so transient an experience. The recurrence of the ritual assures them that the feeling once was there and may come back again. This is, of course, the principal function of the rituals of family relationships—wedding anniversaries, birthday celebrations, and family reunions—and of all those ceremonies where we attempt to reconstitute ritually a feeling that exists but that may lack any immediate power of expression. It is a second function of ritual all over the world.

At the present time, those who are working within the liturgical movement are seeking to produce an all-embracing form, a form that will gather into one whole all the peoples on earth, all the disciplines through which man learns, and all the places where we may go, and, in so doing, will illuminate the events of our time—the civil rights meetings, events taking place on the farthest island of the seas, and the celebration of Easter at the Holy Sepulchre in Palestine. Responding to the present, the liturgical movement can draw on our contemporary knowledge of human capacities and our recognition that the cosmic sense can be studied and understood and related to the rituals we shall build. And now at last the old argument between science and religion can be replaced by a dialogue in which all that we know scientifically from the study of man, especially from the study of children, will be illuminated by the historic and the contemporary inspiration of the Church.

---

* Margaret Mead, "Ritual Expression of the Cosmic Sense," *Worship,* 80; 2 (February 1966): 66-72; also published in *Twentieth Century Faith: Hope and Survival,* (New York: Harper and Row, 1973): 152-160.

PAULA VELÁZQUEZ DE ÁLVAREZ

(1903-1987)

Paula Velázquez de Álvarez (1903-1987), teacher and first elected president of the Episcopal Church Women in the Diocese of Puerto Rico, was born of a rural family in Penuelas, who moved to the city of Ponce to provide for the education of their five daughters. She received a B.A. from the University of Puerto Rico. In 1927, "Paulita" became a missionary teacher to St. Catherine's School. She married an Episcopal priest, Lorenzo Álvarez, and they had a son, David Andrés Álvarez, who became the bishop of the Diocese of Puerto Rico. Paula and her husband established the Mission of the Annunciation in Yauco; they also served St. Andrew's parish in Mayaquez and the parish of St. Mary the Virgin in Ponce, Puerto Rico.[1]

The following document was written by Paula Velázquez de Álvarez to commemorate the twentieth anniversary of the founding of the Women's Auxiliary in the Diocese of Puerto Rico.

NOTES

[1] Biographical information was provided by the Rt. Rev. David Andrés Álvarez.

PAULA VELÁZQUEZ DE ÁLVAREZ
A Short History of the Organization of the Episcopal Church Women in the Diocese of Puerto Rico*

In 1792 the Episcopal Church created a special committee to help finance missionary work. Church women helped very much in that effort. The General Convention, celebrated in 1871 in the city of Baltimore, created a women's organization to help in this missionary work. This is how the Women's Auxiliary was formed which in the triennial meeting of 1958 changed its name to the Episcopal Church Women.

Work in Puerto Rico had begun in 1872 under the Diocese of Antigua and the jurisdiction of the Church of England. With the passing of this jurisdiction to the Episcopal Church in 1901, groups of the Women's Auxiliary began to be formed. This functioned in a non-organized way for many years. In 1948 Bishop Boynton appointed Mrs. Edna H. Villafane as diocesan president. She started organizing the existing groups in the diocese. In March of that year, a group of women met to formalize the plans for this organization. I was one of them.

Plans were made for the first Women's Auxiliary convention which was held in the Holy Trinity Parish in Ponce on April 18, 1948. We had delegations from seven branches and other interested women. Mrs. Villafane held the position as president and I was elected as secretary-treasurer. I held this position until the convention in 1954 when I became the first president elected by the church women. From then on, we continued to elect our officers every three years. In 1959 we approved our by-laws. After that, Mrs. Villafane was elected president and was followed by Mrs. Catin Ruiz who was elected in 1964 and Mrs. Hortensia Troche who was elected in 1967.

It was under the presidency of Mrs. Villafane that we started the Diocesan Project that has helped in special needs of our missions. At the same time, we started participating in the United Thank Offering. Our contribution has grown from $400 to 1949 to $4,000 in 1967.

All this has been achieved due to the dedication of the officers and all the women in Puerto Rico. As we celebrate today our 20th Anniversary of our work, all Episcopal Church Women of Puerto Rico give thanks to Mrs. Villafane and dedicate to her this convention.

---

* This history was written by Mrs. Paula Velázquez de Álvarez for the 20th Annual Convention of the diocese of Puerto Rico celebrated on April 21, 1968, in the parish of St. Mary the Virgin, Ponce. The English translation was provided by The Rt. Rev. David Andrés Álvarez.

DORA PHYLLIS MEEKINGS CHAPLIN

(1905-1990)

Dora Phyllis Meekings Chaplin (1905-1990), musician, educator, theologian, was born in Essex, England in 1905.[1] Her father was a small landowner and her mother was a collateral descendent of Oliver Goldsmith. During her early years, Dora Phyllis Meekings wanted to become a concert pianist. She studied piano at the Royal Academy of Music in London and received a Gold metal, the equivalent of a degree. Chaplin also taught at the Metropolitan Academy of Music in London. However, due to post-polio effects—she wore braces on her legs—Dora moved into music education, thus beginning a long and distinguished teaching career. Chaplin was afflicted with polio as a child and was challenged from post-polio effects throughout her life. She retired from her formal teaching career in a wheel chair.

In 1922, Dora married Frederick James Chaplin of the Royal Air Force. Chaplin was a brilliant man and a members of the intelligence forces. Yet, he suffered psychological traumatic stress after service in two wars, from which he never fully recovered. The couple had two daughters—Ann, a social worker, who lived with her mother until her death in 1990, and Elizabeth, who married an Episcopal priest, John Janney Lloyd, and served with her husband as a missionary in Japan. When Dora Chaplin departed for the United States with her daughters, her husband remained behind; he died in England in 1953.

Once in the United States Dora Chaplin began her work at Church of the Redeemer in Chestnut Hill, Massachusetts. She also attended Episcopal Theological School (now Episcopal Divinity School) and studied Christian education with Adelaide Teague Case. During her long career, Chaplin was also active in a number of other parishes in New York and Connecticut.

Dora P. Chaplin had a gift for communicating the Christian faith, and she understood the importance of interpreting faith and the church within contemporary context. She summed up her philosophy of the mission of Christian education for the General Convention in 1946: "We are being told that we are living on the spiritual capital of our ancestors, and capital unreplenished does not last forever.... most of us enjoy the Christian legacy without stopping to think where it came from...We had better realize it before it is too late that Christianity is locked in a desperate struggle: it is not enough for us to stand and cheer on the fight, we had better enter the lists – parents, teachers, Everyman."[2]

During the 1950s, Chaplin served on the National Department of Christian Education, offering workshops and seminars across the country. A frequent presenter at the College of Preachers, Chaplin's vision of Christian education also influenced two major curriculum series designed for the Episcopal Church, the Seabury Series and *Living the Good News*.

Chaplin was the first full-time residential female professor at the General Theological Seminary in New York City where she was a member of the faculty of pastoral theology for 20 years. She received an S.T.D from Bexley Hall and a D.D. from the General Theological Seminary. A prolific writer, Chaplin published several books, including *Children and Religion* (1948), *We Want to Know* (1957) and *The Privilege of Teaching* (1962).

Besides her active professional life, Dora Chaplin lived a personal life filled with her children, grandchildren, and great-grandchildren. She had a vibrant sense of humor and kept up an active correspondence in her later years.[3] She died from a heart ailment in 1990.

Dora P. Chaplin was a member of the Society of the Companions of Holy Cross, and was intensely interested in aesthetical theology and the life of prayer. The following excerpts from *The Privilege of Teaching* are from chapters on "The Teacher and the Life of Prayer," and "What Does The Teacher Believe?"

NOTES

[1] Biographical information of this article was provided by Elizabeth Lloyd. Also, see her obituary, *Gannett Westchester Newspapers*, September 18, 1990.

[2] The General Convention, 1946.

[3] Helen Barron, "Visionary Teacher: Dora Phyllis Chaplin," *The Living Church* (June 20, 1999): 10.

DORA P. CHAPLIN
Excerpts from The Privilege of Teaching
The Teacher And the Life of Prayer[1]

Difficuties And Excuses

I suppose our most frequent excuse is, "I don't have time." If we care enough, we shall find time, if only a little. The busy mother of several children will obviously have less opportunity for formal prayer than the older woman whose family is grown; the homemaker who also works at a paid job outside the home is hard put to it to find a quiet time and a quiet place; there are marriages in which one partner prays and the other does not—I am aware of all of these factors. Most of us lead driven lives, and there is plenty of noise, distraction, interruption, and worry to complicate them still further. But these are not the reasons why most of us are negligent, or irregular, or superficial in our weak response to "God's outstretched hand." These conditions are not the real explanation for the fact that we simply do not do the most important part of our Christian work efficiently, while we pride ourselves on efficiency in a hundred other ways. Prayer is the most important thing there is, and if we believed this we would find time for it.

We have only to add up the hours of work, leisure, and sleep in our days and try to analyze honestly where the hours go to discover that we do find time for what we find either inescapable (like earning a living or cooking dinner), or enjoyable (such as television, or magazines, or chattering to friends, or whatever our pet diversions are), and of course, for some necessary sleep. All of these things are good in themselves. It is only when we indulge in them to such an extent that more important things become peripheral, and these central, that they can destroy. If we had discovered the central place of prayer we would find time for it. Thousands of people have never been told; others have not heard; and some of us who ought to know better are not always so diligent as we should be.

Although I am going to turn you over to other teachers for this most important side of your life, I would like to mention briefly what are a few of the hindrances to prayer today. First—and this we have already mentioned—our ignorance. We may know little about the nature of God, and we have not known that He waits for us. We have prayed, perhaps, in a self-centered way. Or we may never have been taught about prayer as a necessary part of our Christian life, except when it has been referred to in sentimental or childish terms. We may have thought that parsons, old ladies, and "shut-ins" are the only ones who give considerable time to it; the whole dimension of worship may have been nonexistent for us.

Perhaps we once started out in the right way and were lazy: we did not discipline ourselves to put first things first. Or we may have lost heart during the "dry" times and given up. We may have "grown out of it," thinking it a very doubtful activity in the light of our new scientific or psychological knowledge. We may have thought that the only time one can pray is when one is kneeling by a bed, or in some equally formal position. We may not have heard of the many ways of praying, some of which may perfectly well be done while our hands are busy at other things, or while we are travelling.

Many convince themselves that they are too tired for either prayer or Bible reading, because the only few minutes they save for God are when they get into bed at night. When we come to care, we shall find, somewhere in our crowded days, a time when we are more alert than that. I know a number of mothers who have several school children who say that when the front door closes on the last of them they try to find a few quiet minutes before the day rushes on [....]

Finally—

When Evelyn Underhill was asked to address a great gathering of teachers of religion she talked to them about sheep dogs. You may well ask what the connection is between a sheep dog's vocation and that of the teacher, especially if you have never been to the "trials" held in some parts of the country where these wonderful animals are used to encourage the sheep to go into the right meadows, to bring back the disobedient ones, and generally to watch the flock. They are extraordinarily intelligent and even learn to pick out and then persuade a certain number of lambs to go into a particular enclosure, all at the shepherd's bidding.

Miss Underhill noticed a number of things about the dogs and their masters which we may do well to imitate: they enjoyed their work, their tails never ceased to wag, they never "fussed" or hurried, and they spent a lot of time simply sitting still looking at the shepherd....

If we do not take time to find out what the Shepherd's commands are, through "listening prayer" and faithful study of His Word, if we lose patience with the exasperating lambs in the flock, or give way to endless reproval of their parents, we shall be very poor sheep dogs and the lambs will wander off.

If it is easier for you to think of yourself as a member of an orchestra, someone who has to keep an eye on the Conductor and subjugate his own whims to His guidance, then keep that picture in your mind instead. All that matters is that we shall be obedient.

[...]

What Does The Teacher Believe?
Facing Reality

From time to time we hear a person assert that he has come into the Episcopal Church "because it is so free, one can believe as one likes." What this person is really saying is that to him the Christian religion is a cafeteria. He may have had all the great doctrines spread out before him, but instead of choosing to eat a balanced meal, he has helped himself to a few delectable side dishes and left the substantial ones untouched. We have among us a great many people who have chosen only little fragments of the truth which they find easy to live with, ones which make no demand on their present way of life. They want to be left undisturbed, and they delude themselves that they have "all this and heaven too."

Every modern Christian has presumably been influenced by contemporary secular education. We live in an era in which man has spent a lot of time trying to understand himself and his behavior alone and in groups—the great era of psychology. In much of this thinking there has been no consideration of what God meant man to be. "Experiences" and "felt needs" and "adjustment to the group" were (and still are in much current writing and thinking) the watchwords. Those who are captivated by this jargon have lost sight of the fact that there must be an "absolute," that is, an absolute standard of values, or else it is not possible to evaluate experience. Experience for experience's sake is a pathetic trap; our "felt needs" may not be our real needs; and why must one adjust to the group if the group is doing the wrong thing? This is no place for a long description of rationalism versus positivism, and the many philosophies of education; it is merely an occasion on which to say to the teacher in passing that not everyone who is now teaching religion was prepared to face life as it really is. Most of us made ready for a mysterious "good life" which was supposed to be normal. We did not learn in school that man is God's highest creation, that he has a great destiny, that he is a disobedient creature and falls far short of what he was meant to be: most of us were fed on idealism and the pursuit of happiness. It was the Church which had to step in, perhaps rather late, to teach us first to look sin in the face, and then to know by whom and through whom it is conquered.

But the "everything-will-be-all-right-soon" philosophies have left their mark upon us, and we shall have to work hard to force ourselves to see that the children we teach are creatures of the atomic age, that civilization is changing and will change more. We must not hand out a lot of nonsense about a beautiful world in which all the good people will be safe, and all the bad people will be suppressed. If we do this we shall be like the babbling jokers on the plane and be unable to surround our students with the power of love and true hope which is rooted and grounded in Christ. One of the reasons why mature Christians have a certain kind of (perhaps hidden) gaiety about them is that they know our Lord did not promise anyone happiness; He promised them fullness of joy. Because they are aware of how utterly inadequate we are alone, they have gained a sense of perspective which, as we saw at the end of the first chapter, is really a sense of humor. And have you noticed that real love and real humor go hand in hand?

[...]

Christianity is not built on wishful thinking and pious hopes; nor is it founded on inspired guesses and "unlimited tolerance." Its unshakeable foundation is the revelation of God in Christ. As we saw earlier, we can often observe a sentimental and uncritical devotion in some persons who have compromised with the truth, but this does not stand up under great stress. If we refuse to think, or are afraid of where the thinking may lead us, we are disobeying the command, "Thou shalt love the Lord thy God with all thy heart, and with all thy soul, and *with all thy mind.*" The Christian Faith is for the whole person, which means that the offering of our emotions alone is not enough.

In several recent books I have found that a famous quotation from Simone Weil is used: "The danger is not lest the soul should doubt whether there is any bread, but lest, by a lie, it should persuade itself that it is not hungry."[2] The statement is indeed true of many, but I wonder if in this country we might not also turn it around and say, "The danger is not that the soul should doubt that it is hungry, but lest, by a lie, it should persuade itself that there is no bread." Is that not true of many starved people in our parishes? They simply do not know how nourishing the bread is; they have received only the crumbs and they think they have the whole loaf.

The writer of the Book of Job bids us see that we have touched only the fringe of what is offered: "Lo, these are but the outskirts of his ways...But the thunder of his power who can understand?" (Job 26:14, R.S.V.). And St. Paul says sternly to his pupils, "Examine yourselves, whether ye be in the faith" (II Corinthians 13:5).

I am not making the unpractical suggestion that we should try to produce an army of exceedingly learned instructors. I make a plea for two things: first, that we examine ourselves in the *basic doctrines,* through reading and thinking, alone and sometimes in groups, turning to the clergy for help when necessary; and second, that for the rest of our days we never cease to consider how these doctrines affect every moment of our working lives. I promise you that if you try to discover the faith and teaching of the Christian Church in this way, you will find that there is no more rewarding search that any man or woman can make: it never ends, for the treasure you come upon spurs you to go on and look for more. Our old fumblings and rather misty beliefs, which when we began looked rather like the jumbled pieces of a jigsaw puzzle, suddenly begin to make sense to us. A clear picture is formed. We find ourselves living rather than existing.

---

[1] Dora P. Chaplin, *The Privilege of Teaching* (New York: Morehouse-Barlow Co, 1962): 73-76; 79-84.

[2] *Waiting for God*, translated by Emma Craufurd, G. P. Putnam's Sons, New York, 1951, p. 35.

SARAH PATTON BOYLE

(1906-1994)

Sarah Patton Boyle (1906-1994), civil rights activist and opponent of racial segregation, was born on her family's farm outside
Charlottesville, Virginia. Her father, Robert William Patton,
was an Episcopal priest who worked to provide improved education
opportunities for African Americans. Though Patton exhibited the
paternalistic attitudes that many whites brought to their educational
work, he was considered progressive for early twentieth-century
Virginia. Yet his ministry and values had little impact on his daughter.
A distant father who often worked away from his family, Boyle felt
he never was around enough to influence her values or beliefs.[1]
More influential was her mother, Janie Stringfellow Patton, who
believed that lady-like behavior mandated a distance between herself
and African Americans, especially African American men.[2]

Like other upper-class southern women, Boyle was schooled at
home. She learned to read as a teenager due to an undiagnosed
learning disability. But she excelled at art and in 1926 studied painting
at the Corcoran School of Art in Washington, D.C. In 1932 she
married a drama professor, E. Roger Boyle II, and the couple had
two children. After her marriage, Boyle supplemented the family
income by selling paintings and articles to women's magazines.

In the late 1940s and early 1950s Boyle sought a new sense of
calling. She returned to the Episcopal Church of her youth after

explorations in other forms of spirituality. The catalyst for her conversion was African American attorney Gregory Swanson's successful suit for admission to the University of Virginia Law School. Her attempts to show support for Swanson led her to weekly re-education sessions regarding race relations with journalist and editor T. J. Sellers.

The results of Seller's influence were not immediate; Boyle continued her writing, speaking, and organizing for the NAACP and other organizations. The opposition against her escalated when an article she wrote entitled "We're Readier Than We Think" appeared in *The Saturday Evening Post* under the headline "Southerners Will *Like* Integration." The article caused intense opposition to Boyle from across the country, including a burning cross on her lawn. It took the actual closing of schools in 1958 to temper Boyle's optimism and her faith in the belief of a white majority opposed to the injustices of racial segregation.[3]

Sarah Patton Boyle published the story of her spiritual transformation—her change of heart—in *The Desegregated Heart* (1962). The book was a critical success and read widely in church groups, suggesting Boyle's importance as a spiritual leader and perhaps, as an unrecognized lay theologian.[4] Soon after the publication of *The Desegregated Heart,* Sarah Patton Boyle received a number of prestigious awards from organizations such as the NAACP and the Southern Leadership Conference.

Though ultimately a transitional figure in the civil rights movement, as one of the few mature white women engaged in the struggle, Sarah Patton Boyle was a significant role model for younger white women who later joined the movement.[5] After her divorce in 1965, she moved to Arlington, Virginia and sought to retire from public life and the civil rights movement. A woman of deep faith, Sarah Patton Boyle's final years were devoted to the eradication of ageism—a story told in her final autobiographical work, *The Desert Blooms* (1983).

The following excerpts are from *The Desegregated Heart* and mark the shifts in Sarah Patton Boyle's gradually shifting racial consciousness.

NOTES

[1] Sarah Patton Boyle, *The Desegregated Heart: A Virginian's Stand in Time of Transition* (Charlottesville: University if Virginia Press, 2001): x.

[2] Ibid.

[3] Ibid, xi-xvii.

[4] Joanna Bowen Gillespie, "Sarah Patton Boyle's Desegregated Heart," in *Beyond Image and Convention: Explorations in Southern Women's History*, Janet L. Coryell, et. al., ed. (Columbia: University of Missouri Press, 1998): 158-183. Dr. Gillespie gracious provided her input on Sarah Patton Boyle for this entry.

[5] Boyle, *Desegregated Heart*, xx-xxi.

ℭℛ

SARAH PATTON BOYLE
"Jeffersonian Americans":
An Excerpt from The Desegregated Heart[1]

As I moved confidently into 1953, I believed that the white half of the Southern Dream was true. We really did love "our Negroes," and appearances to the contrary were just an evil illusion. Although the "Sellers Course" had taught me that our expressions of this love often were offensive, I didn't question the high quality of the love itself.

I believed, too, that the other half of the Dream had been true and could be true again. Negroes had once loved us.

Since the deepest desire of every heart was to love and be loved, I reasoned, it was impossible that two peoples could live side by side, interwoven as we were, and not love each other. Once I would have added, "Especially two peoples like us, that are as complementary and supplementary to each other as are men and women." But that would have been before I suddenly realized in the early summer of 1951 that Negroes and whites are the same.

For a long time I had been saying that they were alike—and thinking that I thought it. But one day something in me tangibly dissolved, and afterwards I knew it was a partition which had made me feel that Negroes and whites are *alike* without feeling that they are the *same*. I had had a "we" and "you" feeling which now was gone.

Some immediate rewards followed the dissolving of this barrier. I felt as you feel when you have knocked out a wall between two small rooms in your house. The result isn't just one of the little rooms made twice as big, nor is it simply the two little rooms brought together. It is a new and altogether different room. When the partition between two races comes out within yourself, you haven't just got two races brought together. You've got humanity. If segregationists realized this, they mightn't mind the idea so much. It's the "brought together" concept which seems to distress them most.

I felt whole. This filled me with wonder, for I hadn't known I was divided. I felt relaxed, not having known that I had been tense. I felt co-ordinated and was surprised to discover that I had been confused and torn by feeling one way, thinking another, and behaving still another.

The change probably wasn't as visible to others as to me. Outwardly I continued for a long time to move in my old patterns. Probably I still move in some of them. Even inside me, the change wasn't as clear-cut and permanent as knocking out a plaster wall. My race partition reappeared and vanished like the point of a busy knitting needle. But my over-all view of people showed noticeable alterations from that day.

Some penalties went with the rewards. I saw Negroes more accurately but I saw them unadorned with raiment which once I had found lovely. Their weaknesses became for me merely those of any people subjected to their history—their strengths likewise. They were separated from the blanket virtues, as well as from blanket faults, which I had attributed to them. "They" were no longer lovable. Only some were. There was nothing special about "them" any more. They had just the same old tedious faults and virtues that all the rest of us have.

My relationship with them was realistic—and shorn of magic. Gone was the distinctive flavor which had made it fun just to be with them; gone the mysterious magnet which had drawn my heart toward the whole group. Once sight of a Negro either in the distance or near at hand—any Negro or any number of them—had made me feel tender and flowing, as the sight of any child does to some people.

In one sense, the wall in me which had separated us was a garden wall. I had looked over it to them as a child might look over a stone wall into a forbidden garden of some mysterious neighbor. In that other garden he sees more beauty and lure than in his own. He may long to be rid of the wall, but if it is removed, mystery and lure will go, too. The garden now runs right into his own. He misses the dramatic reaches of good and evil which his mind had found in the forbidden garden. The witch and the fairy who had lived there are really just a sick old woman and her pretty granddaughter—and where is the fun in that?

Just so, my heart had lost the garden that my feet had gained.

The importance of a lost romantic vision should not be underestimated. In such a vision is power as well as joy. In it is meaning. Life is flat, barren, zestless, if one can find one's lost vision nowhere.

Most of us realize the loss we all sustained when the wall went down between men and women. Our discovery with the aid of science that psychological differences between men and women are not as great as they were once thought to be represents a fact, a truth, which we would not consent to replace with old errors. It is not true that man is brave, strong, aggressive, just, objective, and so on, while woman has a set of different and complementary virtues, such as tenderness, humility, purity, compassion, patience. We all know that the most physically feminine woman is likely to come up with the "masculine" virtues if placed from childhood in circumstances which call for their cultivation, and the same is true of a man.

Yet wasn't there something sweetly wild and stirring in the belief that a great chasm of difference forever separated the sexes, bridged only by wide reaches of the soul? How satisfying to be able to look up to members of the other sex for heightened merit in areas where you believed you could claim little. Your heart went out and up to them because they could supply so much that you lacked, and still you knew that you could fully repay them because you, too, as their other half, had much to give. The whole relationship was one of exchange on many levels in which each completed the other and in doing so gave and received joy.

Facts are facts, and as we learn them we creep nearer to a larger truth, so we can't wisely regret having learned how little different men and women are. Yet we want to think of the other sex in these special ways. We are not complete without chasms across which we can soar only on wings of love and worship. We need the distant as well as the close at hand, the mysterious as well as the familiar, the mountain as well as our level front yard.

So I lost magic and found wholeness when my inner wall went down. I lost the Negro race and found the human race. I was sad but I was healthy. I was willing and anxious to go on from there.

My understanding of what I had gained was much clearer than of what I had lost. I only very vaguely grasped at this time how great and varied is the unconscious exploitation of Negroes by Southern whites. For not only have we exploited them physically and economically to bring ease to our bodies and our purses, but also we have exploited them emotionally to bring us many sublimated satisfactions. Our relationship with Negroes is a many-stringed instrument upon which we play melodies to replenish all the empty places in our hearts.

Or you might call our relationship with Negroes a gigantic psychodrama, in which we act out satisfactions for all our basic drives. Whites who live in realms far above carnal exploitation, nevertheless play a sublimated sex role in the "complementary exchange" with Negroes—which in our imagination is mutually satisfying, because satisfying to us.

The parent-child relationship is almost consciously acted out, with the obedience, seeming respect, and acceptance by "our Nigras" going far toward soothing heartaches for the rebellion, arrogance, and rejection we must endure as our real children seize their own lives from us in adolescence. Even the reverse, the child-parent role, is sometimes filled, as we play the part of babyhood helplessness, satisfying immature longings to be waited on and taken care of.

Finally, we constantly act out the role of the noble-hearted, with a minimum cost in sacrifice and moral effort.

But my need to keep as much of the Southern Dream as I could made me skirt any such analysis as I've just made. To sustain what was left of the Dream, I had to search constantly for the most golden motive I possibly could squeeze between the facts of everybody's known conduct.

In carrying on my crusade to bring the Dream fully into fruition, my primary job among whites was, I thought, to help each realize that he wasn't an isolated, helpless liberal, but a member of a great, silent fellowship of good will. My secondary job was to educate them concerning the modern Negro's character and needs.

In addressing Negroes my primary job was to make them see how we really felt about them, and my secondary job was to give them whatever aid and moral support they appeared to need.

In my efforts to do my primary job with Negroes my motives were even more misunderstood than I realized at the time. In all my articles and speeches addressed to them I stressed assurances (1) that they were not abhorred or regarded with contempt to the extent they thought, and (2) that far from being singled out for such treatment, they were only one of many victims of a universal human yearning to feel superior.

My purpose in this was clean-cut and single: I was trying to increase their sense of belonging, to undermine their unconscious fear that just maybe the loud-voiced segregationists were right in their accusations of inferiority. But with hardly any exceptions, they interpreted my words as efforts to defend whites and—worse!—to belittle their own problems and burdens.

A large part of the misunderstanding certainly can be laid at the broad door of semantics, for many words, phrases, and concepts still had strictly white Southern overtones for me, far different from those they had for Negroes. But undoubtedly, too, an important part was played by the Negro's psychological stake in believing the worst of whites. My more convincing points sometimes created real fear, I now feel sure—for many Negro leaders felt that belief in the good will of whites would reduce their own striking power in the fight for freedom from the white man's rule.

My task would have been easier had I not begun it several years before the Montgomery bus strike and Martin Luther King's historic appeal to Negro intellectuals and simple folk alike to love their enemies, since in this lay both their own spiritual salvation *and their best weapon.*

Until Dr. King marshaled and dramatized the irresistible forces of brotherly love, the trend among thinking Negroes—at least those I knew—was to identify loving the white man with Uncle-Tomism. Uncle Tom, of course, was the chief character in *Uncle Tom's Cabin.*

He symbolizes the "good Nigra" who is loyal to his "masters" and thinks it his duty to bear, rather than to combat, oppression. Uncle Toms are about as popular with the new Negro as good, loyal Tories were with American Revolutionaries.

This comparison of Negroes with the Fathers of America is no casual analogy. In Gregory Swanson first, in T. J. Sellers especially, but also in almost every educated Negro I contacted, I was confronted with a Jeffersonian grasp of the American ideal of liberty, justice, and equality for all which made me feel like a visiting tourist talking to a native citizen who is proud of his land.

In the past, references to "our founders," "our great freedoms," "American democracy," "the great ideals of this nation," and so on, had reached me simply as clichés, reeled off by the yard in political speeches in election years. When small, I had learned our important historic documents by rote, and in daily conversation since, it was rare that anybody in my circle said anything about our form of government except to complain about its wastefulness in action or about how much it had gone down hill since the wrong political party had been in power, or how hopeless it was for the right party to try to get the mess left by the wrong one straightened out in one short administration.

But Negro leaders talked often about our founding fathers, our ideals, and our democratic principles, and although they used the same familiar phrases, these were comparable to what I was used to hearing in the same way that a man is comparable to a figure in a wax museum. I came alive inside with the realization that in the Negro's mouth these phrases were not clichés or excess verbiage, but straightforward expressions of vibrant, living truths. Breathlessly I listened and felt rising in me an undreamed of response to, and understanding of, what our nation is supposed to be.

In the fall of 1951, when I attended my first Virginia State Conference of the National Association for the Advancement of Colored People, I was confronted with a virile idealism, an awareness of what man must have for manliness, dignity, and inner liberty which, by contrast, made me see how easy living had made my own group into childishly unthinking people. The Negro's struggles and despairs have been like fertilizer in the fields of his humanity, while we, like protected children with all our basic needs supplied, have given our attention to superficialities.

The average white American of today never thinks about the innate dignity of man because he has never had his dignity challenged. He probably has never known even one man who has. Since such a thing is outside his experience, it cannot be for him a living issue.

Against the unmolded clay of my inner American citizenship, I now felt the impress of those for whom the dignity of man was a vital truth. It was the same with the principles of freedom, equality, and the right to chosen pursuits. I had never been aware of the rich nature of these fulfillments, because my experience had never included a lack of them.

I think it was during a speech by the Rev. Francis L. Griffin[2] of Farmville, Virginia, that I suddenly saw how the situation of Southern Negroes in many important ways resembles that of white Americans before the Revolution. England oppressed and discriminated against us in some instances much as whites now oppress and discriminate against Negroes. And the result has been the same—a fierce awareness of the dignity of man, of the rights of every individual, and a certainty that brotherhood is the destiny of the human race.

It was this awareness, born of oppression and hardship, which gave to Jeffersonian Americans the spiritual brawn which made our nation great. But it has grown weak among us. As our memory of oppression faded, the awareness faded, too. Only in our minorities, oppressed as our colonies were once oppressed, does it still have the powerful thrust which originally drove its expression into our constitution. Our minorities alone are in a position to know what the fathers of our democracy were talking about.

I looked at the dark, intent faces around me, and I heard old phrases made new because they were understood, believed, and lived by. Here was an America more real, more alive, more lovable, than the country I had always vaguely and complacently called my own.

---

[1] Sarah Patton Boyle, "Jeffersonian Americans," in *The Desegregated Heart: A Virginian's Stand in Time of Transition* (Charlottesville: University of Virginia Press, 2001): 167-75.

[2] The perceptive Negro minister in Prince Edward County whose parishioners were the plaintiffs in the original suit against segregated public schools which resulted in the historic Supreme Court decision of 1954 outlawing segregation in public schools.

ELIZABETH "RACHEL" HOSMER, OSH

(1908-1988)

Elizabeth **"Rachel" Hosmer, OSH (1908-1988)**[1], religious, priest, and founding member of the Order of Saint Helena, was born in Everett, Massachusetts, of a New England family. Her father was an unbeliever and her mother an Episcopalian. Though neither parent was a churchgoer, they chose to have their daughter christened in the Unitarian Church. Elizabeth Hosmer was exposed to Christianity through the Girl Scouts and a revival she attended with friends. On the last night of the revival the preacher asked for those who just accepted Jesus as their Lord and Savior to stand. Elizabeth Hosmer stood.[2] She returned home and told her mother that she wanted to attend church, and eventually made her way to St . John's Mission in Sharon, Massachusetts one Easter morning. At the age of sixteen she was confirmed in the Episcopal Church.[3]

Sister Rachel was a brilliant woman. She had a diverse academic background that included study in English literature, history, philosophy, and ancient languages. A gifted artist, she attended St. Mary's School in Peekskill, New York, where she received individual classes in painting and drawing. She also followed her passion "to be a great painter," at Smith College and the Boston Museum of Fine Arts. She later completed her degree at Boston University.

Rachel Hosmer lived out her call to the religious life through a rich and diverse ministry. She lived among various religious communities and deeply appreciated their distinctive vocations. Originally, she made her Life Profession in the Order of Saint Anne in 1935; from 1934 to 1939 she was principal of Margaret Hall, the order's school in Versailles, Kentucky. During these years she, along with some of her sisters, began to feel a call to live a more monastic form of the religious life. With the support of Alan Whittemore of the Order of the Holy Cross, the sisters in Versailles—until then an autonomous house in the Order of Saint Anne—formed the Order of Saint Helena in 1945. Rachel Hosmer became sister-in-charge.[4]

After her retirement as principal of Margaret Hall, Rachel Hosmer returned to the Convent of Saint Helena, Vails Gate, New York, and lived a semi-enclosed contemplative life. She then spent three years at Holy Cross Mission in Bilahun, Libera, West Africa. Sister Rachel was novice mistress at Vails Gate from 1965-1966, resumed graduate study, and returned to West Africa as principal of the Bishop Freguson High School in Cape Palmas, Libera.

In 1972, Rachel Hosmer began her active ministry in New York City. She established residence in the order's house there, taught at the Baptist Education Center in Harlem, and began her long association with the General Seminary. In 1976 she received the degree of Master of Sacred Theology from seminary, where she also served as associate director of the Center for Christian Spirituality, tutor, assistant professor of ascetical theology, and adjunct faculty. She was ordained to the diaconate in 1975 and priest in 1977. She received a D.D. from the General Seminary in 1978, and her second D.D. from Seabury-Western in 1984. She died in New York City in 1988 and is buried at the motherhouse of the Order of St. Helena in Vail's Gate, New York.

Throughout her long ministry, Rachel Hosmer, OSH, was a popular retreat leader, spiritual director, teacher, writer and lecturer. She was active in civil disobedience and the peace movement. Besides her autobiography, *My Life Remembered*, published posthumously in 1988, she wrote *Living in the Sprit* (1977) with Alan Jones, a volume in *The Church's Teaching Series*. Her book *Gender and God* was published in 1996.

In the following excerpt from *My Life Remembered*, Rachel Hosmer,

OSH shares some of her early reflections on her vocation and the three years she served at Bolahun, Liberia, West Africa.

NOTES

[1] Biographical information on Rachel Hosmer, OSH, was provided by Sister Ruth, OSH and drawn from the biography that her order has on file. Also see, Rachel Hosmer, *My Life Remembered* (Cambridge: Cowley Publications, 1991), 1-15.

[2] Hosmer, 13.

[3] Hosmer, 13-15.

[4] Hosmer, 38-43.

❦

ELIZABETH "RACHEL" HOSMER, OSH
Excerpts From My Life Remembered*

As I think about my growing sense of vocation in the religious life during that time, my mind goes back to my first impressions of women religious whom I met—first, to Sr. Martha of the Order of St. Anne with whom I once went shopping to buy those dreadful raspberry jam-filled doughnuts called "bismarcks," much enjoyed by Mother Louise. I caught a glimpse of Sr. Martha's face in repose, sunlit, framed by her starched white Second Order veil. She seemed to me to be transfigured, a beautiful image of peace and wholeness.

[...]

Then there were the Sisters of St. Mary, whom I met, of course, at St. Mary's School. I already had a bond of loyalty to the Order of St. Anne because I had become an Associate before I went away to school, and perhaps this kept me from fully appreciating the very different spirituality of the Sisters of St. Mary. At school the Sister Superior, who was also the principal, and our own corridor sisters took strict care of us. One I loved especially was Sr. Mary Vincent, "Little Sister" as she was called. She was gentle and understood us and our pranks enough not to resort constantly to punishments. Sr. Mary Antony, the Sister Superior, was impressive, with her dark eyes and an almost coquettish manner along with a certain imperial quality. I can see her yet, bowing to each girl separately as we entered the refectory for dinner each night, each of us bowing in return. Her look was penetrating and her command of the school almost complete.

There were, however, ways of getting around the rules, even the honor rules. For instance, tightly fitted blouses were not allowed, but we used to pin our middies tightly around ourselves on one side only because we knew Sr. Mary Christine would stand on the other side of the line to inspect us as we filed into the refectory each day!

Our corridor sister, Sr. Dominica, took us very seriously and managed to put everything, including contraband and untidy rooms, into a theological perspective. I enjoyed debating it with her. I respected these women and had a sense of the depth of their vocation and their faithfulness, but I never felt drawn to join the Community of St. Mary. Nor did I commit myself to anything after graduating from St. Mary's School beyond a year of college before going to art school. Those years at Smith and the Boston Museum School of Fine Arts were, for me, experimental and marked by inner conflict about my future.

I am not sure quite how my monastic vocation revealed itself. I came to know the Sisters of St. Anne in Boston at Bowdoin Street through my discovery of the Church of St. John the Evangelist during my rambles around the city while still at the Girls' Latin School. My confessor was at that church and encouraged me. Little by little it became clearer and dearer that none of the other things I had tried were really what God was calling me to do. So I burst upon my family the astonishing news that entering the Order of St. Anne was what I wanted to do. It was one of the most terrible experiences of my whole life, because they were utterly shattered. My father felt that I was rejecting all that he had ever done for me, and one of my deep regrets is that I was never able to let him know how much I appreciated all that he did. My mother was heartbroken; like him she wanted to give me the best things in life and could see no sense at all in this crazy idea. I think she clung to the hope that I would not persevere with it.

In the end, in spite of everything, I packed a little bag one August day in 1928 and went to Boston to begin my novitiate at the Convent of St. Anne on Temple Street. My father was totally unable to accept it, disinherited me, and never saw me again, but my mother stayed with me. However much pain it gave her, she saw me through. Until my life profession she hoped and argued with me whenever she could to come home and come out, but after that she never tried again. She expected me to take my obligation as seriously as she herself had done in her marriage vows. And so I entered my life as a member of the Order of St. Anne.

[...]

I was duly made a postulant, clothed as a novice, and given the name Rachel. I would have kept my own baptismal name, but since there already was a Sr. Elizabeth in the order, I was required to change it. I rejected a little list of fancy names offered me by the Father Founder, Fr. Powell, SSJE. Marie Antoinette was one of them! Another was Paula Penelope. I took Rachel because it was from the Old Testament, it was short and simple, and sounded down-to-earth.

There were about twelve or fifteen of us in the old house on Temple Street, located near the West End section of Boston where really poor people lived. For me there was a special lure in the idea of poverty. I began to take my share in the work of the convent, including learning to set type. At the back of the Temple Street house there was a printing press on which we published *Gems*, our little quarterly, along with a few other things.

I also learned to cook just a little, and every Saturday night I took part in our weekly expedition to the Boston Market. We carried baskets with us and stood silently at each barrow just before the market closed, hoping for handouts of what was left over. We always brought home enough for our needs and for the soup kitchens and the feeding programs of the Church of St. John the Evangelist. It was during the Depression years, and we tried to reach out to the poor and hungry in our neighborhood. I had never before seen poverty like that and had never experienced want.

I was quite happy doing all of that; at the same time I was able to carry on my interest in Latin. In 1930, two years after entering the convent,

I was sent back to school, to Boston University, for my sophomore year of study in ancient languages. As I walked to school through the Common, I saw men wrapped in newspapers who had slept on the benches all night. I was deeply moved by this and thought guiltily, "I've been called to poverty, but I have a nice clean, warm bed.

[...]

Soon after my arrival, I was assigned, perhaps because it was the only useful thing I could do at that point, the job of watching beside the body of a baby who died a few hours after her birth and baptism. As I watched and prayed there, keeping the children and dogs away, I began to feel a little sense of doing *something* within the life of Africa and the life of the mission, a sense of the fullness of God's special presence there with some of his very poorest children. Eventually I did become more knowing about African ways, more mannerly according to their customs, but I never forgot those early months, when all my taken-for-granted status vanished and left me naked: "Who is she, this white woman, and what can she do?"

Taking over proved to be a large order. We helped at the hospital and shared in "God palaver"—that is, teaching religion to illiterate adults. The Sisters of the Holy Name had organized this "God palaver" for the two language groups, Bandi and Kisi. They had compiled a Bandi word list, collected a library, organized much of the evangelistic work in the surrounding area, going on treks into the bush with the Holy Cross Fathers. Sr. Hilary had put in years of skilled and devoted work in the hospital. Sr. Mary Prisca, who remained with us a few months to help us in the takeover, was in charge of the girls' boarding compound. Her knowledge of the inner workings of the mission was extensive. She knew everyone's name, of course, and also all of their families and their family history. She was also very conversant with African customs.

It is not surprising that when we first landed in Bolahun, the Africans expected us to be equally competent; we were compared to our predecessors and found wanting. The English sisters did it all so much better! It was painful and humiliating for us, and it took a long time to live through, but eventually we began to learn both how to do our own work along traditional ways and how to bring our own special experience and insight to the work. Since Sr. Mary Michael had already had two years of experience in Bolahun as a missionary, she was not as green as we were. When Sr. Frances and I arrived, she had already begun to make some changes. One dramatic change had to do with laundry. The sisters had been responsible for the priests' laundry for years. They brought their great bundles down from the monastery—sheets and habits and all the linen—to be washed by the women from the town and hung out on our back porch in the dry season and in the attic in the rainy season. The men tended to be late about all this, holding up the whole process and keeping us from going about our appointed business. One day Sr. Mary Michael laid down the law: "The next time you bring the laundry late, it isn't going to get done." The inevitable happened, and we transferred the laundry from our shoulders to theirs!

Sr. Mary Michael also began to modify the systems of control over the life of African Christians. No longer did a nun sit at the back of the church on Sunday to take roll call, and no longer was there a system of rewards—in the form of gifts of clothing—for those adult Christians whose church attendance and marital situations met the missionary standards. Another custom that tended to separate us from the townspeople was the requirement that anyone wishing to see the sisters was not allowed to approach the convent building, but had to stop at a small "palaver house" at the edge of the convent grounds and ring the bell. Someone would go out to speak with them there. Instead, we began inviting the Africans who worked with us at the mission and could speak some English to come onto the front porch and to share afternoon tea with us there. Eventually, when Fr. Connor Lynn became prior, the mission adopted two further customs intended to change our relationship with the Africans to one of more equality and mutual respect. He "put a law" that no mission party should include one race only, and he also instituted a common breakfast party after Sunday Eucharist for all who wanted to come. The convent, the monastery, and the missionary families took turns hosting this breakfast. Slowly the reforms were accepted, and eventually the contributions of the Americans began to receive some tentative approval.

[...]

One of the most abiding memories of my time in Bolahun has to do with the assassination of President John F. Kennedy. Shortly before I was due to go home on furlough, I was down in the girls' boarding compound one evening in their dining room where they had pushed back the tables and benches and were dancing to a victrola. A messenger came to me from the monastery to tell me that the President had been shot and killed, and the Governor of Texas had also been shot. I spun around to face the blackboard, then turned off the victrola, and slowly turned back to face the girls. I repeated the message I had been given: "My president has been killed. Will you come to the chapel with me and pray?"

We went silently into the chapel, an open structure with a thatched roof and parapet, and knelt down on the mats. The children crowded around me quietly, pressing their bodies against mine to give comfort and support. I felt so much at one with them, as I was aware of their grief for me. It was only later that I learned that they too felt grief over that assassination. As I was leaving the mission for furlough soon after, one of the young teachers said to me, "Sister, we think he died for us," and pointed out that for the first time in history, African flags were lowered as a sign of respect for a white man.

After we had prayed, I rose and started up the hill to the convent. I looked back in time to see the head girl throw back her head and start the wailing; it went on and on. The next day I suppose everybody, certainly everybody of importance in the village, came to say *"Bene ho,"* the Bandi words used for catastrophes great and small, for the stubbing of a toe, for the death of a mother. It means "Never mind," or "Cease to be upset," or "Be comforted," or "I am sorry."

Three days later, when I went down to the girls' boarding compound again to do my usual job of calling the roll, the head girl interrupted me. She asked, "Sister, is your president dead?" I said, "Yes, Rosina, my president is dead." "Is he buried?" she asked. "Yes," I said, "he's buried." She asked me a third time, "Is he buried in the earth?" I said, "Yes, Rosina, he's buried in the earth." Then she said, "Then you must not grieve." This was her way of calling me back for the whole school community. It is customary among the Bandi people that when, for instance, a woman is bereaved, she may go back to her own people to grieve, but when the time of grieving is ended, somebody is sent from her village to call her to return. Grieving is controlled by custom. It is provided for, and it is also limited. I found it very helpful to be called back to my girls on the compound.

After two and a half very happy years in Bolahun, I was recalled by my community to return to the mother house at Vail's Gate. It was a great blow. On my way out, my luggage in the truck, I said to the driver, "Don't take me past the school—I can't bear to see it again! Drive me through the hospital grounds." As we did that, I left Bolahun in tears. At my farewell banquet Chief Foday had mentioned something I had said to the teachers when I first arrived: "I've had a lot of experience in education, but I come from a different country, and I'm not sure how much help I can be to you. This is your country, these are your children, and I will not tell you what to do. We can talk about it." At the banquet, Chief Foday quoted this to me and added, "Now we know that she meant it." It was a wonderful send-off, a great help to recall it as I rode away from the school. They were sorry to see me go and, I think, resented it, but there was nothing anyone could do about it.

---

* Rachel Hosmer, *My Life Remembered* (Cambridge: Cowley, 1991): 18, 20-21, 59-61, 65-67. Permission for publication from the order St. Helena.

CYNTHIA CLARK WEDEL

(1908-1986)

Cynthia Clark Wedel (1908-1986),[1] ecumenical leader and the first woman to serve as president of the National Council of Churches, was born in Dearborn, Michigan in 1908. Wedel held a number of prestigious ecumenical appointments. From 1955-58 she was president of United Church Women, from 1965-1969 she was associate general secretary for Christian Union, her term as president of the National Council of Churches was from 1969-1975, and from 1975-1983 she was president of the World Council of Churches. In addition to these appointments, during the first half of the 1960s, Cynthia Clark Wedel was an official observer at the Second Vatican Council, and was appointed by President John F. Kennedy to the Commission on the Status of Women.

Cynthia Clark Wedel earned bachelor's and master's degrees from Northwestern University. From 1931 to 1934 she served as director of Christian education at St. Luke's, Evanston. She went to New York to serve as a field worker in 1934 and became the director of youth work at the National Council of the Episcopal Church a year later.

In 1939, Cynthia married Theodore O. Wedel, then director of the Episcopal College Division. The couple left New York shortly after their marriage for Washington, D.C. when Theodore Wedel was appointed warden of the College of Preachers. Cynthia Wedel immersed herself in civic affairs and innumerable social welfare organizations in Washington, D.C., and taught religion at the National Cathedral School for Girls, 1939-1948. Her career of service to the Episcopal Church continued with stints on the national board of the Women's Auxiliary, 1946-1952, and as a member of the National Council, 1955-1962. She completed a doctorate in psychology from George Washington University in 1957 and was a lecturer at American University.

During her tenure as president of the National Council of Churches, Cynthia Clark Wedel was a consistent voice for justice and peace. She spoke out against violence, the death penalty, racism, and was a staunch advocate for church unity. As a national and international church leader, she brought creative leadership, dynamic intelligence and prophetic insight to all her work. Throughout her ministry, Cynthia Clark Wedel encouraged church leaders to think critically about their faith and the place of religion in the modern world: "Every church has within its leadership and membership many people who act and talk as though God is dead. They are the ones who look constantly back to some good old days when God was in charge, people knew their place, stayed in it, and behaved properly....Those of us who really care about our faith and the Church have a tremendous responsibility to think critically about our own faith, our belief in God, and our reaction to the present world and to share this with others."[2]

The Wedels retired in 1969. In retirement, Cynthia Clark Wedel preached and lectured widely, and continued to write for national publications. In 1978, Wedel became the first woman to speak from the floor of a Lambeth Conference. She was a member of the Church of the Resurrection, Alexandria, Virginia until her death in 1986.

The following document is a sermon delivered by Cynthia Clark Wedel in the National Cathedral in 1971, during her term as president of the National Conference of Churches in 1971, at the YWCA event, "Come Alive to Combat Racism."

NOTES

[1] Biographical information on Cynthia Wedel from "Cynthia Wedel Loses Fight With Cancer," September 4, 1986, Diocesan Press Service.

[2] Cynthia Clark Wedel, "The Challenge of the Church and its Educational Resources," Lecture given at Notre Dame University, June 22, 1979.

❧

CYNTHIA CLARK WEDEL
A God For All People*

It seems appropriate, in this great house of prayer, to center our thoughts on the God to whose glory it is being built. For our text I would like to use some familiar phrases from the very first chapter in the Bible—the beginning of the Book of Genesis. "In the beginning God...";—then the account of the creation events with the repeated refrain, "And God saw that it was good"; and finally the climax of the creation story—"God created man in his own image—male and female he created them."

In an age like ours of great scientific and technological development, there is a real danger that many people will jump to the conclusion that we no longer need God. Man seems to be conquering nature and learning to bend the laws of the universe to serve human ends. Even Bonhoeffer's striking phrase: "Man come of age" has been misunderstood to mean that man has outgrown God. Yet nothing could be farther from the truth. As society becomes more global and more interdependent, problems of relationships between nations, races, and individuals increase. In a simpler era when most of us had to deal only with people very much like ourselves, it was possible to have relatively simple rules and codes which governed our dealings with one another. This is no longer true. It is far more important in our kind of a world that we develop a coherent philosophy—a sense of meaning in the universe and in our own lives—which can guide us through the perplexing changes we have to face.

I don't intend to take time here to present arguments for the existence of God. Since I find it quite impossible to believe that this complex universe, and we creative, free human beings, all just happened by chance, I have to believe in a power beyond us—and to me the Christian God is the one which makes the most sense.

And if we believe in God as the beginning—the creator and ongoing ruler of the universe—we need to look at what is happening to our world today in the light of that belief. God is still there. There is no evidence that He is dead, or that He has resigned. Therefore, He must be in the midst of all this change and turmoil. Our task is not to keep looking backward to some mythical "good old days" when God was active; but rather to try to discern his hand in what is going on today.

And what is going on is, of course, radical and wide-spread change—so radical that we can call it revolution. We see it in the new nations of the world demanding a share in the power and wealth of the world. We see it in the economic revolution being demanded by the poor; the social and political revolution being demanded by oppressed peoples everywhere; the educational revolution being demanded by the young; and in the domestic revolution being called for by the women's liberation movement.

For many of our friends—if not for us—this is very threatening, and very hard to understand. The majority of us here today are middle-class Americans. Few of us are wealthy. Many of us probably think of ourselves as poor when we look at some others whom we know. The first thing we need to do is to become *really* aware of the fact that we are part of a very, very small group of the most privileged people who have ever lived. Very few of us have known real poverty. Very few of us have had to face starvation. Very few of us have had to watch our children die of malnutrition. Few of us have had to live all our lives with no comforts, no conveniences, no medical care, no education.

But almost 90 percent of the people of this earth have always suffered all these things—and are doing so today. Do you for one moment believe that the God who created the world and "saw that it was good" intended this? Can you imagine that he meant the "goodness" just for a very small number of his children? I cannot guess why He has allowed these conditions to exist for so long. The only explanation I can find is that God does not measure time as we do—so maybe in the light of eternity it doesn't seem so long!

But it seems pretty obvious that God has now decided that the time has come for all people to share in the riches of the good earth. He has, in recent years, allowed men to discover many of the secrets of his universe which he had long kept hidden. From this has come modern science and technology; the productivity of our day; new forms of transportation and communication; fascinating new knowledge about man himself and his potential for growth. God himself is right in the midst of change. God is the author of the revolution of our day.

Let's not get "up-tight" about the word revolution. Fear-mongers like to imply that it has to be violent. But revolution is actually just another word for change—a turning around. The trouble comes not from those seeking change but from the entrenched and privileged who fear any change. When they fail to read the signs of the times—signs which God himself may be raising—and when they refuse, often with contempt and disdain, to listen to the cries for help from the oppressed, they often force the oppressed to take overt action to call attention to their plight. If this is a demonstration, or a strike, or a "sit-in," it is often met by the force which only those in power can assert.

And violence can, indeed, erupt. But I think it is safe to say that most oppressed groups only resort to violence when they have tried many other forms of protest—or when violence has been used against them.

These are hard things to say, but the situation today is too critical for us not to try to be honest. And one other thing needs to be said. This is that uprisings of the oppressed only come when there is some "hope" in the world. When repression is complete, the response is despair, hopelessness and apathy. It is the hope that things can be better that makes it possible for change to come.

If we who are among the privileged and the powerful can realize first the fact that God is in the changes of our time, and secondly that they are signs of hope, perhaps we can begin to be less anxious, less fearful, and can begin to look for the ways in which we can work together with God to make this more nearly the kind of a world He wants it to be.

I believe that this is what we in the YWCA are trying to do—and we have a lot going for us. A first need is for growing world fellowship—really getting to know people of other lands, other cultures. God obviously likes variety. There is no reason to imagine that he wants any nation, or race, or society to make everyone over into its image. We need to remember that he is the God of and for all people—every human being is the image of God. It is, therefore, blasphemy not to respect the rich variety of images—in persons, cultures, political and ideological differences. Our world fellowship, in the YWCA is doing this—but it needs to be vastly expanded. We who have so much must go much farther than we have in sharing with our sisters around the world.

Through modern technology the world has suddenly become very small. Just a generation or two ago, few people could know those of other nations and cultures. The world beyond one's own town was vast and unknown. Events in far-away places were heard of only months after they happened. Today, a celebration or a disaster half a world away appears, in living color, in our living rooms as it happens. We in the YWCA have been ahead of many in our world wide contacts and friendships. We now have a responsibility to help others catch up. And our basic motivation can be that God has certainly always intended all of his human children to be brothers and sisters, children of one father. For the first time in human history there is a possibility today of a world of brotherhood, mutual caring, and peace. And you and I are the lucky ones who can help make this possible.

A second urgent need of today is new patterns of human relationships. For far too long, people have assumed that only a small number had the qualities of leadership—power, ability, education and wealth. We took it for granted that a few made the decisions and everyone else stayed in his place and did as he was told. This was the way it had always been in government, education, business, the Church. We even sanctified such arrangements with phrases like "the divine right of kings."

But many things are changing this aspect of life. New discoveries of the latent abilities which many people never use; increased education; growing knowledge of how other people live are causing many to question why some people should make decisions for others. Are we not all "made in the image of God?" This is undoubtedly what our founding fathers meant when they said it was "self-evident" that all men are created equal. And so, today, oppressed groups of every sort—those living under colonial rule (including the citizens of the District of Columbia); the poor; the black, brown and yellow races; the young; the female, are rising up to demand the right to determine their own destinies, to make their own decisions. And doesn't it seem to you that this is what God wanted all the time? It is not to replace one dominant group with another—but to let all share in the decision-making. That some group must be on top is a false assumption. When I talk about women's liberation, someone often says "Oh, so you want women to run the world, do you?" I don't want women to run the world—nor do I want men to do so. I want us to work together to make a better world.

We have lived so long in a world of scarcity with not enough food or shelter or medical care or opportunity to go around, that we have come to accept competition as an innate part of human nature. But today we have the know-how to produce enough so that everyone could have a decent life. It is no longer necessary to put others down that we may keep what we have. The crying need today is to unlearn competition and learn how to cooperate to produce and to distribute the goods and services which are needed.

Again, it seems obvious that this is what God would want. All the uprisings and demands of today are signs that more and more people really have hope that the world can be a better place. There have been times in the past which all of us can agree were great periods—turning points in history—giant steps forward for mankind. The renaissance, the reformation, the industrial revolution, the political revolutions of the end of [the] late 18th Century are among these. We look back on them as wonderful times. God seemed to be very active—moving his creation toward the goals he had for it. Yet I suspect that people who lived in those times found them very upsetting. They probably said, "What is the world coming to? All the old certainties are being destroyed."

I hope you share my conviction that you and I are living in such a time. A hundred, or five hundred, years from now people will be saying, "Wouldn't it have been wonderful to have been alive in the last third of the twentieth century, when so many great and good things came to pass." As we sense God's good purposes—pulling and pushing us toward a world of understanding, peace, human dignity and opportunity, let us make our faith in him and our trust in his plans evident. Let it show in our openness to change, our ever-widening relationships, and our inconquerable conviction that the God in whom we believe is, indeed, a God for *all* people.

---

* Preached at the YWCA World Fellowship Observance, Washington Cathedral, November 14, 1971. The annual YWCA event was on the theme "Come Alive to Combat Racism."

EMILY GARDINER NEAL

(1910-1989)

Emily Gardiner Neal (1910-1989)[1] leader of the healing ministry in the Episcopal Church, deacon, journalist, was born to an affluent family in New York in 1910; neither of her parents were believers. She was a trained concert violinist and studied at Brearly School, Santa Barbara School for Girls, and David Mannes College of Music. She married Alvin Neal, a graduate of the United States Naval Academy, in a Park Avenue church, "because it was the socially acceptable thing to do."[2] Alvin Neal later became an executive for Gulf Oil Corporation, and the couple had two daughters. During these years, Emily Gardiner Neal had a successful career as a free-lance journalist, publishing over fifty articles in popular magazines such as *Look, McCalls,* and *Redbook.* "Who needed or wanted God? Only the poor, the suffering, the weak, and we weren't any of these. And then I inadvertently attended a healing service ....my life was to be forever changed," she wrote.[3]

Emily Gardiner Neal began to study the phenomenon of healing with the tenacity and skepticism of a reporter. "My faith came not as a sudden and dramatic conversion," she wrote, "but by means of a rather torturously-arrived-at intellectual conviction."[4] In 1956 she published her first book on the subject, *A Reporter Finds God Through Spiritual Healing.* In 1961, Neal was appointed to the Episcopal Church's Joint Commission on the Ministry of Healing. She wrote the commission's report to the 1964 General Convention; the document remains the official position of the Episcopal Church on the ministry of healing.

During the early years of her ministry, Neal worked closely with the founders of the Order of St. Luke, John Gaynor Banks and Ethel Banks. She participated in healing services at Calvary Episcopal Church, Pittsburgh, before joining the staff of St. Thomas Episcopal Church, Terrace Park, Ohio in 1976. For the nearly 30 years, Emily Gardiner Neal served as an international leader of healing missions; she also counseled and lectured widely. Neal supported ecumenical healing ministries. She became a member of the Third Order of St. Francis, and was ordained deacon at Trinity Cathedral in the Diocese of Pittsburgh in 1978.

Emily Gardiner Neal resisted the label of "healer" in reference to herself, rather "she saw herself simply as an instrument that is used for *God's* healing purposes." Neal more readily accepted the definition of her ministry as that of an "enabler of healing," thereby making no claim to divine powering relation to herself.[5]

The Episcopal Healing Ministry Foundation was founded in 1987 in honor of Emily Gardiner Neal, and she served as its first president. The foundation encourages healing ministry in parishes and recommends the teaching and training of clergy to conduct the ministry from a sound historical and theological basis. Neal's later works include *The Healing Ministry: A Personal Journey* (1982), and the posthumous *Celebration of Healing* (1992). In the later years of her life Neal lived at the Convent of the Transfiguration in Glendale, Ohio, where she was an associate of the community, attending the Eucharist daily and counseling and leading a weekly healing service. (Her husband died in 1961). She died in 1989.

The following document from *The Healing Power of Christ* (1972), relates the story of one of Emily Gardiner Neal's healing missions.

NOTES

[1] The main biographical source is Emily Gardiner Neal, *The Reluctant Healer: One Woman's Journey of Faith* (Colorado Springs: Shaw, 1992). Biographical information also provided by Jean S. Kinmonth and The Episcopal Healing Ministry Foundation, Christ Church Cathedral, 318 East Fourth Street, Cincinnati, Ohio 45202; episcopalhealing @att.net or www.episcopalhealing.org. The foundation offers a number of publications related to and by Emily Gardiner Neal and the ministry of healing in the Episcopal Church.

[2] Emily Gardiner Neal, *The Healing Power of Christ* (New York: Hawthorn Books, 1972): 9.

[3] Ibid.

[4] Neal, The Reluctant Healer, 36-37.

[5] Ibid, 8-9.

EMILY GARDINER NEAL
Excerpt From The Healing Power of Christ:*
The Long Road Begins

Glancing at my watch, I noted that within half an hour the plane would be arriving at my destination—a city far from home—where I was to lead a three-day healing mission. The stewardess was serving coffee to the passengers, when the plane hit rough weather. I smiled to myself at the seemingly inevitable simultaneity of air pockets and coffee-serving. As the "Fasten Seat Belt" sign flashed on, I started to reach out for my cup but quickly changed my mind. The plane was pitching and plunging too much to risk a shower of hot coffee. The stewardess, undaunted, walked past me, struggling to keep her balance.

As the plane hit another air pocket I tightened my seat belt, and at that moment a small child, sitting a few seats in front of me, escaped from his parents and began to run up the aisle. The plane gave a lurch and the child started to fall. Instinctively I twisted quickly in my seat to catch him. That sudden movement of my body, confined as it was by the seat belt, wrenched my back in such searing pain that I thought I would faint.

At the time of the initial injury to my back, six months earlier, I had had to cancel one mission, fortunately the last of that season and the first I had ever had to cancel. It had been a difficult summer of lying flat on my back for weeks on end, but by the grace of God I was up and around once more, and had recently completed several missions. As I sat in my plane seat now in excruciating pain, I could only pray; "Lord, if I am to do this mission, You'll have to make it possible."

The plane landed, and with superhuman effort I got myself down the ramp, where I was met by the smiling rector of the mission church, who was full of plans for the mission which was to begin the next day. I said nothing about my back until we arrived at the hotel where I was to stay. Unable to get out of the car, I was forced to tell him what had happened.

I will long remember his kindness. Instead of being upset over the probable cancellation of the event planned two years before and widely publicized, his sole concern was for me. After a short prayer, he called a physician who, after a cursory examination, said that I must be hospitalized at once.

"But what about the mission?" I asked.

"Forget it," was the response. But this was an unrealistic order, for how could I "forget" it when I knew that busloads of people were arriving from far-distant points, that hundreds would be bitterly disappointed, and that there was no time to procure another missioner?

Early next morning while I was still groggy from Demerol, the physician and rector stopped by my hospital room. Before either could speak, I said, "I'll do the mission." The physician demurred but was understanding albeit skeptical.

"All right," he said, "if you think you can. But of course you'll have to return to the hospital immediately after each session. Have therapy as often as possible, and we'll try to keep you free from pain."

An hour before I was to leave for the church for the opening service that evening, three nurses came in to dress me. A back brace had been hastily fitted, and while one nurse was strapping me into it as I lay on the bed, another was pulling on my stockings. The third nurse stood by my head and said, "Mrs. Neal, please don't try it. You'll never make it."

I knew better than anyone that I could never make it on my own—but I also knew that I could "do all things through Christ which strengtheneth me" (Phil. 4; 13).

When I was finally dressed but still lying flat, the physician came in with a packet of pain pills. "Take one of these now," he said, "and carry the others with you. You can sneak one into your mouth as you take a sip of water from the pulpit,"

I refused the pills, afraid to take them lest they befuddle my mind, and the physician left the room.

To my surprise and joy, the nurses stood around my bed, and one of them said, "We'd like to pray for you before you go." Deeply grateful and greatly strengthened, I managed to get off the bed, and I was taken to the church.

As I stepped into the pulpit, the first person I saw was the kind physician, who had taken time off to come to the service; he was waiting to catch me if I fell. However, stronger hands than his were to hold me up that night.

The church was packed, and only the rector and I were to administer the laying on of hands. According to usual custom we divided the altar rail, he taking one half and I the other.

The line of people streaming up to receive the healing rite seemed endless. Each time I finished my section of the rail, I turned toward the altar with the silent prayer, "Lord, let Thy strength be made perfect in my weakness." Little did I know that night that this would be the burden of my prayer for years to come, as during mission after mission I could not under my own power stand on my feet.

By the time the last group came up to receive the laying on of hands, I had been standing for nearly four hours, and I could scarcely walk. Reaching down to hang on to the altar rail, I suddenly felt a firm hand under my left elbow and then an arm around my waist, which held me up straight and strong until the last supplicant had been ministered to. The service over, I slipped out the back door and into the waiting car which returned me to the hospital.

Next morning the rector telephoned and I thanked him for supporting me at the rail the night before. With some embarrassment I felt compelled to add, "I certainly needed your help last evening, as I was about to collapse, but tonight could you please get us more clergy to help with the laying on of hands? I managed last night because you held me up and I am grateful, but please don't do it again. It seems hardly suitable at a formal service to have you with your arm around me supporting me!"

There was a long silence at the other end of the telephone—and then, in a small voice, came his words: "Emily, I didn't touch you during that service. I was finished before you, and during the last fifteen minutes I was kneeling before the high altar."

Then I knew: Not only had Christ upheld me, He had quite literally held me up. And so it was to be in the years that lay ahead. At home I was unable to stand for the reading of a psalm, but during a mission I was on my feet for three or four hours at a time, solely in his strength.

During this mission there was a great outpouring of the Holy Spirit, and many healings were reported. The only obligation I could not fulfill was that of greeting people after the services. If the time between the various daytime sessions was short, the rector would take me to his study, where with the door locked I lay on the floor (my back needed a hard surface) until time for the next event. Again, little did I know that for months and years to come, I would have to rest on the floor of the clergyman's study in whose church the mission was being held. I am sure my record is unique in one respect at least: Never has anyone lain on the floors of so many pastors' studies!

I was in the hospital for some days after the mission, during which time several prayer-group members came to visit me. This was a surprise, as I was unaware that anyone other than the clergy knew I was there. As I look back now, it was actually these kind women who sowed the first seeds for this book. One said to me, "Why didn't you let us know your predicament so we could have been praying for you?" My only answer was the true one: It had never occurred to me to tell these people, and I could only wonder why it had not.

The love and concern of these prayer-group members, and the letters I received later, demonstrated once again how God can use any and everything for His glory. Typical of these letters was one which read: "I was miserably ill last week—and then I remembered your doing that mission in the strength of Christ. What an inspiration, as through you we saw the living Christ sustain and enable. Suddenly my own sickness seemed very trivial, and God healed me in record time."

[...]

So it was during this mission led from the hospital, and so it would be in all the missions to come for a long, long time. I thought often of St. Paul, and drew courage from his example.

There was not a day during these years that I did not expect and claim the miracle of physical healing in my own life. As time after time I received the healing rites, at a point at which I felt I could bear no more suffering, the pain would marvelously cease. I would be certain then that the healing had occurred—and so, for the moment, it had. But for reasons I did not know, I could not hold it. Within a short while, the pain would be back; but it was as if by each easement of the pain God was reassuring me of His mercy and love. As a result, I never for a single moment at any time felt abandoned by him, and I was more sure than ever before of His will to heal.

Nevertheless, there was so much I wanted to do in Christ's service which was now impossible that at times I felt almost overwhelmed by frustration. During one such time I was reading Scripture, and Elisha's words to Elijah leaped from the page: "I pray thee, let a double portion of thy spirit be upon me" (II Kings 2:9).

Closing my Bible, I pondered these words, puzzled why they should seem meaningful, since within the context of the passage in which they occurred there was certainly no possible personal application. Still wondering, I reopened the Bible at random, and my eyes fell upon the words, "They shall possess the double: everlasting joy shall be unto them" (Isa. 61:7).

Suddenly a great light shone: Impressed upon my heart was the conviction that the Lord rewards those who are afflicted, by a double portion of His Spirit. This, then, was the secret of the supernatural strength and grace which were mine, making the impossible possible. "I declare that I will render double unto thee" (Zech. 9:12). He has— and my gratitude, as my joy, is everlasting.

Through it all—the long hours spent in bed lying perfectly flat, unable to read because holding even a paperback book caused painful strain on the back; the months that ran into years during which I could be up only four hours at a time—I was to learn much by the teaching of the Spirit, much of prayer, and what it meant to be alone with God. And I was to learn that whatever *He* wanted me to do, He would make possible, and that which I thought I should be doing was often not at all necessary. That I have been able to continue to work and have never had to cancel a mission since that first hospitalization has been the continuing and marvelous evidence of the power of the Holy Spirit.

I was to learn what it was to be stripped of pride—so often, between connecting planes, I would be forced to lie down in airport waiting rooms, and on many occasions, on the floor of the airport's ladies' lounge.

I was to learn patience—and this in itself was a minor miracle, for by temperament I am impatient, hard-driving, hard-working, and filled with energy.

I was to learn a new compassion for all who suffer, for one who has not himself suffered cannot possibly fully comprehend it.

I was to learn experientially the validity of what I have so long taught: that when one is healed in spirit, the healing of the body is no longer of primary importance. Thus when people would say accusingly, "Why don't you ever speak of your back?" I could honestly reply, "Why should I? It's not that important."

[…]

During the fall of 1956, when my first book was published, I was invited to speak at the International Order of St. Luke Conference, a religious conference in Philadelphia, which was attended by numerous clergymen. I received many requests to speak on the healing ministry and began to accept them. As my children were young and at home, I refused to leave them overnight, and wherever I went I managed to fly home the same day on which I spoke. There was one exception to this: I received and accepted an invitation to lead a three-day mission at an Episcopal church in a far-distant state.

At that time I had no idea what a "mission" was; all I knew was that I was to give three addresses on successive nights. When I arrived I was informed that each evening address was to be followed by a healing service at which I was to administer the laying on of hands with the participating clergy. I demurred strongly, never before having laid on hands or prayed for the sick. However, my protests were in vain, and in fear and trembling, I did what I was told.

The rector of the church was a firm believer in the healing ministry, but his new assistant did not share his sentiments. The young priest made abundantly clear his disapproval of both the ministry of healing and of me, a woman, performing a sacramental rite.

At the end of the second healing service the rector knelt in moving humility to receive the laying on of hands from me. Under the circumstances, the assistant rector could hardly fail to follow suit. As I laid hands on him, there was a loud crack, almost like a bomb exploding. I jumped, having no idea what had happened. Fifteen minutes later the mystery was solved: The crack had been the sound of a long-dislocated bone in the young man's body snapping back into place. It need hardly be added that the young assistant became at that moment one of the great champions of the healing ministry, and from that time on, I became increasingly involved in the ministry.

As I realized what was happening to my life, I fought, I kicked, I ran; but surely and relentlessly God pursued me. He caught and held me fast in the net of His love. Holding me there enmeshed, He transformed my life by His touch. He drove me to my knees not by force but by love. And by His love He has kept me there, no longer struggling, but now in complete happiness and joy.

I was to learn over the years that it is by love that God works. Love is His power to convert and change lives, His power to heal and to mend all brokenness. His love enables us to say, "I will not be offended in Him" (Matt. 26:33) no matter what happens, and His love calls us to obedience and makes it our joy to obey, no matter how rough the road or difficult the way.

I was to learn, as I had never even remotely conceived before, the fullness of the truth that God's grace is indeed sufficient, and that His strength is made perfect in weakness.

I was to learn that His grace and His strength never fail, and that with Him all things are indeed possible. And I was to have reaffirmed for all time the greatest of all His promises: "Lo, I am with you always, even unto the end of the world" (Matt. 28:20).

---

* Emily Gardiner Neal, *The Healing Power of Christ* (New York: Hawthorn Publishers, 1972): 1-5; 7-8; 9-11

ANNA PAULINE
"PAULI" MURRAY

(1911-1985)

Anna Pauline "Pauli" Murray (1911-1985)[1], the first African American woman ordained to the priesthood, lawyer, educator, writer, poet, was born in Baltimore, Maryland. Her father, William Henry Murray, was an educator and high school principal and her mother, Agnes Georgianna Fitzgerald Murray, was a nurse, and one of the first graduates of Hampton Institute. Pauli Murray was always proud of her ancestry—African American, American Indian, and European—and believed that racial and cultural differences were a potential source of enrichment, rather than obstacles to relationship and community.[2]

After her mother's death, Pauli Murray was raised by her maternal grandparents and an aunt in Durham, North Carolina. She received a bachelor's degree from Hunter College (cum laude) in New York City in 1933. Rejected for graduate study by the University of North Carolina in 1938 because of her race, Pauli Murray became a lifetime activist for racial and gender equality. Her own experiences of racism and sexism, along with her indomitable spirit, strengthened her resolve to oppose oppression.[3]

In 1944, Murray sued Harvard University for refusing to admit her because she was a woman; she attended Howard University, and wrote a thesis challenging the "separate-but-equal" premise of racial segregation. Pauli Murray went on to earn several more degrees in her legal career; a masters degree in law at the University of California, Berkeley (1945), and a doctorate in constitutional law from Yale (1965).

Throughout her career, Pauli Murray held many prominent positions in law and education, including: deputy attorney general in California in the 1940s; lawyer in a private New York City firm in the 1950s; and, professor of American Studies, law, and political science at Brandeis University from 1968 to 1973. Many sought her counsel, in particular in the areas of racial and gender discrimination, including Eleanor Roosevelt. She was a founder of the National Organization for Women.[4]

Pauli Murray left her teaching position at Brandeis University in 1973 to enter the General Theological Seminary in New York to study for ordination. She was ordained deacon in 1976 and, in January 1977, was ordained to the priesthood in Washington Cathedral. Pauli Murray was the first African American woman ordained to the priesthood in the Episcopal Church. After her ordination, Murray served in the Church of the Atonement in Washington, D.C. After her "retirement" in 1982, she served in a variety of pastoral capacities and assisted at her home church, Holy Nativity in Baltimore. She died of cancer in 1985."[5]

Pauli Murray was a prolific writer and throughout her long career was much in demand as a lecturer and conference speaker. Before and after her ordination, Pauli Murray was also much in demand as a preacher. She wrote many technical articles for journals and books, as well as a book of poetry, *Dark Testament and Other Poems* (1970). Her books include: *Proud Shoes: the Story of An American Family* (1978), and *Song In A Weary Throat: An American Pilgrimage* (1987).

The following document is the text of an inaugural sermon delivered by Pauli Murray on the First Sunday of Lent in Emmanuel Church, Boston. At the time Murray was a candidate for Holy Orders.

NOTES

[1] For biographical information see, Pauli Murray, *Song in a Weary Throat* (New York: Harper & Row, 1987).

[2] Ibid, 1-13.

[3] Ibid, 1-14; 114-129.

[4] Ibid, 113-149; 117-188; 189-368.

[5] Ibid, 415-437.

CR

PAULI MURRAY

Women Seeking Admission to Holy Orders—As Crucifers Carrying the Cross*

Text: Isaiah 61: 1-4

I have selected this passage for our reflections because it seems to describe more eloquently than anything I can say to you this morning where I am and where many women of our Church are who are seeking admission to Holy Orders as their vocation. Six months ago, you sent me forth as a member of your congregation with your blessings and prayers to begin my training for the Sacred Ministry. This is my first opportunity to return to my home parish church and give an account of myself. I must confess I am torn between the joy of being back in my sponsoring parish and the nervousness of any first year seminarian called upon to proclaim the Word of God from the pulpit.

One of the first lessons we learn at Seminary is a profound sense of our own unworthiness and the awesomeness of the task we have set for ourselves in tension with a commitment which will not permit us to escape the pain, the doubts, the fears that assail every confessed Christian in moments of personal crisis.

Secondly, we learn that every Christian baptized into our Church is admitted to membership in the royal priesthood of Christ and has a ministry, whether one is male or female, old or young, white or black, lay member or clergy. Those of us who feel a special call to seek Holy Orders do so, not because we are better Christians or more able than our brothers and sisters, but because something has happened to us and there has taken place a radical shift of God's moving from the periphery to the very center of our lives. We dare to answer this call because, in a very real sense, we have no choice in the matter. God has spoken to us through an event or through a series of events which point us in one direction— toward full time service of God. Like the prophet Isaiah and the other prophets of the Old Testament, we are compelled to believe that sinful, rebellious, broken as we are, God is using us as instruments of his will— not ours—to love and serve him and our fellow human beings to the greater glory of God our Creator and Redeemer.

This decision makes us vulnerable to hurt, to heartache, to sorrow and suffering—for our very striving to be open to God's will intensifies our sensitivity to the tragedies of the human condition and we soon learn that without the love of God we are all lost, rudderless, without direction—an aircraft out of control and without a pilot. We have made the choice to reject our human drive to be self-sufficient and self-dependent and to follow the example of Jesus Christ in utter dependence upon God and radical obedience to God's will, not our own. Each day as we try to follow this example, we are chastened and humbled by our own shortcomings, our own self-willed disobedience and sinfulness and excessive self-centeredness in which state of being we hurt others and fail to live up to our commitments. Each day we are made more acutely conscious of how difficult it is to be a Christian, even in a small intimate community of committed Christians headed by twenty-three or more ordained priests.

Our failures, our weaknesses would overwhelm us were it not for the fact that each day we gain a growing sense of God's infinitely tender love and mercy and the gifts of grace bestowed upon us impel us to sing out spontaneously in hymns of joy, thanksgiving, and praise.

Because I am a woman, I must speak of this *call* through the experience of a woman—my own experiences and those of other women seminarians who have shared their hopes and dreams and tears of heartbreak with me.

Why is it that at this particular moment in the history of our church and of other faiths women are beginning to rise up and seek the ordained priesthood with such determined insistence? Is it a product of the Women's Liberation movement as others suggest? Cannot women be content to serve as members of the royal priesthood of Christ as they have served from the beginning of the Church? Why do they clamor to be admitted to all levels of the clergy—the Diaconate, the Priesthood, the Episcopacy? Why, in the face of the devastating rejection at the Louisville General Convention of last October, 1973—a rejection which Bishop Paul Moore of New York has called the violation of the very core of their personhood— [have they] only increased their determination to enter the higher levels of the clergy? And why must their *call* no longer be denied?

As I have pondered these questions since I left you last August and searched for answers, I find myself reflecting upon human history and looking at comparable periods in the long pilgrimage of humankind toward God, our Creator, Redeemer and Savior from death and nothingness.

The God of the Christian faith and the God of the Prophets of Israel moves, acts, and speaks in history through events and through individuals. Throughout all human history—today as well as 2500 years or more ago—our God is active in the affairs of humankind to bring us to redemption, salvation, and reconciliation with Him, the source of our being. We were created in His image and are the objects of an ineffable love which passes or transcends all human understanding. But we were also created with the freedom of will—the choice to love God and obey him or *not* to love God. Being human, finite, and therefore imperfect, *each of us, all of us,* from the dawn of human history, cannot resist the temptation to try to be God ourselves, to set our wills, our goals, our selfish interests above the will of God.

The more our cunning brains invent and the more dominion we achieve over the world we live in, the more our tendency is to rely upon ourselves, and even to shift the blame for our own sins and shortcomings upon God. How often have we heard skeptics say, "How could a loving God let such terrible things happen in the world?" In our drive for possessions, for dominion over nature, for power, status and prestige, we too often forget that our relation to the earth is that of stewardship—not ownership; that our destiny is not limited to our finite life; that we continually stand in God's judgement, and that we can escape the terrible consequences of our many failings only through God's grace; that we are engaged in a pilgrimage toward a higher and better life—toward union with God—and that this life we now live is a stage of our preparation for this higher destiny.

This radical departure from our Godward destiny has been particularly evident in certain periods of human history and has produced crises which have destroyed whole nations and peoples. The United States of 1974 is frighteningly like the people of Israel with their divided kingdoms in the 8th and 7th centuries B.C. In both periods of history we see certain common features: a comparatively advanced civilization[,] militarized dominion over weaker peoples, governmental intrigues, political assassinations, exploitations of the poor by the rich, neglect of the weak and defenseless, dishonesty and deceit in the marketplace, bribery and corruption of public officials and of the administration of justice, the drive for affluent living, carousing, and lavishment in food and drink, the jockeying for supremacy by the international great powers—and above all, the apostasy of the chosen people—the falling away from God. In the 8th Century B.C., the people gave lip service to Yahweh and took for granted that as the *elect,* God's chosen people, they would be saved. In the United States of the late 20th Century, we have relied upon our military strength, our bountiful natural resources, our "America First" mentality and our historical ethos of "Manifest Destiny."

And we are now in a deep and pervasive national crisis not unlike the crisis the 8th Century prophets and their successors foresaw in their own era. In such periods of human crisis, God has called forth prophets who will not be silenced, who will not be coopted by the established hierarchies whether they be clerical or secular. The role of these prophets is to call the people to repentance, to a return to the God of salvation. Their message is two-fold. They speak of the awful judgment of God's anger and the infinite tenderness and mercy of God's love. They proclaim that the gloom which attends the devastation will be followed by salvation and joy and the rebuilding on the part of those who remain faithful to God.

I believe that today God has chosen his messengers to warn of God's judgment upon a sinful and rebellious people and simultaneously to bring a gospel of hope and joy to those who will listen and have faith. I believe that God is choosing these messengers from the ranks of the dispossessed, the oppressed, and from those who have listened to his Word and are open to feel deeply the sorrow of the human condition. And I believe that many women of all ages are answering that call because they have suffered and endured and are particularly vulnerable to human sorrow and need.

Nothing less than the urgency of their mission, born of the depths of our moral and social crisis, could impel them to face the incredible barriers which have existed for thousands of years, to endure the ridicule and even violence of their detractors, and the continual heartache of rejection which blocks their path and makes their burden almost intolerable. I believe that these women are in truth the Suffering Servants of Christ, "despised and rejected," women of sorrows and acquainted with grief. They are answering to a higher authority than that of the political structures of our Church, and in the fullness of time God will sweep away those barriers and free the Church to carry forward its mission of renewal as a living force and God's witness in our society.

As I have already said, the remarkable quality of the Old Testament prophets is their dual message of judgment and salvation. It is this hope of reconciliation with God and our sisters and brothers which is the Christian joy—an ebullient, loving, giving and forgiving joyousness which we experience in our beloved associate rectors, Al Kershaw and Jack Greeley. (I hope you will forgive my irreverence when I tell you that I call Al Kershaw an outsized Pixie and Jack Greeley the Jolly Green Giant!) We see it in those great spirits like the late Eleanor Roosevelt, and others who have endured many agonies of loss, or privation or even oppression, but who, sustained by an abiding faith that they are children of God and the objects of his love, grow through their trials and radiate a spirit of loving kindness to everyone.

I sense this joy in the women of our Church who, supported by their own faith and by the open and sincere concern of many of their brother clergy, realize that tears sown in this night of temporary despair will bring joy in the morning. As I have watched my sisters in Seminary serving as acolytes at the altar; as crucifers carrying the cross, as lay readers and intercessors, as senior seminarians leading the morning prayer and evensong, as they carry on their ministries to one another, to their male brethren, to the sick and the dying, I am brought back to the words of Isaiah and the prophecy which will be fulfilled when the Church recognizes their full humanity:

1. "The Spirit of the Lord God is upon me; because the Lord hath anointed me to preach good tidings unto the meek; he hath sent me to bind up the broken-hearted, to proclaim liberty to the captives, and the opening of the prison to them that are bound...

3. "...to give unto them beauty for ashes, the oil of joy for mourning, the garment of praise for the spirit of heaviness...

4. "And they shall build the old wastes, they shall raise up the former desolations, and they shall repair the waste cities, the desolations of many generations."

Let us pray.

---

* Pauli Murray, "Women seeking Admission to Holy Orders." Sermon delivered on the First Sunday of Lent, Emmanuel Church, Boston, March 3, 1974. Pauli Murray Collection. Schlesinger Library, Radcliffe College. Cambridge, Massachusetts.

PHYLLIS ANDERSON STARK

(1911-1993)

Phyllis Anderson Stark (1911-1993),[1] clergy spouse and author, wrote about her experiences in the book, *I Chose A Parson (1956)*, and later in the unpublished manuscript, *I Married A Bishop*. Phyllis and her husband Leland served two small congregations in Minnesota, at Calvary Cathedral in Sioux Falls, South Dakota, and Epiphany Church in Washington, D.C., before his election as Bishop Coadjutor of the Diocese of Newark, New Jersey, in 1953. Leland Stark served as the sixth Bishop of Newark from 1958-1974.

Phyllis was born in Braham, Minnesota, in 1911. She attended Gustavus Adolphus and graduated *summa cum laude* from the University of Minnesota. Phyllis and Leland Stark were married in 1934 and had two sons, and eventually four grandchildren. Leland died in 1986 and Phyllis died in 1993 after a long illness.

As her writing suggests, Phyllis Stark had a long and active ministry in partnership with her husband. Wherever the couple served, Phyllis Stark gave speeches, taught classes, worked for charitable causes, and participated in the life of the local community. In the diocese of Newark, Phyllis and Leland Stark participated in the civil rights movement and worked for social justice in an era when urban issues and the war in Vietnam were prominent concerns. A beloved figure throughout the diocese of Newark while her husband was bishop,

Phyllis Stark exercised an influential ministry of her own in her local church community and beyond.

The following excerpts from *I Chose a Parson* depict Phyllis Stark's perspective on the clerical life.

NOTES

[1] Biographical information for this article provided by Linda Stark — Phyllis Stark's daughter-in-law – and Kitty Kawecki, director of the Bishop Anand Resource Center, diocese of Newark. An obituary on Phyllis Stark appeared in the *Montclair Times* (December 30, 1993).

❦

PHYLLIS STARK
Excerpts from I Chose A Parson*

The Sunday before Christmas was to be long remembered by our small congregation in Sleepy Eye. As was their custom, the faithful Marthas of the parish had assembled the previous day and cleaned the church and burnished its simple brasses and then decorated it for the Christmas festivities. Never had the little church of All Souls, Sleepy Eye, looked lovelier.

After the nine o'clock service there, we returned to New Ulm for an eleven o'clock service. We were just beginning our Sunday lunch shortly after one o'clock when the Junior Warden at Sleepy Eye telephoned.

"Leland," he said, "I've got bad news. The church has just burned down. It's a complete loss."

Right then they set a parish meeting for three o'clock that afternoon at his home.

Few sights are more melancholy than a burned church, and the spectacle made me numb all over. Only a portion of the outer walls remained standing. In the sanctuary the floor had not given way, and the altar still stood, but it was hopelessly charred. What remained of the church gave off the sickening odor of wet ashes.

All twenty-six members of All Souls Church were present at the meeting. As Leland began with prayer, it was a sad little company that knelt to ask for guidance. The prayers ended, one of the men explained what had caused the disaster. The fire marshall, he said, had discovered a long crack in the chimney between the inner and outer walls, and a hot finger of flame had probed its way through and almost certainly was burning unbeknownst to anyone by the time the morning service had concluded.

The Senior Warden then rose ponderously to his feet. He was eighty-six, and while admittedly there had been times when he had wearied us by the vigor with which he reiterated, upon the slimmest pretext, that he had voted the straight Republican ticket since the days of Ulysses S. Grant, that same tenacity was to stand the little church in good stead in its hour of tribulation. The insurance was inadequate, and the people were all of slender purse, but when our morale was at its lowest, he staunchly maintained that of course the church must be rebuilt. And so we adopted a tentative plan for a modest new church on the foundations of the old and gave ourselves two years to get it done. In the meantime, we would gratefully accept the generous offer of the Congregational Church across the street from our own; the fire had been at its height when their service was concluding, and even while it raged, their minister and trustees had met to offer us the use of their church.

Leland has always tried to preach sermons that would answer people's specific questions and problems, and the week following the fire, he interred himself on the sunporch of our apartment, which doubled for a library, and for his sermon to be preached in all four of his missions, pounded out one on the old problem of evil: to be specific, why should a church, dedicated to all that is good and holy, burn down while a nearby tavern, openly flaunting religion and decency, flourishes and abounds? The people, I think, really felt somewhat consoled the next Sunday by his theological explanation of the ways of God with man. But they would have felt considerably more secure had the matter dropped there. Instead we were awakened early Monday morning by the fire apparatus clanging down the street en route to the tavern directly across the street from our apartment. It was shortly reduced to cinders and broken bottles. Theologically at least, the score was even.

[...]

But religion in the home is not of course insurance against adversity, and sometimes, swiftly and unpredictably, come times of testing.

One such time came upon us very suddenly when our younger boy was almost ten. One morning we had to rush him to the hospital for what appeared only a routine attack of appendicitis. In this day an appendectomy doesn't cause too much concern, and as we upheld him in our prayers and waited eagerly for his return from the operating room, we had no reason to suppose the surgery would take more than the usual forty or fifty minutes. It was not, however, until two and a half hours had passed that he was brought back, and shortly thereafter the doctor came in to tell us that the appendix, which had been satisfactorily removed, was not the major problem but that an internal prenatal complication had necessitated a bowel resection. This had turned into a major operation. As was to be expected under the circumstances, the child was very ill, but then instead of the usual pattern of improvement, it became evident on the third day that an obstruction had set in. His abdomen continued to swell despite all kinds of tubes, he writhed in constant pain, and his general condition steadily deteriorated. Everything known to medical science was done by his own and consulting physicians, but by the sixth day it was clear the child could not live unless a second major operation could be successfully performed.

At ten o'clock on the night of the sixth day, the poor lad was taken to the operating room again. His surgeon, a most capable man and a dear friend as well, had told Leland that if this second operation took more than an hour, he would be fearful of the outcome. Time seemed to stand still that night but somehow one hour and then two went by before the boy was brought down from surgery. At least he was still alive but desperately ill. In the days and nights that followed, we could scarcely tear ourselves away from the hospital, even for a few hours of rest, for fear he would slip away and we not be there. He was of course in an oxygen tent and had nothing but intravenous feedings for ten days, and the equivalent of thirty-four pints of blood were given him in regular and albumin transfusions.

I hardly need say that we prayed with an earnestness our prayers seemingly had never had before. The people of Epiphany and of several other Washington churches were also remembering the lad in their prayers. Our Bishop was a real "Father in God" to us, and we were all mightily upheld by the prayers of our families and also by Leighton's godparents, Alice and Cleve Main, who called each day from Sioux Falls, South Dakota, to inquire and encourage.

Although at first it seemed we could not give him up, there came a time when both Leland and I could pray unreservedly that God would grant our petitions as He alone knew best. While understandably we desired nothing so much as the sparing of our child's life, we were gradually given grace to pray that God would overrule our judgment if He had reasons which we did not understand for wanting to fulfill the dear lad's life not here but in His nearer presence.

That Thursday morning at four o'clock, both Leland and I woke from light and fitful sleep and felt we must go at once to the hospital. When we got there, we learned that Leighton's doctor had been called shortly before. By now Leighton was sleeping the restless sleep of delirium, but at least the flame of life was still burning. All day long we watched for some sign of change. Late in the afternoon, when he seemed to be resting more quietly, we slipped down to the hospital cafeteria.

When we returned, his nurse met us at the door. Her eyes were misty, but it was the trace of tears of joy! The crisis was past—the child would live!

Though he was so thin he scarcely looked human, he slowly began to improve, and then came the day when the doctor said, "Our surgical difficulties are largely over now; from here on it is more a matter of bringing him back from starvation, and I think if he got home to his own room with his own things and his dog, we could more quickly rebuild his body."

A few minutes later we asked Leighton with studied casualness whether he would like to go home.

"Would I!" he cried, his eyes opening wide and a half-smile of incredulous joy on his lips.

And so we brought home our little bag of bones. By fall he was completely recovered, the glorious answer to a prayer to which God answered yes.

During his illness it had been necessary to have three special nurses, and we had been fortunate in getting perfectly splendid ones. The night nurse was very young, and Leighton looked forward to her coming each evening. His morning nurse was a wonderful Christian woman, but it was the afternoon and early evening nurse whom he liked the best. She was a French woman, not young, but gay and always quietly doing things to make herself ridiculous in an effort to amuse him.

Since we have always prayed together as a family, Leighton, when he was able, took part very naturally in our brief prayers with him each night, and joined faintly in the benediction (which we always say in unison, changing the wording to "The Lord bless us and keep us," etc.). His nurse was often present, but she made no comment. Then a year later when I had to have major surgery of my own and needed a special nurse, Leland called her in the hope that she might be able to care for me. Unfortunately she was on a case and could not come, but she said: "I've intended for a long time to call you or Mrs. Stark to thank you for what you did for me during Leighton's illness. You didn't know it of course, but I hadn't said a prayer for years. But when I saw that dear child so ill and saw how confidently you all prayed, I started to pray too, and now I am back in the church, and prayer is a part of my daily life."

Perhaps, after all, every Christian family does have a few "rarefied" moments.

[...]

To be sure, we had never been free of financial problems, but we had always had a house to live in, and we certainly hadn't starved. A good many of my friends had had more to spend on clothes, but I hadn't had to be dowdy. We had managed to travel a little and to buy books. And lots of good people had voluntarily lightened our financial load in various ways. Friends had given us wonderful gifts, doctors had gone all the way from subtracting a generous discount to writing off the whole whacking bill, and even merchants had sometimes given reductions. When we were first married, I often used to wonder whether this practice of clergy discount could claim a kindly, solicitous origin, or whether it came out of a resignation to the inevitable. Be that as it may, it is a quaint old custom which still means a great deal in rectory economy.

Then as I looked back over our life as a clergy family, from quite a selfish point of view, I couldn't think of a single profession in which we would have been treated so kindly in other ways. Most families moving into a new and strange community count themselves fortunate if a kindly individual or two takes some interest in them as newcomers, but from the first moment of arrival, except in the rarest of cases, the new minister and his family become an integral part of a whole host of people who are eager to take them to their hearts and make them welcome. There develops almost at once a bond of genuine affection and a sense of being very special to each other. The congregation from the beginning speaks in terms of "our minister" and "our minister's wife," and the clergy family on its part identifies them as "our congregation" and "our people." Nor is this happy expression of possessiveness only something verbal. It carries with it a sort of family feeling. When, for instance, the young parson's wife brings home the first baby, is any youngster more welcomed than the rectory infant? It all but becomes public property! And is there any profession in which holidays and special occasions are made more meaningful by friends than the ministry? Greetings and good wishes pour in from near and far, and one is overwhelmed by the loving kindness of people who, though one may have left their community long ago, still hold one in their thoughts and affections.

And when trouble comes, I'm sure no profession is surrounded by so concerned and devoted a group as is a clergy household. On this particular Sunday morning as I pictured Leland, Craig, and Leighton kneeling with our parish family at the service, I knew how many of that congregation would also be remembering me just as they always upheld each one of us, especially when we faced some unusual difficulty. As I thought of the courage that had come to us from their loving support in other times, there came to mind now an incident Leland had spoken of in one of his sermons a few Sundays before. It had occurred in a little fishing village in Newfoundland. All the men of the village were fisherfolk, and one day they were out on the fishing banks when a great storm suddenly arose. They were all able to scurry back into the harbor safely save one old fisherman, whose boat was wrecked at the very entrance. There he could be seen clinging precariously to a rock as the thunderous waves broke and swept over him. There was no possibility of launching a boat in that mountainous surf, but his friends did not desert him. When evening came, they built a huge bonfire and then took turns all night long standing silhouetted against the fire, waving their caps in his direction to let him know they were standing by. When morning came and the storm abated, they went to his rescue, and as they took him into the boat, he said in a voice tremulous with gratitude, "I could not have held on except you waved your caps!"

Today I knew our parish family would be waving their caps in my direction.

Phillips Brooks once told a group of theological students, "Among all the good things in life you have chosen the best in choosing the Christian ministry." I was sure that, as a parson's wife, I had chosen the next best.

---

* Phyllis Stark, *I Chose A Parson* (New York: Oxford University Press, 1956): 33-35; 199-202; 235-237.

CARMAN ST. JOHN WOLFF HUNTER

(1921-2000)

Carman St. John Wolff Hunter (1921-2000),[1] missionary, educator, and literacy advocate, was born in Fredericton, New Brunswick, Canada in 1921, and was raised in Melrose, Massachusetts. She spent most of her career as an appointed missionary of the Episcopal Church overseas, and in various high-ranking positions on the national staff of the Episcopal Church in New York. She was the first woman appointed as a departmental director at the National Council when she was named director of the department of Christian Education in 1963. She was also the co-author of a 1979 Ford Foundation study under the auspices of World Education, Inc. that focused on adult literacy in the United States. The study, *Adult Illiteracy in the United States: A report of the Ford Foundation*, examined the implications of poverty, race, and gender in relationship to the low levels of literacy among American adults and suggested implications for national policy.

Carman St. John Wolff received her B.A. *magna cum laude* in 1943 from Western College in Oxford, Ohio. Between 1944 and 1946, she trained at Windham House, a national graduate training center for women in New York City. In 1946 she received an M.A. from Columbia University and Union Theological Seminary. The same year she went to teach English and religion at St. Hilda's School in Wuchang, China. Her next missionary post was in Brazil, where from 1951 to 1959 she directed the Woman's Auxiliary Program, and for three years co-directed, with a Brazilian priest, the entire Christian education program for the Igreja Episcopal Brasileira (the Episcopal Church in Brazil).[2]

From 1959 through the 1970s, Carman St. John Wolff Hunter held various posts on the national staff. In 1959 she was appointed secretary for overseas education, and traveled widely in Japan, the Philippines, and Mexico, as well as numerous other overseas districts. In 1961 she became associate director of Christian Education, followed by her appointment as director in 1963. Carman St. John Hunter was named Deputy for Jurisdictions by John E. Hines, Presiding Bishop in 1972. In this position she administered a wide variety of programs linking the national church with 109 dioceses. Later, as director of national and world mission for the Episcopal Church, she collaborated with other Anglican mission executives to design administrative procedures for working with the churches of Asia, Africa, and Latin America based on a model of partnership and empowerment.

In 1965, Carman St. John Wolff married David R. Hunter, a priest who also worked for the national church and who eventually became deputy general secretary of the National Council of Churches. Together the Hunters made their home in Brooklyn and raised four children.

Before her retirement in 1986, Hunter was a frequenter lecturer and conference leader throughout the United States, Canada, and Asia. She pioneered the concept of participatory literacy education and developed community training programs that focused on literacy, health, and family-planning for an international audience. As a researcher she was known for her perseverance, backbone, analytical skills, and creativity. She believed in the power of literacy to affect social change. In 1978, Hunter translated from the Portugese a book by Brazilian educator, Paulo Freire, *Pedagogy in Process: the Letters to Guniea Bissau*. She also co-edited *Adult Education in China* (1985) for the International Council for Adult Education. Carman St. John Hunter died of cancer in March 2000 in Moorestown, New Jersey.

The following document was published as part of a series in the periodical *Forth*, entitled "Why I Went Into Church Work." The article was also released as a pamphlet by the Woman's Auxiliary. In the article, Carman St. John Hunter vibrantly describes her vocation.

Notes

[1] There are a variety of sources for biographical information on Carman St. John Wolff Hunter. The most comprehensive, include her obituary from the *Philadelphia Inquirer*, March 15, 2000, and the press release issued from the National Council/Episcopal Church, October 18, 1963, when Carman St. John Wolff was appointed director of the Christian education department, and an obituary in *Timelines*, the newsletter of the Episcopal Women's History Department, 20, No. 1 (Spring 2000) 1.3.

[2] Ibid.

❦

CARMAN ST. JOHN HUNTER
Each Day Brings New Joy*

It sounds romantic; four years in the inscrutable East, China at the moment of the lowering of the bamboo curtain, a trip home in which travel folders came alive, Hong Kong, Singapore, Aden, Suez, Port Said, London—and now Brazil.

Where did it start? Why am I here, a professional worker in the Church overseas? There wasn't anything startling about the decision, nor was it the result of long questioning. It was simply the sure response to a call which came at precisely the moment when I was ready to understand it. Everything had combined to make it natural: my own family in whose love there was always security; the parish in which the rhythm of Christian worship and activity laid a foundation. And finally a summer conference for young people. Things said there, lives seen, and the apartness which those ten days brought opened new vistas. The

Church became more than just a place where I felt happy and whole; it became that which can make the world whole.

It was a new discovery bursting on my seventeen-year-old world, this seeing things whole, comprehending the purpose. There were people there who talked of life as growing surrender of self to God, of service as the expression of our life in God, and it made sense. But I realize now that it made sense because the ground was laid. There was no other response possible but a joyous acceptance of this as my vocation, the call to a life of growth in God, expressed where and how He willed. At the time there was a sense that this might mean the overseas field of the Church's work. I talked long hours with a woman worker from Japan.

Each time I was home for vacation, she guided me to turn back and back to the springs of religious experience in sacrament and prayer and helped me to understand the necessity of a disciplined, religious life. She also suggested summer work during my college years: a church vacation school in East Boston, a camp for children from city mission parishes, rural work in Maine, which all proved both prelude and testing ground.

I graduated from college during World War II and taught for a year. Just before Christmas there came a telephone call telling me that a new program was to be set up at Windham House, New York, for the training of women who wanted to enter the work of the Church. At the same time, word came that the Overseas Department wanted to get people ready to go to China as soon as the war was over. There it was. I knew that there could be nothing else that was as right for me.

There followed two years of concentrated study with weekly field work, first in a settlement house and then in a parish, of close living and heated discussions, of fun and growth, which all was grounded in private and corporate devotional life.

In 1946 I went to St. Hilda's School, Wuchang, China, where the plan was that I should teach while learning the language and becoming a part of life in a new culture. Eventually I was to be on the staff of the Chinese training center for women workers.

It is almost impossible to condense the China years. Despite outward strangeness, despite long language struggles, despite extremes of heat and cold, there was never any inward strangeness, never any moment when I did not feel that I belonged there. Colleagues among the teachers, students in the school, church people, young and old, we were part of a community, bound by bonds stronger than nationality and deeper than custom.

Chinese friends taught me what no preparatory course could of the psychological and spiritual demands placed upon the overseas missionary, different from those known to the missionary working among his own people. For most of us, the learning of the language demands sacrificial concentration, but it is only a primary step. Chinese clergy and colleagues showed me how subtle are the things which separate the foreign worker from people and make his task difficult.

When I left China it was with the deepest pain that I have ever known. It was clear that the world situation would prohibit a swift return. I reached home saying that I would not go overseas again until I could go back to China. It seemed clear that I should work among American college students, study Chinese, and wait until I could "go back to *my* work." Brazil was mentioned but it seemed a far-fetched idea. No, I couldn't start all over again with a new language; my work was in China.

For four months I continued with the smug assurance that I knew what I must do. Underneath there was the plaguing question, "*Just what do you mean by vocation?*" And slowly I came to the reply that I had been called not to a specific task in the Church but to a life. I was called to know and to love God, a vocation which is common to all His creatures. The accident that I happened to have started in China had nothing to do with the basic vocation. At about this point there was a weekend retreat. I began it saying, "*If I go to Brazil...*" and emerged saying, "*When I go to Brazil...*"

Even an outline account of these years reads like an adventure story. I have known life in two countries, one with the oldest continuous civilization in the world and the other young and exuberant. I have done a little bit of everything, teaching groups of different ages, races, nationalities, student work, counselling, program planning, dramatics, writing, and social work.

I might have chosen professional church work for any one or all these reasons, but I didn't. Whichever of the manifold parts of the work a given day brings, the vocation is the same: to love God in all things. I have been singularly blessed along the way both in the work and in the close comradeship of Chinese, American, and Brazilian friends. We are bound together eternally in the certainty of our oneness in Christ even when the world's confusions enforce silence and separation. The first response at seventeen was not just to a work which appealed but to a way of life which brought integration and meaning and wholeness. With each day the gladness and the joy are deeper.

---

* Carman St. John Hunter, *Forth* (October 1953): 21-22. Also published as a pamphlet by the Woman's Auxiliary, n.d. Text suggetsed by Fredrica Harris Thompselt.

JEANNE LOUISE McGONIGAL VETTER

(1929-1996)

Jeanne Louise McGonigal Vetter (1929-1996),[1] spiritual director, writer, hotel clerk, housewife, mother, administrative assistant, was born in Queens, New York City, in 1929, the daughter of Violet Gunsburg and James Leslie McGonical.

When Jeanne was five the family moved to Manhattan and began to attend the Church of the Intersession on 155th Street and Broadway; this parish became Jeanne's spiritual home. After her parents moved to the Bronx, and after she prepared for confirmation at the local Lutheran church—in an action quite courageous for a twelve-year-old—Jeanne told her parents that she could not go through with it and wanted to return to Intercession. She was later confirmed there. After her death in 1996, Jeanne returned "home" to Intercession; she was buried in the Trinity North Cemetery just outside the church's doors. Besides the church, her neighborhood on the Washington Heights-Harlem border in New York City was an important part of Jeanne's formation. She said that she would have participated in the "white flight" of the 1960s, but she eventually became grateful that the move remained unaffordable. Jeanne Vetter believed that "the friendships she formed in that time and place taught her how completely irrelevant—*and how deeply relevant*—differences of race and language and gender could be. With her, the social and the spiritual always fed into each other."[2]

Jeanne Louise McGonigal graduated from George Washington High School in New York City, with honors. An enthusiastic learner, full-time college study was not an economic option for Jeanne. She began work in the hotel industry. She completed a semester of night school at Hunter College. In her mid-40s, she went back to school and took courses at New York Theological Seminary and the General Theological Seminary. She also enrolled at Empire State College. Jeanne was a voracious reader and absorbed whatever learning she could, even in the form of typing her daughter's college papers!

Jeanne met her husband, Henry Theodore Vetter, Jr. at the Church of the Intercession where they were married. Within a few years Jeanne quit her job as a hotel clerk to provide twenty-four-hour-a-day care to a family that included her husband, two small children, her father, and her mother-in-law. Jeanne shouldered these responsibilities for over a decade—and fought agoraphobia brought on by isolation—sustained by her rich life of prayer. A woman of deep mystical insights and contemplative disposition, yet enmeshed in a very busy life, Jeanne turned to the one who was perhaps her closest companion, Jesus. She identified with the passage from Julian of Norwich's *Revelation of Divine Love*: "And it has ever been my comfort, that I chose Jesus." Though there were problems in the Vetters' marriage, often because of Henry's struggles with alcohol and financial pressures, Jeanne and her husband prayed together and raised their children to know a loving God. As a young woman, Jeanne Vetter experienced a call to the priesthood—an impossibility for a girl in the 1930s and 1940s. Though encouraged to consider the sisterhood or a vocation as a deaconess, Jeanne was aware that she was not called to a celibate life. After her children were grown and she began to work outside of the home, Jeanne once again experienced a call to the priesthood and had hoped to finish her degree and enroll in seminary even though she had been told that she was too old to proceed to ordination.

Jeanne Vetter taught Sunday school while in high school and in her 20s; she was active in adult education and was a dedicated prayer group leader. Her first published work was in the Church of the Intercession's newsletter, *The Vine*, and she was encouraged as a writer and as a preacher by the clergy there, first Robert Spears (later bishop of the diocese of Rochester), and Frederick Boyd Williams.

During her last job, as an administrative assistant at the Episcopal Church Center, she collaborated with Charles Cesaretti on writing the 1979 "Lent\Easter" issue of *Forward Day by Day.* During her tenure at the Episcopal Church Center, Jeanne was known for lively humor, her quick mind, and for her devotion to her cats, Gabrielle and Ashfurred. At the General Seminary she was encouraged in her ministry of spiritual direction by Diana Lee Beach. Jeanne Vetter was a spiritual director, formally and informally, to many.

Around 1990, the Vetters moved to Staten Island, New York, and joined Christ Church where she established a prayer group and led adult education programs. As her health failed, the Christ Church prayer group met in the Vetter's apartment. The following excerpts from Jeanne Vetter's homilies give a glimpse into the reflections of this woman of faith.

NOTES

[1] Biographical information on Jeanne Vetter was provided by her daughter, Janet Vetter.

[2] Quoted from Janet Vetter, March 11, 2002.

JEANNE LOUISE MCGONIGAL VETTER
Selections from her Homilies*

"Journeying"

I live in Staten Island. One of the few advantages of taking a ferry at 6:20 AM every day is that at certain times of the year one can watch the sun rise. Long before it appears, the light becomes apparent in the sky, and as the boat progresses, looking back at Staten Island it is still dark, while the sky above Brooklyn and Manhattan is already beginning to be light. If I happen to be running late and take the 6:40 boat instead of the 6:20, the sky is already light when I board the ferry, but as the trip proceeds the suns rays become brighter and brighter until suddenly the red ball, like a balloon set free, bounces into clear view above the buildings in Brooklyn Heights. Needless to say the reflections on the water and the light changes in the clouds and sky are sometimes breathtaking.

This week with the end of daylight savings time the sun is already up when I board the ferry so it will be a while before I will view the sunrise again—that glimpse of God's hand at work, of God's Presence in our world.

Last week, on one of the final days I was watching the sunrise, I began thinking about darkness and light. About the dark places in which we find ourselves in our journeying and our moving from darkness into light. About the mortal blindness which limits our vision and holds us in darkness. When, like Bartimaeus, we need God to heal, to lift the veil of blindness so that we can see again. Bartimaeus knew about Jesus, believed that Jesus could heal his blindness; wanted to see Jesus, called him as he went by; and then heard the words, "Take heart, stand up, he is calling you." His request to Jesus, "that I may see again." Jesus' answer, "Go your faith has made you well." And it says Bartimaeus immediately regained his sight, and followed Jesus on the way; received his sight and followed him.

Sometimes when we're in dark places we don't seem to even have the strength to call out as Bartimaeus did. We can't see any way out of the darkness. I've discovered, however, it doesn't have to be a shout if we don't have the strength to call out. It actually takes no more than a breath, a whisper deep within, a sigh that says, "God get me out of the dark—I want to see"; and there may very well be an echoed whisper deep within, "Take heart, stand up, he is calling you."

[…]

We need our blindness healed. The world needs its blindness healed. We need our hearts to hatch. The world changes only as individuals change and learn to love and touch others. With our impaired vision, our mortal blindness, we can't see the whole, yet though imperceptible to us, God is moving—watch a sunrise and you can't doubt it—the Holy Spirit broods. So believe in hatching hearts! Believe we can move from darkness into light! Glimpse the beauty and the wonder, the revelation of God's Presence in a broken world. In spite of the pain, the bitterness and hatred, the horrors yet to be dealt with—with each hatching heart a new light begins to reflect love—reflect Christ's light along the pathway as we move out of darkness into light and follow where his light shines.

Jesus said, "Go, your faith has made you well." Immediately he regained his sight and followed him on the way.

"Take heart, stand up he is calling you".

"Thy love full oft in kindness, hath milk and honey given. Oh heal our mortal blindness, and fix our hearts on heaven."

"Open our eyes Lord, we want to see Jesus."

[...]

"The Marking"

While quietly relaxing one evening, my thoughts wandering at random from past to future, I was brought back to the present by the awareness of a furry little something rubbing up against my leg. It was my cat, Ashfurred, and a wet little nose rubbed against me leaving a wet mark on my skin. I thought to myself, "She's marked me for her own again." Many years ago I read a book on cats which said that when a cat rubs a human with its wet nose it is marking that human with a part of itself, a sign of itself. It is in essence an act which by scent leaves the unmistakable message, "This human belongs to me." I had not read that particular book when we acquired our older cat, Gabby, so I must have been marked for Gabby's own many times without being aware of it, but on this particular quiet evening the affectionate act of a little cat reminded me that we are all marked for God's own without our being aware of it. The words of a half forgotten poem formed on my lips as a prayer:

> *I want to be marked for thine own*
> *Thy seal on my forehead to wear*
> *And to have my name down on that mystic white stone*
> *Which none but thyself can declare.*

We are marked for God's own, every one of us, whether aware of it or not, and this marking makes us part of one family, God's family. This marking makes us part of one another.

[...]

"Prisoner of Love"

When I was in my teens, the song "Prisoner of Love," sung by a very young Perry Como, was a big hit. I remember sitting in the Capitol Theater entranced, listening to the words, "Alone from night to night you'll find me, too weak to break the chains that bind me, I need no shackles to remind me, I'm just a prisoner of love." I was a prisoner of love for Perry Como, but even though my teen-age passion for him was all consuming for a month or so, ultimately I had enough common sense to realize that the chance of our ever meeting or of him reciprocating my feelings was rather dim, so the passion wore off and I began concentrating on more likely candidates nearby. Just for the record, Perry Como's voice still gets to me.

"Prisoner of Love." It may seem strange, but sometimes that song comes back to me when I read the words from today's epistle, but with the words, "Prisoner of love of self". All of us, throughout our lives, are shackled to the kind of slavery that St. Paul talks about, many times unaware of being prisoners—perhaps at times prisoners of ourselves, yet very much aware of a tremendous struggle to act on what we believe is right, on what we believe God is calling us to do. What is the solution?

When we moved to Staten Island three years ago, the morning after we moved in no one could get to the front door there were so many boxes and odd pieces of furniture blocking it. A few months ago when we celebrated three years in the apartment, the door was no longer blocked, but our closets and drawers so neat, after we first moved in, badly needed clearing out. I remember one Saturday attempting to clear out desk drawers, bureau drawers, and a file which we fondly call our "important paper" file, which generally contains anything we can't find another place for at the moment. The attempt was made partly because a hint of premature spring in the air inspired me, but mainly because we couldn't find my husband's Railroad Retirement tax withholding form and could feel the hot breath of the IRS upon us if we didn't locate it. As I went through the drawers and file I was amazed at the amount of unnecessary accumulations we had which left no room for, or messed up, the things we really needed. It was my fond belief that every few weeks I got rid of unnecessary papers and letters, but obviously the amount I thought I cleared out did not agree with the reality of the-accumulation I could see. I couldn't help thinking of the parallel in my spiritual clearing out and how little space I sometimes leave for God in me. I may take a very quick look each day at what is accumulating inside me and what needs to be sorted out, but just as with the desk, file, and bureau drawers, I only do a hurried job.

It sometimes takes being blocked from doing something that must be done, having to find something important that's missing, such as the form for the IRS, to make me do a really thorough search and clearing out. It sometimes takes getting to the point where I fear God is missing and become aware that Christ has no room to get in that makes me do a more thorough spiritual cleaning out. When the struggle between being who I want to be—who God is calling me to be, and the blocks which are keeping God from the door become too great, when the willingness to be emptied so that "God may be poured out through me" is strong enough, then I, by God's grace, with God's help, do a more thorough job.

We don't have to be prisoners. God will unblock and unlock the doors—unlock, as Perry Como's song says, "the chains that bind us" if we take time to look and search within, to discover the locks and blocks and want them removed.

Being who we're called to be is a struggle and will remain so as long as we live. But the unhappiest people in the world are those who realize who they are called to be, yet do not act on growing beyond the blocks. For instance, when we live our lives in slavery to the opinions of others, or, in fear of breaking the chains of conformity, when we don't allow ourselves the freedom to be and to become. Christ came to loose the chains—to give us freedom within his freedom.

---

* Jeanne Vetter's unpublished writings were provided by Janet Vetter and John Ratti.

DOROTHY J. BRITTAIN

(1932-2001)

Dorothy J. Brittain (1932-2001) served the Episcopal Church as a consultant, educator, trainer, and author for nearly forty years. As an expert in organizational development and leadership training, she was responsible for countless conferences, programs, and consultations for local churches, dioceses, as well as denominational boards and agencies. Among other professional publications, Brittain co-authored the widely used training manuals *Women of Vision* (1989) and *Gaining Authority through Education and Service* (1991), and she was a contributor to *Stories from the Circle: Women's Leadership in Community.* Known as an expert facilitator with keen insights and a non-anxious presence, Brittain was called on throughout her long career to work with many groups in complicated circumstances engaged in controversial issues. This work she did with uncommon amounts of grace, strength, and integrity. It is not an overstatement to suggest that she had the capacity as a leader to bring vision and health back to organizations and groups that lost touch with their own values and purpose.

Though less known in church circles, Brittain's professional accomplishments extended well beyond ecclesiastical structures. For over twenty years as a professional consultant with her own firm, she worked with government agencies in the United States and Canada, as well as over 200 human services programs throughout North America. As a recognized professional in organizational development, Brittain specialized in a variety of areas including management and administrative skill building, strategic planning, conflict resolution, system analysis, operations, policy methods, volunteer management, and communication systems. Yet as much in demand as Brittain was as a professional, she always continued her work as an internationally respected leader in the Episcopal Church. As she worked in so-called "secular" environments, she showed her unique ability to bring both genuine love and highly technical skills to those she served.

Dorothy J. Brittain began her professional life as a music teacher in central New York. In 1962-1963, she attended Saint Margaret's House in Berkeley, California and was graduated with an M.A. from the Church Divinity School of the Pacific. Three years as the director of religious education at Trinity Church, Binghamton, New York, was followed by a five-year stint as program executive for the Episcopal Diocese of New York. Beginning in 1971, Brittain began her professional consulting career, including a vice-presidency at Richard Ford Associates, Inc., seven years as executive director of the Association for Creative Change in Religious and Other Systems (ACC) in Syracuse, and as founder of her own firm. In 1995, Brittain was honored with the degree of Doctor of Humane Letters, *honoris causa,* as a tribute to her graceful ministry in the world.

Dorothy J. Brittain died in Massachusetts in 2001 after a long illess. Besides her training publications, she was also the co-author of a popular curriculum on human sexuality. Throughout her career Brittian encouraged the open and honest discussion of values in all areas of human experience and relationship, including human sexuality. The following article represents her thinking on human relationships in the 1980s.

DOROTHY J. BRITTAIN
Intimate Friends: Being Single in the 1980's[1]

This is a story about Friendship. Friendship is the subject of song, story and poetry. Its virtues and benefits have been extolled and perhaps trivialized in this age which has idolized and made sexual consumation [sic] the goal of relationships. I believe that the concept of friendship needs more refreshment, development and understanding as a means of helping adults in our culture adjust to and maximize life giving inter-personal relationships. We are, after all, first and last, single.

My own saga is one of making choices which have only awkward or derogatory names. These names—single, maiden, spinster, old maid, imply that these life style choices are negative. In this article, I share some of my experience as a single woman in a coupled society. I also share some of the difficulties and joys of working through my own and others' acceptance of this life style.

I invite you into my experience, to sense it and to question it with me. Out of my subject "Being Single in the '80's" comes that which for many is a quandary : How to be single or how to relate to single persons both personally and professionally within the context of a society that is devoted to quick and simple answers.

CHOICE OR CHANCE?

As a single woman, flirting with age 50, I find myself taking stock. Have I received my due? Have I given my due? Has life "passed me by" since I have decided to remain unmarried, not to be a parent, but to take this mind, body and soul of mine and invest it in a life that is mysterious to many, envied by a few and pitied by others.

The issues, contributions and worries of the single adult in our society have not been well exposed or explored. It is as if the single state is defined by what it is not, therefore it is characterized as a deficient life style. With increasing numbers of single persons it cannot be ignored.

"Mid-life crisis," is a peculiar plague which has hit our country and many of my contemporaries (voluntarily or involuntarily) have become single once again leading to new interest in this less frequently chosen option. I, for one, welcome this exploration because it feeds into my personal reflection.

The issues that center around choice are important. The validation of *choice* is often denied by a casual explanation of *chance*. Let me illustrate.

"Poor thing, never married" is to be interpreted "Was never asked," "Was never chosen or accepted," "Lost out to someone else."

Or in the case of separation and divorce: "Had the chance and blew it," "Surely was not lucky in love," "Somehow I knew that one didn't have much of a chance."

Or in the case of the widowed, the projection of fragility is heard: "Was left alone and have never recovered."

Singles are often isolated, sometimes by their choice but often by the choice of others for whom relating to them is too difficult, too demanding or too threatening. The script is one that is unwritten and therefore requires risk in working through the details—the lines and cues are largely ad lib.

For me it is imperative to choose and not to be just swept along. The fact that, for some, singleness has been a real choice, comes as a surprise to many newly singled persons. In conversations with these persons, one observes that the discovery that "victim" is only one of many optional scripts is liberating indeed.

PATTERNS, PALS AND PUT-DOWN?

Threatening, uneasy, and unpleasant are words that describe social situations in which the rules do not clearly apply. Awkwardness prevails when an invitation is issued for a social event.

"It will be all couples, bring someone if you like." or "I've invited Dave for you." This is an attempt to accommodate but one which is always offered with embarrassment and uncertainty.

It is clear to me that our society encourages adult persons to embrace and relate to it as heterosexual couples or married persons. It is a goal of our social system to produce stable families, taxable units, sexual outlets that are controlled, controlled competition, winners and losers, ins and outs. "Both/and" is much too complex to work through so we settle for "either/or" terms.

The boundaries of community, the rules of the game, are carefully taught but not always followed. The effect is to produce norms which push against persons who are not in compliance. There is a non-subtle pressure on and mythology about "singles." Contradictions and confusion abound so it is not surprising that stereotypes are found for convenience; yet they are by their very simplicity limited in usefulness for describing the singles' dilemma in terms of relating to the dominant culture.

"Singles swing." Singles are to be pitied, envied, mistrusted because the very state of uncoupledness is either judged by or stands in judgement on the norm of the married. As a single person, I have experienced that which is highlighted about the uncoupled state as drawn in either negative terms, i.e. isolated, bereft, lonely, ineffective, frustrated or in the fantasy terms of irresponsibility, sexual promiscuity and gay abandon. The assumption is curious that with freedom from a marriage contract comes irresponsibility in relationships. The assumption is that single persons are or must necessarily be deprived of close, maturing relationships.

When societies' norms become ends in themselves, that which has the potential to be the dynamic, transforming process, one which could enrich and humanize our lives, is lost. The focus gets shifted from those processes which could produce whole, mature adult persons to the ends. We look at the form (marriage) instead of the function (supported, nourished, challenged adults).

WHERE DO SINGLES MAKE CONTRIBUTIONS?

Having been single all my life, while most of my contemporaries married, raised families and made their contribution to society, I have been viewed largely as a non-contributor at least in terms of the social fabric, the warp and woof of society, or in terms of societial glue, the family.

Certainly my career contributions have been recognized and valued but for many who happen to be both women and single, the inequality of opportunity and remuneration is symbolic of a devalued contribution. The designation "just a homemaker" also symbolizes devaluation and it is seldom applied to single persons, yet it is an important role played by singles. Singles live in homes.

As a single woman, several stereotypes have had great power in my life. I am bemused by my own reaction to these. There is power in these stereotypes, power to define.

A frequently repeated interchange goes like this:

"Do you have children?"

"No, I'm not married."

"Oh, I'm sorry."

"I'm not!"

I say more than I want and then react defensively. Why? Our vocabulary points to marriage as a norm. Apparently marriage is blessed by the church while other relationships are not. No wonder there is power in that stereotype.

In business settings, when it is determined that a single woman is present explicitly sexual jokes are alluded to but not told. This I admit is a mixed blessing. It saves us from bad jokes but again signals an assumption of depravity of experience.

The curiosity about how a single woman manages travel or relates to an all male team does point to some very real, underlying dynamics. Can a person be fully sexual or must sexuality be disguised and diffused. The power of sexuality in a business situation, especially where norms of competition prevail, is not over estimated. It is, however, seldom dealt with openly and helpfully. Much of what is now understood as sexual harassment are, I believe, inappropriate attempts to deal with the power issues related to the sexual energy present in the business place. The social mores define the business transactions and render both the social and business transactions confused and frustrating.

The projections (elevated to virtue) that single persons are completely devoted to their work (expressed, "Married to her job") and that within that devotion are sufficient rewards and satisfactions need to be challenged. Out of those projections come a rationalization for looking only to the dominant ethics of family and work for contribution to and enrichment of society.

The poverty inherent in this narrow view is society's loss. An openness to accept the contributions of those whose life style is outside the norm would require the diverting of energies from pressure to *conform* to a *confirmation* of that which is a different not deficient alternative.

SO, HOW IS THIS A STORY ABOUT FRIENDSHIP?

"Intimate," from the Latin intimatus, means "pressed into."

In our usage the word "intimate" expresses a dual image and a rather contradictory pair at that. Intimate refers to a close associate, close personal friend or illicit sexual relations. In our society which has been preoccupied with sexual relations and under-occupied with notions of friendship, the last meaning has gained dominance.

"Intimate" is a word that I would like to reclaim. It is within intimate relationships that I have learned to live and give. It is obvious that such learning must be vigorously pursued within a marriage; it is less obvious that such intimacy is required for one to mature at all. In order to grow, one must wrestle with self and rigorously work to learn to live and give. For the most part this happens with persons with whom contracts are less open, visible or modeled. Should marriage be the only standard by which maturity is measured? I think not.

Since our society presently does hold marriage as standard, how does one work through to feelings of confidence and wholeness outside a marriage contract? Once you have worked through the self-affirmation needed to feel okay when the dominate [sic] culture refuses to affirm your position, whether it is your choice or not, then you must begin by affirming others who try to relate to you. You must strive to make the relationship a trustful one.

In a helpful little book, *The Gift of Courage*,[2] James Wilkes speaks of the activity, the process, if you will, of healthful relationships: trust, then truth telling (sharing) and then contracting. For the relationships with singles, with so much mistrust and negativity unthoughtfully projected, truth telling and contracting is extremely difficult.

As a single person (and we all are that) I must first risk myself to a relationship, trust enough to enter into a dialogue in which I can then share truth, and out of that context and interaction, share expectations and agreements. Is this not the process of friendship?

Discrimination against single persons is subtle. To characterize the single life style by extremes makes good jokes but bad dialogue. For me, it's more important to recognize the subtle language cues, and then move them from the "deficient" column to the "different" column.

Having done that, many new options will be open to us. Options with potentials for life giving friendship. We can choose from the different; to choose the deficient would be crazy. But many of us are doing just that.

---

[1] Dorothy J. Brittain, "Intimate Friends: Being Single in the 1980s," *Journal of Religion and the Applied Behavioral Sciences*, 2, no. 3 (Summer 1981): 15-17.

[2] The Anglican Book Centre, Toronto, Canada, c. 1979.

ALICIA "CRISTINA" RIVERA, OSH

(1933-1996)

Alicia **"Cristina" Rivera, OSH (1933-1996)** religious and pastor, was born Alicia Rivera in Ponce, Puerto Rico. She spent her childhood and adolescence in Ponce, and trained there as a laboratory technician. Her family's religious background was Baptist; Alicia was received into the Episcopal Church in 1945.[1] When Rivera moved to New York City she worked at Memorial and Roosevelt hospitals as a laboratory technician and hematologist. She entered the Order of Saint Helena (OSH) as a Postulant in September 1959, and was Life Professed in April of 1964.

"Sister Cristina" lived out her religious vocation—a life of prayer and service—in many corners of the world. Soon after her life profession, she was sent for five years to the order's Holy Cross Mission in Bolahun, Liberia, West Africa, where she was involved in leadership training groups, among other ministries. "In Africa [Sister Alicia Cristina] began to understand the true nature of missionary service, not as someone sent to preach or bring Christ to others, but to listen and discover Christ in the life of the people. She was an example of humility, desirous of living a lifestyle similar to the persons whom she served."[2]

Sister Cristina also lived in the convents of Saint Helena in August, Georgia, and Ghana, West Africa, before arriving at the convent in New York City, where she spent the last eighteen years of her life. A multi-talented woman, Rivera was accomplished in yoga, dance, and gardening. She was a founder and pastor of the San Juan Bautista Mission in the South Bronx.

Sister Alicia Cristina's ministry among Hispanic people in the South Bronx was recognized by the Diocese of New York when she was awarded the Bishop's Cross by the Rt. Rev. Paul Moore, Jr. on October 21, 1986: "Nurtured by the Eucharistic, Prayer-Centered Life of her own community of the Order of St. Helena, she came to understand the significance of what could be derived by Hispanic Christians from congregational life under Hispanic leadership; from a Eucharistic assembly in their language, oriented to their culture and their special needs...."[3] The citation for the award goes on to laud Rivera's skill in using the learning of the base community experience; and her contribution to the development of a viable and vibrant team ministry in the South Bronx which supported the growth of other congregations.[4] In addition to her work at San Juan Bautista, Sister Cristina was active on the Hispanic Commission of the Diocese of New York, the National Hispanic Commission, the Episcopal Urban Caucus, and the Coalition of Human Needs.

In her funeral sermon—Sister Cristina died of cancer in 1996—she was praised as a woman "very aware of human suffering and of issues of justice. She fought courageously for what she believed in these areas, and sometimes had difficulty understanding those who were blind to suffering and injustice."[5] In her last letter to her community, Rivera wrote: "I know and sense that life and death are going on simultaneously and I want to have the strength to continue to give of myself."[6]

The following document is a letter from Alicia Cristina Rivera, OSH to community. It was written c1973 while she was called to Jamaica to discern the viability of an Anglican order there.

NOTES

[1] Biographical information on Sister Cristina was provided by Sister Ruth, OSH, and includes a biographical entry written after her death, and a copy of the funeral sermon preached by the Rev. Canon Mary Michael Simpson, OSH. Also included with this documentation is a copy of the citation written when she was awarded the Bishop's Cross from the diocese of New York in October 1986.

[2] Jaime Juan Forme, summarizing an article by Nina Olmedo in *Anglicanos* (April-June 1984).

[3] Paul Moore, Jr., citation, Bishop's Cross Award, October 21, 1896.

[4] Ibid.

[5] The Rev. Canon Mary Michael Simpson, OSH, "Sermon, Funeral of the Sister Alicia Cristina Rivera, OSH, August 26, 1996, Chapel of St George's Church, New York City," *Saint Helena*, 17, no. 3 (Fall 1996): 1.

[6] Ibid.

CR

ALICIA "CRISTINA" RIVERA, OSH
Letter to the Order of St. Helena from Jamaica, c. 1973[*]

Dear Sisters,

Since I had presented an oral report of my work in Jamaica, during the April discussions, it did not occur to me to write it down. So, I am sorry for the delay. I am very thankful to the community for allowing me the time and sparing my presence, in order to pursue a call to live the religious life among the masses of the world.

Although it has been a very frustrating year in many ways, it has been on the other hand a very challenging experience, from which I have learned a great deal. Some of us who have experienced other cultures know that it takes a while to know and understand our differences; the way we think and do things, even the way we speak. So as a result there is always some misunderstanding. I have been 10 months in

Jamaica and there are many people there that do not know that the Anglican Church has Religious Orders. Since I am not living in a Convent, and I work and support myself, many wonder what it is that I am doing. After all, I am not working for the Church.

I thought that I made it clear from the beginning that I was not going to be engaged in any of the usual works that our community performs. However, I did agree to speak to congregations and small groups and especially youth groups, about the Religious Life. However these requests have been very few. The idea was to inform people about the Religious Life with the possibility of helping towards the establishing of an indigenous Jamaican community.

I have been working full time in the Government Medical Laboratory, as a Lab Technician. This work has not in any way interfered with my being available. The idea of the Religious Life is fairly new in Jamaica, and therefore I feel that a great deal of education and information is needed. Those who are familiar with the Religious Life, think of it in the traditional way of the past. The people in Jamaica think of an ideal that is less true today. I have been trying to clarify the position of Religious in the world today, a task that is very hard indeed.

During my first 6 months in Jamaica Miss Cynthia Alexander lived with me. We shared responsibilities, and we prayed together (saying of offices, Mass), Recently Cynthia has decided to enter a contemplative community in England, and is planning to try her vocation in the latter part of September. Our time together proved very fruitful, for both of us, since we learned a great deal from each other. In July I came across a girl by the name of Beverly Johnson. She had been at our first July Conference in Newburgh. She is a pre-med student at the University of the West Indies. The idea of the Religious Life is in the back of her mind, but she is still searching and trying to know what God's will for her is. Anyway, she is with me during the summer, since she is working in the city and also at the same place I work. Beverly is 19 years old, and Cynthia is 51, so you can imagine this would be quit[e] a different adjustment for me.

Jamaica is a beautiful Island and I have been able to enjoy a great deal of the beauty that it has to offer.

The outcome of my stay in Jamaica is very hard to evaluate. For what it is worth I want to inform you, my sisters, that I have found it very helpful. I do not know how to explain the fact that my spiritual life has deepened and my vocation greatly strengthened. I felt from the beginning that this was something God was asking me to do. I've tried to live in the Spirit of the Gospels as I understand the Good News, and I have tried to share this life with others. The time of the experiment is coming to a close and I feel greatly enriched and I thank God and you for caring.

Respectfully submitted,
Cristina, O.S.H.

---

* This letter from Sr. Cristina in from her file at the Convent of St. Helena, Vails Gates, New York and was provided by Sr. Ruth, OSH. The text is unedited with the exception of two spelling corrections.

SELECTED BIBLIOGRAPHY

This bibliography is not intended as an exhaustive account of all the various sources that support the study of the history of Anglican and Episcopal women in the United States, nor does it include all the printed sources available for the study of each subject in this anthology. Rather is it a selection of sources consulted repetitively over the course of research for this book.

PUBLISHED PRIMARY SOURCES

Armentrout, Don S. and Robert Boak Slocum, ed. *Documents of Witness: A History of the Episcopal Church, 1792-1985.* New York: Church Hymnal, 1994.

[Ayers, Anne]. *Practical Thoughts on Sisterhoods.* New York: T. Whittaker, 1864.

Beecher, Catharine E. *An Essay on Slavery and Abolitionism, with Reference to the Duty of American Females.* Philadelphia: Henry Perkins, 1837.

Beecher, Catharine E. *Religious Training of Children.* New York: Harper & Brother, 1864.

Bedell, Harriet M. "Among the Indians of Oklahoma." *The Spirit of Missions*, 85. 4 (April 1910): 271-74.

Black, Allida M. ed. *Courage In a Dangerous World: The Political Writings of Eleanor Roosevelt.* New York: Columbia University Press, 1999.

Bowen, Louise deKoven. *Growing Up With a City.* New York: Macmillan, 1926.

Boyle, Sarah Patton. *The Desegregated Heart: A Virginian's Stand in Time of Transition.* Charlotteville: University of Virginia Press, 2001.

Bradford, Sarah. *Harriet Tubman: The Moses of Her People.* New York: Cornith, 1961.

Chaplin, Dora P. *The Privilege of Teaching.* New York: Morehouse-Barlow, 1962.

Coon, Anne C., ed. *Hear Me Patiently: The Reform Speeches of Amelia Jenks Bloomer.* Westport: Greenwood Press, 1994.

Cooper, Anna Julia. *The Voice of Anna Julia Cooper.* Charles Lemert and Esme Bham, eds. Lanham: Rowman & Littlefield Publishers, Inc.

Delany, Sarah L. with Amy Hill Hearth. *On My Own at 107.* San Francisco: HarperSanFrancisco, 1997.

Delany, Sarah L., A. Elizabeth Delany, Amy Hill Hearth. *Having Our Say: The Delany Sisters' First 100 Years.* New York: Delta, 1993.

Deloria, Ella. *Speaking of Indians.* Lincoln: University of Nebraska Press, 1998.

Deloria, Ella Cara. *Waterlily.* Lincoln: University of Nebraska Press, 1988.

DoBois, Ellen Carol. *Elizabeth Cady Stanton, Susan B. Anthony. Correspondence, Writing, Speeches.* New York: Schocken Books, 1981.

Collier-Thomas, Bettye. *Daughters of Thunder: Black Women Preachers and Their Sermons, 1850-1979.* San Francisco: Jossey-Bass, 1998.

Gilbert, Olive, ed. *The Narrative of Sojourner Truth.* Battle Creek: Michigan, 1878.

Gillespie, Joanna Bowen. *The Life and Times of Martha Laurens Ramsay, 1759-1811.* Columbia: University of South Carolina Press, 2001.

Hale, Sarah Josepha, ed. *Woman's Record; or, Sketches of Distinguished Women.* New York: Harper & Brothers, 1976.

Hosmer, Rachel, and Joyce Glover, ed. *My Life Remembered.* Boston: Cowley Publications, 1991.

Larcom, Lucy. *A New England Girlhood.* Gloucester: Peter Smith, 1973.

Larcom, Lucy. *Life, Letters, and Diary.* Daniel Dulany Addison, ed. Boston: Houghton Mifflin, 1894.

Lili` uokalani. *Hawaii's Story by Hawaii's Queen.* Rutland: Charles E. Tuttle Company, Inc., 1964.

Lomax, Judith, *The Sabbath Journal of Judith Lomax, 1774-1828,* Laura Hobgood-Oster, ed. Atlanta: Scholars Press, 1999.

Mason, Lucy Randolph. *To Win These Rights: A Personal Story of the CIO in the South.* New York: Harper & Brothers, 1952.

Mead, Margaret. *Twentieth Century Faith: Hope and Survival.* (New York: Harper & Row, 1972.

Morgan, Emily M. *Letters To Her Companions.* Adelynrood: Society of the Companions of the Holy Cross, 1944.

Murray, Pauli. *Dark Testament and other Poems.* Norwalk: Silvermine, 1970.

Murray, Pauli. *Song In A Weary Throat: An American Pilgrimage.* New York: Harper & Row, 1987.

Neal, Emily Gardiner. *The Healing Power of Christ.* New York: Hawthorn, 1972.

Neal, Emily Gardiner. *The Reluctant Healer: One Woman's Journey of Faith.* Shaw: Colorado Springs, 1992.

Ovington, Mary White. *Black and White Sat Down Together: The Reminiscences of an NCCAP Founder.* New York: Feminist Press, 1995.

Ovington, Mary White. *Hazel.* Freeport: Books for Libraries Press, 1971.

Reik, Cynthia, ed. *The Harriet Beecher Stowe Reader.* Hartford: Stowe-Day Foundation, 1993.

Richardson, Marilyn. *Maria W. Stuart: America's First Black Woman Political Writer. Essays and Speeches.* Bloomington: Indiana University Press, 1987.

Robertson, Mary, D., ed. *Lucy Breckinridge of Grove Hill: The Journal of a Virginia Girl, 1862-1864.* Kent: Kent State University Press, 1979.

Roosevelt, Eleanor. *The Autobiography of Eleanor Roosevelt.* New York: Da Capo Press, 2000. Reprinted 1961 edition.

Roosevelt, Eleanor. *Christmas.* New York: Alfred Knopf, 1940.

Scarlett, William ed. *Toward A Better World.* Philadelphia: John C. Winston, Company, 1946.

Scudder, Vida Dutton. *The Church and The Hour. Reflections of a Socialist Churchwoman.* Eugene Oregon: Wipf and Stock Publishers, 200. Reprinted from 1917 edition.

Scudder, Vida Dutton. *On Journey.* New York: Dutton, 1937.

Sealander, Bernard and Judith Sealander. *Women of Valor Against the Great Depression as Told in Their Own Life Stories.* Chicago: Ivan R. Dee, 1999.

Simkhovitch, Mary Kingsbury. *Here Is God's Plenty.* New York: Naroer & brothers, 1949.

Simkhovitch, Mary Kingsbury. *Neighborhood: My Story of Greenwich House.* New York: Norton, 1938.

Simkhovitch, Mary Kingsbury. *The Red Festival.* Milwaukee: Morehouse Publishing Company, 1934.

Stanton, Elizabeth Cady. *Eighty Years & More. Reminiscences 1815-1897.* New York: Schocken Books, 1971. Reprinted from 1898 edition.

Stanton, Elizabeth Cady. *The Woman's Bible.* New York: Prometheus Books, 1999.

Stark, Phyllis. *I Chose A Parson.* Wilton: Morehouse-Barlow, 1956.

SECONDARY SOURCES

Anderson, Owanah. *400 Years: Anglican/Episcopal Mission Among American Indians.* Cincinnati: Forward Movement Publications, 1997.

Armentrout, Don S. Robert Boak Slocum, eds. *A Episcopal Dictionary of the Church: A User Friendly Reference for Episcopalians.* New York: Church Publishing, 2000.

Cook, Blanche Wiesen. *Eleanor Roosevelt.* 2 Vols. New York: Penguin, 1998, 2000.

Coryell, Janet L, et al., eds. *Beyond Image and Convention: Explorations in Southern Women's History.* Columbia: University of Missouri Press, 1998.

Darling, Pamela W. *New Wine: the Story of Women Transforming Leadership and Power in the Episcopal Church.* Boston: Cowley Publications, 1994.

Donovan, Mary Sudman. *A Different Call: Women's Ministries in the Episcopal Church, 1850-1920.* Wilton: Morehouse-Barlow, 1986.

Douglas, Ian T. *Fling Out The Banner! The National Church Ideal and the Foreign Mission of the Episcopal Church.* New York: Church Hymnal, 1996.

Howard, Jane. *Margaret Mead: A Life.* New York: Simon and Schuster, 1984.

James, Edward T. Janet Wilson James, Paul Boyer. *Notable American Women: A Biographical Dictionary.* 3 Vols. Cambridge: Belknap Press, 1971.

Lesser Feasts and Fasts (2000). New York: Church Publishing, 2001.

Lindley, Susan Hill. *"You have Stept out of your Place": A History of Women and Religion in America.* Louisville: John Knox Press.

Metraux, Rhoda, ed. *Margaret Mead: Some Personal Views.* New York: Walker and Company, 1979.

Perkins, Frances. *Madame Secretary.* Boston: Houghton Mifflin, 1976.

Peterson, Barbara Bennett. *Notable Women of Hawaii.* Honolulu: University of Hawaii Press, 1984.

Porter, Boone. *Sister Anne: Pioneer in Women's Work.* New York: The National Council, 1960.

Prelinger, Catherine M., ed. *Episcopal Women: Gender, Spirituality and Commitment in an American Mainline Denomination.* New York: Oxford University Press, 1992.

Riggs, Marcia Y., ed., with Barbara Holmes. *Can I Get A Witness? Prophetic Religious Voices of African American Women: An Anthology.* New York: Orbis Books, 1997.

Ruether, Rosemary Radford and Rosemary Skinner Keller, eds. *In Our Own Voices: Four Centuries of American Women's Religious Writing.* San Francico: HarperSanFrancisco, 1995.

Schultz, Rina Lunin and Adele Hast, eds. *Women Building Chicago, 1790-1990*. Bloomington: Indiana Univerity Press, 2001.

Sicherman, Barbara, Carol Hurd Green. *Notable American Women: The Modern Period*. Cambridge: Belknap Press, 1980.

Sklar, Kathryn Kish. *Catharine Beecher: A Study in American Domesticity*. New York: W.W. Norton, 1973.

Tomes, Margaret A. *Julia Chester Emery: Being the Story of Her Life and Work*. New York: The Woman's Auxiliary, 1924.

heryl A. Kujawa-Holbrook, Episcopal priest, is associate professor of pastoral theology and director of Congregational Studies at the Episcopal Divinity School in Cambridge, Massachusetts. She received doctoral degrees from Boston College and Columbia University. She current teaches Episcopal history and polity, and a variety of courses in congregational development, educational ministries, and pastoral care. Kujawa-Holbrook is currently the chair of the Anti-Racism Committee of the Executive Council of the Episcopal Church.